CHANGING NORMAL

To Cindy,

May God do his "changing normal" work!

Jolene Kinser
周珍

March 2026

PRAISE FOR *CHANGING NORMAL*

Jolene Kinser has written a wise and very practical guide to breaking through the barriers that stand in the way of pursuing peace with others. While the context from which she writes is the Chinese Christian community, Jolene's approach to thinking biblically about cultural obstacles can be applied in any setting. *Changing Normal* is a vibrant affirmation that with God all things are possible. I am grateful to her for reminding us of this truth.

Ken Sande
Founder and President of Relational Wisdom®360
Author of *The Peacemaker, A Biblical Guide for Resolving Personal Conflict*

Jolene Kinser, an American deeply immersed in Chinese culture, provides invaluable insights into conflict resolution by integrating cultural awareness with biblical principles. This approach proves beneficial for Christians navigating conflicts with spiritual depth and cultural sensitivity.

Kinser compassionately addresses the intricacies of Chinese social interactions, adeptly navigating face-saving and power dynamics with scriptural guidance. The book encourages reflection on the teachings of Christ in both actions and attitudes.

Her experience of 31 transformative stories from individuals in mainland China illustrates the life-changing power of Christ in conflict resolution. By fostering a deep, empathetic engagement with others, Kinser transcends surface-level communication, revealing the profound effects of truly understanding and connecting with people's interests. This approach strongly resonates with me, echoing the empathetic communication skills central to my work.

I wholeheartedly recommend Changing Normal for Christians to those seeking to foster healthier relationships and deepen spiritual understanding. It serves as a guide to embody Christ's teachings not only in our personal lives but also in ministry and reconciliation.

Agnes Ip, PhD
Founder & CEO of Presence Quotient®
Intergenerational and Multicultural Community Specialist,
Seminary Instructor, Leadership and Relationship Consultant,
and Marriage and Family Therapist

Real-world, insightful, conversational, *Changing Normal* is a must-read book for anyone desiring to learn how to navigate conflict biblically and heal broken relationships in a different cultural context—both at home and abroad. Jolene Kinser's keen insights, practical guidance, and personal stories transcend beyond Chinese culture and applies to many other cultural frameworks. This excellent resource will enable willing peacemakers to sharpen their understanding regarding status and respect issues, shallow apologies, cultural traditions, and power imbalances. This book is ideal for anyone doing ministry cross-culturally anywhere and values Jesus' words: "Blessed are the Peacemakers, for they will be called children of God" (Matt. 5:9).

Laurie A. Stewart
CEO & President of Peacemaker Ministries

Dr. Kinser is a highly respected "honorary" Chinese among her colleagues and friends. Her book is culmination of years of research towards a vision for holistic "peacemaking" in Chinese culture.

Reading as a 3rd generation diaspora Chinese, this book hits all the notes of the pervasive dynamics of being stuck in cycles of conflicts. Dr. Kinser describes explosive forms of conflict, a "no-no" in Chinese culture and highlights a "passive-aggressive" form of conflict that does not get at heart level reconciliation. She astutely identifies the core issues of face, status, power, and cultural expectations that perpetuate conflicts among individuals. Personal observations suggest that these core issues also apply to the primary drivers of long-lasting conflicts between opposing groups within Asian church and Christian communities.

The book's primary value lies in its message that achieving peace and reconciliation starts with individuals choosing to break down barriers and initiate conversation. Dr. Kinser builds upon rigorous academic research to present profound concepts and insights in a relatable way. Enhanced by heartwarming stories and solid biblical guidance, each chapter invites readers to reflect and create space for peace.

Rev Dr Lim Siew Pik
President, Alpha Omega International College, Malaysia

With decades of faith-informed, Chinese-language-based, peacemaking practice in mainland China, Kinser offers a must-read, step-by-step, how-to guide for in-Christ transformation of relationships from energy-sapping conflict to grace-filled joy. Brimming with lived Chinese examples, Biblical evidence, the latest Chinese research, and Spirit-matured wisdom, *Changing Normal* lights the way for everyday Christians, pastors, and lay leaders to real, experienced peace not only in Chinese cultural contexts but in any context, particularly cross-cultural contexts. When the going gets tough, reach for *Changing Normal's* insights, chapter summaries, illuminating prayers, and questions for reflection that provide the skilled support we all need for heart-transforming reconciliation, inter-relational harmony, and Holy Spirit-led serenity.

Dr. Diane B. Obenchain
Director of the China Initiative 2014–2021
Senior Professor of Religion, Fuller Theological Seminary

Jolene Kinser begins *Changing Normal* with the rhetorical question: "Why is a white American writing a book on Chinese culture and peacemaking?" My answer to her is: "Why not?" A Chinese adage wisely says, "Participants in a situation are often confused, but onlookers may have a clearer view." (當局者迷,旁觀者清.) As we all know, Chinese culture emphasizes the collective over the individual; social norms and rules are well developed to maintain interpersonal and collective harmony. However, for Chinese persons entrenched in this highly complex structure, these very same norms and rules, such as "face" issues and rigid social hierarchy often become obstacles to resolving conflicts when they arise. Kinser, being an outsider free of the entrenchment, is in a better position to "see more clearly." Moreover, her knowledge and experience accumulated in 24 years of ministry among the Chinese in Mainland China as well as the Chinese diaspora, have helped her develop this practical guide based on sound Biblical principles as well as insightful social and cultural analysis for peacemaking in the Chinese culture. I myself, as a Chinese church leader with more than 40 years of local church and mission ministry, have benefitted from Kinser's excellent work. Her interviews with Chinese Christians involved in actual conflicts are most helpful to me. I recommend this book to all who are involved or interested in peacemaking in the Chinese context, other cultural contexts, and intercultural situations.

Wing Ning Pang PhD
Co-Founder of Christian Leadership Exchange

In *Changing Normal*, Jolene Kinser challenges the assumption—common across cultures—that we must simply learn to live with unresolved conflict and broken relationships. By uncovering the roots of interpersonal conflict, exploring the obstacles to reconciliation, and presenting case studies of real-life relationships that have been restored, Kinser lays out a hopeful roadmap for change, beginning in our own hearts and extending to the lives of those we care about. Rooted in Scripture and borne out of her own lived experience in the Chinese context, Kinser's well-researched approach provides a unique perspective on applying biblical principles cross-culturally. By illuminating the challenges posed by her particular cultural milieu and how Chinese Christians have overcome these, Kinser highlights the importance of learning from diverse voices within the global church. Throughout the book, Kinser's humble, prayerful posture invites readers of all cultural backgrounds into deep personal reflection, the necessary first step toward thriving in relationships.

Dr. Brent Fulton
China Source Founder
Author of *China's Urban Christians*

Changing Normal is a valuable and much-needed resource in understanding and applying biblical peacemaking in the world and churches today. Jolene, through her years of experience and research, helps bring fresh understanding of how biblical peacemaking is understood outside of a Western cultural context and specifically in Chinese culture. This book brings to light new ideas and insights on how to apply biblical peacemaking and understand peacemaking through a non-western cultural lens. A valuable and commendable read for anyone wanting to broaden their understanding of living out biblical peacemaking, particularly in the Chinese cultural context.

Wayne Forward
Pastor and CEO PeaceWise, Australia

Conflict is endemic in Christian communities throughout the world yet poses unique challenges in contexts of high-face sensitivity. Jolene Kinser tackles this challenging yet critical topic head-on with this new book. With rich ethnographic detail, Kinser deftly demonstrates how fundamental face and face concerns are for Chinese and other face-sensitive cultures. Her many years of practical experience in face-laden and conflict situations enable Kinser to provide a deep theoretical understanding of face, honor, and shame brought into concrete and practical situations. *Changing Normal* is more than merely a strategy for reconciliation. It offers a biblically grounded personal and communal Christian face ethic. This book is a welcome addition to the growing literature on shame and face issues and fills a gap for the global church in conflict literature, as most current materials in that area are written from a Western context, operating with Western frameworks and assumptions. Though particularly helpful for those who work with Chinese, the lessons from Kinser's work are critical for anyone engaged in intercultural service. This book is a fantastic gift to the global church!

Christopher L. Flanders
Professor of Missions, Graduate School of Theology,
Abilene Christian University, USA

Appreciate very much Jolene Kinser's passion and effort in tackling such a challenging yet subtle issue in the Chinese context. Being raised in a shame-oriented culture, in times of conflict, the Chinese tend to ignore it or normalize its impact. Kinser introduces Changing Normal, based on the teaching of the Bible, as a positive way of strengthening and restoring personal relationships. She also provides a process for personal growth, being empowered by the Holy Spirit, to become a peacemaker. I highly recommend it to every Chinese church pastor, lay leader, and parent, both first and second generation.

Aaron Tang
Executive Director, Canadian Chinese Alliance Churches Association

Changing Normal is a wise book that should be of great value to anyone practicing or teaching peacemaking, especially those who live and work in a Confucian-influenced culture. Drawing from her many years of cross-cultural ministry and exercising considerable theological sensitivity, Jolene Kinser helps us think through such thorny issues as the role of "face" in interpersonal relationships and the importance of genuine apologies in the pursuit of reconciliation. Her discussion of face is especially enlightening, as she shows that the concern to preserve face may express a legitimate awareness of the value God places on each individual. Face, she explains, is not the issue. Instead, we must ensure that we make God himself, not other people, the ultimate source of our affirmation. This sense of the "face" we have from God by virtue of our creation in his image gives us the courage to admit our contribution to conflicts and take steps that can lead to genuine peace with others. Highly recommended.

Rev. David Clotfelter, PhD
Former Chaplain, Tunghai University, Taichung City, Taiwan

Regardless of our culture of origin, it is a huge and difficult paradigm shift to comprehend and begin living first and foremost as citizens of the Kingdom of Heaven rather than as citizens of the land of our birth. God's Kingdom is trans-cultural and at odds at multiple points with every human culture. This is an important book because it is an informed attempt to help our Chinese brothers and sisters in Christ "get beneath" the surface of Christian principles and understand in their own language and nuances what a very alive God is trying to do at their heart level to transform them into citizens of His Kingdom. Stories are of people who took the big leap to begin living as citizens of God's Kingdom and the transformational effect that it had in them. May these stories and this book be contagious and read voraciously by all looking for a deeper walk with the Lord!

Rick Stein
Alliance Peacemaking Director
The Christian & Missionary Alliance

CHANGING NORMAL

Break Through Barriers to Pursuing Peace in Relationships

JOLENE KINSER, PHD

PUBLISHING

SEASIDE, CA

© 2023 by Jolene Kinser

All rights reserved. No part of this publication may be reproduced without written permission from Jolene Kinser. Contact Azure Seas Publishing for permission. www.azureseaspublishing.com.

All Scripture quotations, unless otherwise indicated, are taken from the Holy Bible, New International Version®, NIV®. Copyright ©1973, 1978, 1984, 2011 by Biblica, Inc.™ Used by permission of Zondervan. All rights reserved worldwide. www.zondervan.com. The "NIV" and "New International Version" are trademarks registered in the United States Patent and Trademark Office by Biblica, Inc.™

Scripture quotations marked NLT are taken from the Holy Bible, New Living Translation, copyright © 1996, 2004, 2015 by Tyndale House Foundation. Used by permission of Tyndale House Publishers, Inc., Carol Stream, Illinois 60188. All rights reserved.

Scripture quotations marked AMP are taken from the Amplified® Bible (AMP), Copyright © 2015 by The Lockman Foundation. Used by permission. lockman.org

Scripture quotations marked BRB are taken from the The Reader's Bible (www.ReadersBible.com) The Reader's Bible © 2020 by Bible Hub and Berean Bible. Used by Permission. All Rights Reserved.

Scripture quotations marked (ESV) are from The ESV® Bible (The Holy Bible, English Standard Version®), © 2001 by Crossway, a publishing ministry of Good News Publishers. Used by permission. All rights reserved.

Scripture quotations marked NASB are taken from the (NASB®) New American Standard Bible®, Copyright © 1960, 1971, 1977, 1995 by The Lockman Foundation. Used by permission. All rights reserved. lockman.org

Scripture quotations marked NLT are taken from the Holy Bible, New Living Translation, copyright © 1996, 2004, 2015 by Tyndale House Foundation. Used by permission of Tyndale House Publishers, Inc., Carol Stream, Illinois 60188. All rights reserved.

Scripture quotations marked NRSVue are taken from the New Revised Standard Version Updated Edition. Copyright © 2021 National Council of Churches of Christ in the United States of America. Used by permission. All rights reserved worldwide. https://nrsvue.scribenet.com

Cover design: Linda Hucks

Back cover photo: Ray Mok

Names: Kinser, Jolene, author.
Title: Changing normal : break through barriers to pursuing peace in relationships. / Jolene Kinser.
Description: Includes bibliographical references. | Seaside, CA: Azure Seas Publishing, 2023.
Identifiers: ISBN: 978-1-950058-08-2
Subjects: Christian Living / Family & Relationships. Christian Living / Spiritual Growth. Christian Living / Church Leadership.
Library of Congress Control Number: 2023924609

Printed in the United States of America

First edition

DEDICATION

For my Chinese brothers and sisters in Christ whose stories inspired this book as well as the many others who are courageously following Jesus as peacemakers in everyday life.

And for Jim Malone, who believed in this peacemaking work and opened the door for me to begin research.

CONTENTS

Introduction 1

PART 1: LOOKING BACK TO MOVE FORWARD

Chapter 1:   It's Not Working 13

Chapter 2:   Why We Feel Stuck 29

Chapter 3:   Can We Live Differently? 55

PART 2: THE COMPLICATIONS

Chapter 4:   Face Matters... 87

Chapter 5:   Status, Power, and Cultural Expectations......... 115

Chapter 6:   Looking Out for Interests 145

Chapter 7:   Confession-Apologies 171

PART 3: WHAT GOD MAKES POSSIBLE

Chapter 8:   Bearing Fruit 199

Chapter 9:   Initiating Coversations 217

Chapter 10: Finding and Being a Helpful Conflict Companion ... 243

Chapter 11: Cultivating an Environment of Peace............... 265

Final Thoughts	287
Acknowledgements	291
Appendix A: Feelings Reference Guide	295
Appendix B: Universal Human Needs	301
Appendix C: Conversation Space Ideas	305
Appendix D: Apologizing FAQs	311
Appendix E: Resources	317
References	321

PREFACE

SET AGAINST A CHINESE CULTURAL BACKDROP, *Changing Normal* provides a practical guide for all who desire to strengthen or restore personal relationships suffering from unaddressed conflicts. Why is a white American writing a book on biblical peacemaking in the context of Chinese culture? This is a fair question, and its answer requires some background. For over twenty-five years, stemming from my days as an undergraduate at UC Davis, I have had countless meaningful and life-enriching friendships with Chinese people. These relationships began when I joined my college's welcoming team for international students. As life continued, I developed more friendships among the first, second, and third generation Chinese diaspora living in the United States and Canada. When I moved overseas to China to learn Mandarin, I got to know individuals living in their own homelands: mainland China, Taiwan, and Hong Kong. From 1997 to 2020, I worked in China for fifteen years, regularly spoke Mandarin for seventeen, and for over twenty years was a member of a Chinese church in the United States.

During my first year in China, I experienced the unconditional love of a Christian Chinese couple who took me under their wing and became my family there, despite my inability to communicate beyond the most basic Chinese. I also lived with an incredibly hospitable Chinese family during my second year of studying Mandarin, learning some of the ins and outs of that region's food, culture, and relational communication dynamics. Later I learned the traditional Han Chinese storytelling art of *pingshu*.[1] Learning this cultural art form warmed people's hearts to me as it is seen as an indication of a deep understanding of Chinese culture. Although being so immersed in another culture hasn't always been easy, I have deeply enjoyed learning and growing in a better understanding of Chinese culture and language.

While in China, I ran an organization with team members diverse in age, culture, and ethnicity. I was particularly attentive to observing relational dynamics and felt needs. I discovered that, just like in the United States, many interpersonal conflicts in China are left unaddressed and unresolved with individuals, organizations, churches, and families suffering as a result.

I became keenly aware of both a personal and community need for further discipleship and spiritual formation in living out biblical, relational principles when handling conflict arising from differences, offense, and misunderstanding. For myself, I needed to learn how to respond to personal slander and team conflict. On my team, two Chinese colleagues resisted working together due to past conflict that had never been addressed. In the greater community, a local Chinese church leader told me she didn't know how to help two worship team members who weren't speaking to one another. Another local pastor told me about a pastor and elder of a church who didn't speak to one another for months due to a church split. And these are just a few of the many conflict situations in my direct sphere.

Other general examples I have observed in both China and the United States include:

- People who avoid addressing conflict issues, resulting in untrusting, distant, or dissatisfying relationships. Unaddressed conflicts remain under the surface, taint future conversations, and sometimes grow bigger. Wounds remain and often people leave.
- Conflict which has exploded resulting in angry words, broken relationships, and people who don't know what to do next. They either ignore each other, keeping surface-level harmony for the sake of the group, or leave. Sometimes relationships end.
- Intergenerational family or church members with conflicting values and ways of thinking and doing things. When experiencing conflict, they don't know how to bring up or talk about the root issues behind the conflict.
- Older people in a church or organization who feel ill-equipped to bring change or are resistant to change. They stay in power because of age and status, but the younger people who want to contribute feel unheard. As a result, younger generations are leaving local churches and even the faith.
- Relationships characterized by resignation and maintaining distance: "Some people are just impossible to serve together with." "We are too different." "He never listens." "She talks too much."

In response to opportunities that opened up as people shared relational challenges with us, my team and I began facilitating interpersonal peacemaking workshops, retreats, and small group studies in Mandarin.

The peacemaking curriculum that we introduced was eagerly received, and we saw many transformed lives.

Yet, I was troubled. Even though the principles in our peacemaking curriculum were biblical and people were growing spiritually and relationally, the examples and the framework for the material were from a Western social and cultural context. I kept thinking we need a biblically-based, relational reconciliation curriculum for those specifically living in a Chinese social and cultural context. I wondered if there was any way that I could contribute to this endeavor and began considering conducting research. Hearing some small group participants make statements such as, "These principles only work in Western culture," "It's too hard to live this out in Chinese culture," and "We need examples that bridge Chinese culture," only reinforced the urgency I felt to see additional materials created.

I discussed doctoral research ideas with several local pastors, noting that most conflict-related research in Chinese contexts has explored how people manage conflict but not how genuine, from the heart, reconciliation happens. I asked various pastors if they could introduce me to any potential interviewees who had experienced significant conflict and reconciliation. They responded, "If you want to hear stories of people who are in the middle of unresolved conflict, I can introduce you to many research participants. Stories of reconciliation? Those are far more rare." This further motivated me to find reconciliation success stories that would help me better understand what factors impact relational reconciliation from a Chinese cultural perspective, which then became the focus of my dissertation. Thus, a white American is writing a book in which I share my discoveries about what makes biblical peacemaking possible in a Chinese cultural context.

My prayer is that whoever you are and whatever background you bring, as you apply what you learn from God while reading this book, you will experience a *changing normal* process that leads to personal growth, restored relationships, and conflict culture change in your family, church, or workplace.

— *Jolene Kinser*

INTRODUCTION

PART ONE OF *CHANGING NORMAL* explores the question: Why do people so often feel stuck in conflict? An exploratory look at four conflict-impacting cultural norms, followed by a consideration of heart issues and other external factors, allows us to start answering this complex question. However, just understanding *why* we feel stuck in conflict does not resolve problems. We need God! Experientially understanding God's reconciling and forgiving heart provides the foundation for fundamental spiritual and emotional shifts to take place in our own hearts.

Part two deep dives into some of the most challenging complications that make proactively addressing conflict so hard for many people: face matters, status, power dynamics, cultural expectations, apologizing, and the instinct to look after one's own interests. Analyzing such complex issues will help us better navigate the dark depths of conflict.

Part three presents the voices of thirty-one men and women from mainland China whose stories demonstrate what God makes possible for individuals when they live according to His reconciling Kingdom-culture norms. These individuals, ranging in age from late twenties to seventies, are all committed Christians, have been through a peacemaking small group study, and have experienced radical life change as a result of applying what they learned. In interviews with me, they poured out their hearts, describing their conflict stories and the actions they took to pursue reconciliation in obedience to the Lord. Not every conflict has been resolved, not every relationship has been reconciled. There is still pain. But there is also joy in relationships that have been reconciled and are now stronger than ever.

I am excited to share their lessons of biblical peacemaking principles in action in order to instill hope for what is possible. These everyday people have been empowered by the indwelling Holy Spirit and have broken through spiritual, emotional, and cultural barriers. They have *changed their normal* and now proactively deal with conflict issues instead of avoiding them. We can, too!

WHO CAN BENEFIT FROM READING THIS BOOK?

I have written *Changing Normal* with a few different groups of people in mind.

- Chinese church leaders, organization leaders, and parents — 1st Gen
- Chinese & Asian Diaspora — 1st & 2nd Gen
- People in cross-cultural relationships — churches, families, teams, workplace

- As a leader in your family, church, or workplace, learning how to proactively address conflict is critical.

- As a person facing conflict in a relationship with someone a generation older or younger than you, learning new ways to approach the relationship can be a game-changer.
- As someone in a cross-cultural relationship in which you hope to work, serve, play, and live life better together—be it a marriage, a church leadership or ministry team, or as a neighbor—this book will help you get there.

Whether from a Chinese culture or not, as you read, you may find yourself saying things like, "That's true here, too!" or "That's similar, but it's a little different," or "This helps me understand my colleague better!" May this content be fodder from which the Holy Spirit draws as God moves you forward in proactively addressing conflict in God-honoring ways.

A FEW NOTES, EXPLANATIONS, AND DISCLAIMERS

Culture, God's Kingdom-Culture, and Chinese Culture

Throughout this book, I will be talking a lot about culture. There is great diversity in how the term culture can be used and defined. Culture can refer to the arts, music, literature, or history of a particular society. I am not referring to this type of culture in *Changing Normal*. Rather, we will focus on the applied definition of culture: "The rules for functioning and living in society."[2] According to this definition, every person on the planet has culture. And as culture includes the "cumulative deposits of knowledge, beliefs, views, values, and behaviors that are acquired by a large group of people and passed on from one generation to the next,"[3] each of us begins to learn culture from the time we are born.

Culture often affects us unconsciously, teaching us the rules of life, the how and what to think, as well as what value to ascribe things (beautiful, ugly, appropriate, inappropriate). It provides the guidelines that help us know when to do what. For example, in the culture in which I grew up, when you are a guest in someone's home and they ask if you would like something to drink, it's polite to say, "Yes, thanks!" if you are indeed thirsty. If you say no, the host will assume you are not thirsty and will not ask you again for a while. In addition, to indicate to the host that you liked a meal, you eat everything on your plate. To have all the food on the table eaten causes the host to feel proud.

However, in the culture to which I moved overseas, when you are a guest in someone's home and they ask you if you would like something to drink, the polite thing to do is to say no three times before accepting the drink, even if you are thirsty. The host is expected to repeatedly offer a drink. Also, it is polite to leave some food on your plate or in the serving dishes when you are finished eating. To completely eat everything on the table indicates that the host has not provided enough food which would be shameful.[4] We all follow such unspoken, subconsciously understood rules in order to function, be accepted, and be successful in our family and society.

Culture also imparts to us a sense of identity and belonging. From the time we are young, we learn that we belong to a particular family, school, sports team, religion, etc. We are instilled with the understanding that we belong to a particular ethnic group—Chinese, Chinese American, Thai, Brazilian, German, South African—and we learn socially appropriate behavior for that cultural group or how to navigate between what is socially acceptable in multiple groups if living in a multicultural family or community.[5]

So when I refer to God's Kingdom-culture throughout the book, keep these explanations about culture in mind. When individuals join God's family, they now have a new identity and sense of belonging. Christ-followers begin learning the love and grace rules of God's Kingdom-culture and how to function in this new family. Living by Kingdom cultural norms can transform relationships.

There's Not Just One "Chinese Culture"

I have already frequently referred to "Chinese culture" in the first few pages of this book. Some of you may be thinking, "But there isn't just one Chinese culture!" Indeed, there is great diversity in Chinese cultures depending on urban/rural settings, political institutions, and history. The numerous regions in mainland China, Hong Kong, and Taiwan, as well as the societal pockets of Chinese diaspora worldwide, have stark differences as well as striking similarities.

The research forming the backbone of *Changing Normal* is based on interviews with Christians who came from thirteen different urban city churches in China, so the perspectives shared here are from this particular cultural context.[6] Even so, I have been deeply encouraged by Chinese Americans, both first and second generation, as well as Taiwanese and Hong Kong Christians, who have affirmed that the topics raised in this book are also relevant for their contexts. For ease of writing, I will continue to speak of "Chinese culture," but I am fully aware that there are discrepancies among the various Chinese cultures and that the perspectives shared here are limited.

Beyond Chinese Culture

Even though *Changing Normal* looks specifically at relational reconciliation in light of certain aspects of Chinese culture, I am not suggesting that

Chinese culture is exclusive in the particular cultural norms, mindsets, and behaviors that this book highlights. These reflections easily characterize many other cultures as well.

In addition, regardless of the culture we are born into, personal growth as a peacemaker involves multiple mindset shifts, starting with a fundamental change in focus away from fixing others and their problems and toward Jesus. Jesus instructs us to remain in Him (John 15:1–12) and empowers us through the Holy Spirit to do so. Remaining in Jesus enables healing to happen and develops within us the wisdom, love, and courage that makes living as a peacemaker possible for anyone, even for those of us who are in family or cultural contexts where it seems impossible.

FACE IN CHINESE CULTURE

Throughout this book, I talk about *face*. If you are Chinese or Asian and you hear me say, "The topic of face is quite complex," not only will you most likely nod your head in agreement, you might sigh and shake your head saying something like, "Face is a really big issue." You instantly know what I am talking about. However, if you are from a Western culture, you might look at me blankly and ask, "What is *face*?" When I ask if you have heard any of the phrases, "lose face," "give face," or "save face," you may have flickers of recognition and begin nodding.

For the sake of being on the same page regardless of background, I will briefly describe the concept of face as experienced in Chinese culture.[7] There are two Chinese words for *face*, each referring to different aspects of face: *mianzi* and *lian*.[8] English has only one word: face. For the sake of simplicity, I am going to combine the meanings of both *mianzi* and *lian* in my description of face.

Think of face as your perception or awareness of your reputation in the eyes of others.[9] Your perception of how others view you forms the basis for your personal sense of integrity, honor, shame, prestige, and dignity.[10] As human beings, we all, consciously or unconsciously, have an awareness of what public image others have formed about us based on our performance or moral conduct.[11] We also, consciously or unconsciously, have an idea about how qualified we are in each relationship and situation to claim respect or deference from others. In face-conscious societies, to lose face is a serious issue and can affect one's ability to function effectively socially.[12]

Face is also something that can be given to you by others based on your relative positions in your social networks and on how well you conduct yourself in those positions. To give or save face shows respect and boosts one's self-esteem. People commonly give face to others through compliments on diligence, status, beauty, wisdom, or elegance, and by complying when asked to do something.

When critiquing someone's performance, people save the face of others by avoiding direct criticism, using tactful or ambiguous words instead. Showing respect for someone's suggestion or position, even if one does not agree with the person, also saves face.[13] The common thought is that by saving face for others, one can prevent conflicts, and by giving face to others, one can enhance interpersonal relationships. In his interview, Li Jie, explained:

> In Chinese culture, face is very important, especially for men. A man is supposed to display his position in society, so from those in the very top of the government to the very lowest in the household, men especially want face. As a result, face has caused a lot of conflicts.

I pretty much have never truly reconciled with someone. Every time our reconciliation has strictly been to maintain face, meaning that on the surface level, everything looks fine, and we are speaking with one another, but in fact, we have not reconciled.

In the relationship with my work partner who cheated me financially, we still have tea and eat with each other, but the relationship is completely based on face. Our behavior lets a third party see that it looks like we are still friends. But in fact, we no longer have the friendship we once had; our relationship is strictly a business relationship now.[14]

This description begs the question: To what degree does giving and saving face as a way to deal with conflict contribute to or hinder reconciliation? We will more thoroughly explore this question later, but for now I will make two research-based comments: (1) Giving and saving face can be helpful practices at times and can contribute to both preventing and escalating conflict, and (2) Giving and saving face may be limited in their ability to move a relationship to a place of real heart-level reconciliation.

ADVANTAGES AND DISADVANTAGES OF NOT BEING CHINESE

Finally, I recognize that not being Chinese has its advantages and disadvantages when it comes to researching and writing a book that is built so specifically around Chinese cultural, spiritual, and relational practices. The advantage of growing up in one culture and then spending significant time in another is that I can more easily see the nuances of the differences and similarities between these two cultures.

Yet the disadvantage of not being Chinese is that any conclusions I draw most certainly will be colored, to some degree, by my own white, middle-class, American, cultural experience. As human beings, we all have blind spots. A researcher can't avoid such limitations. Over the years, as I have grown in Chinese cultural understanding and linguistic ability, I have occasionally had to revise my own inaccurate interpretations or conclusions. I will always be a learner and my learning will never be complete.[15] In order to help mitigate such pitfalls, I have asked readers with a diversity of backgrounds—Hong Kong Chinese, Taiwanese, and mainland Chinese, as well as Euro-American, Chinese-American, and Chinese-Canadian—to read this book prior to publishing. However, I take full responsibility for what I introduce here and welcome your responses and thoughts. I see this book as a small contribution to a greater work that is already in progress.

PART 1

LOOKING BACK TO MOVE FORWARD

WHEN CONFLICT HAPPENS, WE ALL HAVE our normal ways of responding. Avoid. Defend. Argue. Blame. Smooth things over. Frustratingly, many of our typical responses do not foster the trust, cooperation, understanding, and support most of us long for in our relationships. Our responses don't make things better because they don't lead us to address the core issues that led to the conflict in the first place.

Discovering the root of conflict often requires looking backward and noticing our own mindsets, longings, and response patterns, becoming aware of the reasons behind why we allow uncensored words to boil over in anger or why we break off relationships through silence. Understanding our own cultural background, family background, and personal experiences can also prepare us to do the sometimes uncomfortable, hard work that may be needed to begin a reconciliation process with someone.

But unlike anything else, looking back at what God has done for us, recognizing our need for Him, and returning home to God provides the foundation and strength to begin. Embracing a new identity and beginning in Christ, experiencing God's Kingdom-culture, learning God's reconciling ways, and being empowered by God's Spirit enables each of us to courageously take a new approach to conflict and begin *changing normal*.

ONE

IT'S NOT WORKING

WHEN OUR PHONES, CARS, OR COMPUTERS glitch or break down completely, many of us panic and go into fix-it mode because these items are of critical importance for smoothly functioning lives. We look to pinpoint the cause and then repair or replace the broken part. Sometimes we need professional help because we are unable to resolve an issue on our own. There is always huge relief when the problem is discovered and fixed and life returns to normal.

Similarly, when a relationship breaks down, we sometimes panic and go into fix-it mode. Life has been disrupted and the conflict consumes our thinking and energy. We often seek to pinpoint the cause(s) by looking at the other person, hoping to repair or replace their broken part. Something in the other person may indeed need fixing, but this repair work is a work that only God can do. Realistically, we all have areas in our lives that God wants to reveal and work on. A friend once said that conflict leads us to see our own helplessness. In and of ourselves, we can't fix people—ourselves or others.

Take a moment now to reflect on your own fix-it approach when relational breakdown happens:

- What is your standard response to conflict?

- When, why, and how do you typically apologize to others?

- How do you view yourself and the other person when conflict happens?

As you read in this chapter about conflict approaches that are failing others, I invite you to ask the Holy Spirit to reveal to you what aspects of your approach to handling conflict need God's repairing, adjusting, or replacing work.

In and of ourselves, we can't fix people—ourselves or others.

MY STANDARD CONFLICT RESPONSE ISN'T WORKING

When someone tells you, "No," or you experience a value clash, point of disagreement, or feel hurt, disrespected, offended, sinned against, misunderstood, unheard, or neglected, does your in-the-moment response look anything like one of these?

Just Set It Aside—Wang Jia's Response

> The two of us would shelve the issue for a while, trying to avoid causing an even bigger conflict. Setting the issue aside was our way of handling the problem. Whether we remained friendly in appearance

but estranged at heart didn't matter as long as visual conflict wasn't occurring. [Wang Jia, describing herself and her mother when in conflict.]

Avoid and Keep My Distance—Li Min's Response

No matter whether or not a person is a Christian, when we personally feel hurt, I think the majority of Chinese people react in a similar way: "Well, alright then, I just won't say anything to you, but I'll keep my distance from you." People respond this way out of fear of being hurt again. Behaving this way doesn't mean a person has a great personality; rather, it simply reflects their choice to endure or put up with the situation. There will come a day when they will no longer be able to endure.

Build a Wall—Wang Fang's Response

My relationship with my male, Christian colleague didn't have any big conflicts, yet at the same time, it didn't improve at all after the offense happened. We just built a wall between us. When problems came up, emotions would surface. We looked like everything was peaceful, but in reality, the waves were choppy under the surface.

Be Reserved; Don't Share Your Views—Chen Dandan's Response

I think the method that Chinese people use to handle conflict is rather reserved, or maybe I'm just that way. If it's possible to not get into conflict, then we work hard to avoid the conflict. But there is a downside to this: we lack communication. Our communication is not thorough. Sometimes I think that if we keep talking about something, we'll end up in a conflict, so I'll just not talk about it.[16]

We fear expressing a different view. If I hold a different view from you, that means that I am negating you and don't respect you. If I agree with you, this means that I love and respect you. However, in my heart, I don't necessarily hold your view, so this is a very big problem.[17]

Just set the issue aside; avoid the person and keep your distance; build a wall; be reserved and don't share your true feelings and views. Though these ways of responding to conflict are instinctive and may even seem legitimate in the moment, they don't resolve issues or restore relationships.

SAYING I'M SORRY ISN'T WORKING

For some people, another instinctive reaction to conflict is to quickly say *I'm sorry*. Instead of apologizing to admit a wrong, at times we apologize to give face in order to preserve a relationship, even if just superficially. As Zhao Cheng put it: "I apologize; you then apologize; we have both given face and are now reconciled at least on the surface level." The semblance of relationship is maintained—but at what true cost?

We might also apologize to try to quickly normalize a relationship, saying what we think the other person wants to hear. Chen Dandan described this phenomenon: "In most relationships, if I apologize, I say something like, 'Okay, okay, I was wrong,' for the purpose of returning the relationship back to normal. I don't admit to actually having done something wrong." Such apologies are built on a desire for non-confrontation and not from a true understanding of the situation. In fact, Chen

Dandan reveals, some apologies are entirely fake:

> Some people are just going through the motions when they apologize. It is perfunctory; they apologize to satisfy the other person. That type of apology is fake. Its only purpose is to make the relationship better faster, but in reality the person doesn't want to admit their mistake.

Liu Haifeng identified a similar issue:

> Sometimes I apologize because I want the situation to pass as quickly as possible and not influence my mood, but I don't feel like I truly owe the other person an apology. I say *I'm sorry*, but the apology backfires and the other person criticizes me in response. The situation gets worse instead of having the effect that I set out for.

While the person making the apology wants to return the relationship back to normal, the person receiving such an insincere apology feels like the other person is just making excuses. Defending themselves. Trying to prove why they were justified in their behavior. The end result is that the apology makes the conflict situation even worse!

A forced apology also tends to backfire. As a teacher, Chen Meizhen once required one of her culinary students to apologize to another student after that student brandished a knife at him. When apologizing, he avoided the other student's gaze and mumbled, "I'm sorry. I guess I was wrong; I'm sorry." The apology ended up having no effect because the student was not truly sorry for his behavior. Forced apologies were mentioned in a number of interviews, yet none of them had a positive effect on the relationship.

Criticizing while apologizing also proves to be ineffective. Choosing to avoid criticizing in such moments may seem obvious and simple, but it can be surprisingly difficult. After Wang Jia and her mom's intense conflicts, they would apologize but only while also pointing out each other's faults. One time Wang Jia got so frustrated by this that she angrily said to her mom, "If your purpose for apologizing is to create an opportunity to tell me once again that I am wrong, then you don't need to apologize; we don't need to apologize. I didn't want to reconcile with you anyway." And once again, the ineffectiveness of apologizing without the right motivation becomes evident.

When we have experienced enough of these failed apologies (whether given or received), we may find ourselves more hesitant to apologize in the future. It is easy to start thinking that apologizing doesn't help or that it even makes conflict worse. Keep in mind that these types of "apologies" are not genuine apologies at all, so of course they don't restore relationships. At best, they enable a superficial reconciliation.

"GETTING THE SALT" ISN'T WORKING

Yet what about the times when we are truly sorry and want to apologize? How do we go about apologizing and making amends? As you think about these two questions, consider what was modeled to you by your family when you were growing up.

Liu Haifeng learned the following action-apology method:

If you and I have a conflict and it seems that I am in the wrong, I will proactively help you with something to apologize, but I will never say *I'm sorry*.

For example, if I see my older sister cooking, and we had been in a conflict where I was in the wrong, I would apologize by saying, "Does that need a little salt? I'll get the salt for you."

Then I would check her expression. If her face still looked dark, if she didn't look at me at all, or if she said, "Go away!" then I knew things hadn't blown over yet. But if her expression was somewhat warm, friendly, and demonstrating goodwill, then I knew that things had returned to a good enough place relationally.

When Liu Haifeng shared this example with me, I was intrigued and asked him, "Does this method work? Does it really mend the relationship?" He laughed and replied, "It has a little bit of an effect because in the surrounding environment, everyone behaves this way." But Liu Haifeng went on to say that this type of apology doesn't resolve the problems:

> Even though we say that we have forgotten about the situation, in fact, no one has forgotten about it. We just aren't willing to mention it again. But the next time we run into the same thing, we will argue again. Not only that, when we argue, we will bring up the details from the previous time.

For many of us, an "I'll get the salt" action apology is the only type of apology that was modeled to us or expected from us growing up. While this type of non-verbal apology is commonplace, it unfortunately does not address the root cause of a conflict. Many people feel stuck in relationally distancing or damaging communication patterns as a result.

MY MINDSET ISN'T WORKING

Not only do ineffective apology methods keep us from restoring relationships, but self-justifying mindsets such as, "I'm right," "I'm a good person," and "I didn't make a mistake," also keep many of us, including me, from addressing conflict issues. Holding tight to unexamined views of ourselves and our positions can be a big blind spot for all of us.

"I'm Right"

When you disagree with someone, do you find yourself rigidly digging in your heels on your own position? Describing her previously conflicted relationship with her younger sister, Li Na said, "My sister and I had lots and lots of conflict because she felt we should do everything her way while I felt that I was right." Similarly, when reflecting on how she used to never apologize, Wang Fang said, "In the past, I wasn't willing to apologize because I didn't think I had done anything wrong. I felt I was right!" At the moment of disagreement, and even later on, unbidden thoughts can easily flood our minds and bodies:

"I'm right. I'm going to prove it to him; I'll convince him."

"My way of thinking on this is right; hers is wrong."

"I didn't do anything wrong!"

Yet focusing on who is right and justifying ourselves while not listening only heightens conflict. Min Lei once shared a story with me about how another woman in her prayer group, Chen Li, had been deeply offended and hurt by something she had said. When another prayer group member shared this with Min Lei, she was shocked and even upset. She hadn't intended to hurt Chen Li! She had spoken with the best of intentions. How could Chen Li have interpreted her words in that way?

When the prayer group member suggested that Min Lei call Chen Li to talk and possibly apologize, Min Lei at first refused. She felt she hadn't done anything wrong. But as Min Lei spent time praying about the situation, God helped her see that the issue wasn't about right or wrong, whether her words were justified, or her motivation pure. Rather, the issue was whether Min Lei would be humble and compassionate enough to call, ask Chen Li to tell her how Min Lei's words had hurt her, and apologize for causing hurt.

So Min Lei called her. Chen Li was quite upset as she shared what Min Lei had said that was so hurtful. As Chen Li shared more, Min Lei realized that her words had triggered a past wound. Min Lei was able to see just how hurt Chen Li felt by what she had said. God moved her heart to compassion, and she genuinely apologized for having hurt Chen Li. Chen Li was able to forgive her and their relationship was restored. They even became close friends! To accomplish all this, Min Lei had to move past focusing on being right, a mindset that would have kept her stuck relationally.

> Focusing on who is right and justifying ourselves while not listening only heightens conflict.

"I'm a Good Person"

When we know at a gut level that we messed up, made a mistake, or sinned, sometimes we find ourselves minimizing or justifying our behavior, thinking, *I meant well. I'm a good person; this isn't worth losing face over.* Yang Lin expressed such a mindset:

> We think we are good. Deep inside, we think, *even if I am not perfect, at least I am better than the average person.*
>
> Even if we hate someone in our hearts and distance ourselves from people, we think we are still good: *At least I didn't argue with her!* and *I am being polite to her!*

The human ability to self-justify is quite impressive! As we hold on to our thinking, *at least I didn't argue with her*, we feel so justified and right. Sometimes we don't even reflect on whether we have done anything wrong.

Such evasion of responsibility is not an unusual reaction to conflict. I have found, even as Christians, we are tempted to think that in some way, apart from Christ, we can be and ought to be good in and of ourselves. Subconsciously we want to believe that we don't need to apologize because we have some form of goodness which can justify our condemning thoughts, words, behaviors, and attitudes toward others.

We are tempted to think that in some way, apart from Christ, we can be and ought to be good in and of ourselves.

"I Didn't Make a Mistake"

Sometimes we so deeply feel the need to preserve face that we don't acknowledge our wrong to anyone, not even to ourselves. Why is it so difficult for us to accept our imperfect selves? Huang Jingjing's description of feeling justified in her anger and having face-preserving reasons for not apologizing gives some clues:

> I used to rarely apologize to my husband or child. For one, I felt there was a reason for my anger toward them. Two, there was also my face. Even though in my heart I felt conscience-stricken and ashamed of my words, I still would not apologize. I would think, *Just wait for a while; it will pass.*
>
> I think a lot of people, like me, really want face. It is extremely hard to take the first step and admit our mistake or wrong; we fear that others will think poorly of us, or even attack us. I have this worry.

I fake thinking I am correct, that I am very strong, because I don't want to admit I am weak. I feel like apologizing proves I have failed or done something wrong. This demonstrates that I'm no good.

Notice Huang Jingjing's equation:

doing something wrong or failure = **negative self-worth ("I'm no good")**

Her gut response, even to herself, was to prioritize saving face above all else, to fake being strong, and to not admit any weakness. If we equate doing something wrong, failing, making a mistake, etc., with our self-worth, no wonder we instinctively avoid thinking about whether we might be wrong, never mind publicly acknowledging being wrong!

Wang Jia so aptly found words to describe what many of us feel unconsciously:

> If you are really going to deal with the conflict, you need to address your part of the problem; I am not that willing to face myself, that I sin, that I did something wrong. I'm not that willing to face this problem; if I do face the problem, it will cause me to feel ashamed.

Particularly when facing a conflict in which we know we have blame, we often emotionally hide and just try harder to be good. We feel ashamed. Something deep inside moves us to ignore the issue entirely. Instead of humbling ourselves, acknowledging our contribution to the problem, and confessing our sin to God and the other person, we revert to acting like nothing is wrong in order to preserve face and protect our own sense of goodness or self-worth.

CALLING SIN "A MISTAKE"

At times we also get stuck relationally because we consciously or unconsciously hide *sin* behind the word *mistake* in order to feel better about ourselves or to evade responsibility. We sin when we substitute our own will for God's will. In those moments of substitution, our actions, words, or attitudes are contrary to God's heart and purposes; our behavior stems from self-reliance, self-focus, self-importance, or self-protection, not from a God-focus and rooted identity in Christ.

Sometimes, at the moment of sinning, we don't realize we are sinning. We are caught up in the emotion of the moment. We haven't planned ahead of time to break God's law of love by withholding love or harming someone (Matt 22:37–38; Gal 5:14). Afterwards, we may think, "I messed up!" It feels like a mistake, so we default to calling it a mistake and excuse our behavior. We don't want our sin to carry the gravity that is does. Yet 1 John 1:8 reminds us: "If we claim to be without sin, we deceive ourselves and the truth is not in us." Sinning is part of our reality.

Calling something a mistake implies that what was said or done was unintentional or accidental; it was wrong based on an error in judgement, misunderstanding, inadequate information, distraction, or carelessness.[18] Genuine mistakes do happen. So talking about making a mistake feels less damning, less shaming, and socially more acceptable than talking about having sinned (though in face-saving cultures, admitting to either can feel equally shameful).

Even though a clear distinction exists between *mistakes* and *sin*, many of us blur the concepts. You will see throughout this book that those I interviewed often interchange the terms. This blurring occurs for many reasons: both sin and mistakes can be described as *doing something wrong*, they both leave others feeling hurt, and both require admitting to and taking responsibility for words and actions.

However, I am inclined to believe that we avoid using the word *sin* because of the greater shame and condemnation that we associate with it, which is in part due to our forgetfulness as Christians. God's good news for us is that no sin can separate us from His love, for "if we confess our sins, he is faithful and just and will forgive us our sins and purify us from all unrighteousness" (1 John 1:8–9).[19] We can draw courage from these truths, face our sin squarely, change our standard response, and do as God instructs us: confess our sins. What joy to be able to confess to God—knowing Jesus has already paid for our forgiveness—and be shown grace and mercy in a secure relationship. One aspect of *changing normal* is choosing to believe what God has done for us and in us.

CHAPTER WRAP-UP

As Proverbs 21:2 (NIV) says, "A person may think their own ways are right, but the LORD weighs the heart," so our way of responding to others often seems right to us. We defend and justify ourselves when in conflict, but the Lord looks at our hearts to see what is motivating our responses. We all have blind spots and need the Holy Spirit's revelation of mindsets that are hindering us from addressing issues with others. Only then do we begin to see how often our typical response patterns are laced with sin; how often our apologies are not a sincere conveying of genuine sorrow over something we have done; and how our views of ourselves, in relation to others, are often inaccurate and harmful to everyone involved.

All people have value because we were all created in the image of God (Gen 1:27). But goodness comes entirely from being in Christ. Yet, even though as believers in Jesus Christ we have been given a new identity and source of goodness (Jesus), we still struggle to live in this reality. In response to continuing to sin, disappointing, or offending others, we unconsciously fall into self-absorbed, justifying, or condemning thoughts. We fear that if we apologize or admit weakness, others will label us as *sinner* and condemn us. We might even fear that our sin condemns us to being just that—sinners.

Even though we still sin, the label *sinner* no longer defines us. We are no longer condemned or bound to sin because of our old sin nature; rather, we each have been given a new, not-yet-fully-formed-in-us nature in Jesus Christ (Rom 8:1–2). Instead of clinging to our old ways of self-reliance, we can begin to *change our normal conflict responses* through relying on the Holy Spirit and believing that Jesus' death on the Cross fully provided for the cleansing of our sins.

A PRAYER

Oh Lord, help me! More than anything, I want to be good. Yet the reality is, I keep sinning. I don't like to admit that I sin. It feels shameful, so I ignore my weakness and failure. I focus on putting forward a strong front and letting people know that I am right and they can count on me. But I confess, this isn't working, and it's not Your way. In fact, the extremes of insisting that I am right all the time or condemning myself for sinning does nothing to change my situation for the better.

Relying on my own striving is the exact opposite of what You have said is the source of my goodness. I am hating and condemning the wrong things when I condemn myself—someone who is now in Christ. I cry out with Paul, "What a wretched man I am! Who will rescue me from this body that is subject to death? Thanks be to God, who delivers me through Jesus Christ our Lord!" (Rom 7: 24–25).

And so I declare, "There is now no condemnation for those who are in Christ Jesus" (Rom 8:1). Thank You, Lord, that I can come to You, knowing that I am no longer condemned. I can admit and repent of my sin without shame and turn from it with Your help. My goodness is in You. I rest in You. In Jesus' name I pray, amen.

REFLECTION QUESTIONS

1. What is your standard conflict response when you experience a value clash; have been told, "No," by someone; or disagree, feel hurt, disrespected, offended, misunderstood, unheard, or neglected?

2. Do you or those around you expect you to superficially reconcile and maintain a relationship even if the real issues haven't been addressed?

3. At times, when you have said *I'm sorry*, what motivated you to apologize? Do you see any of the above-mentioned motivations (to preserve or normalize the relationship) in yourself?

4. How do you typically apologize? Do you "get the salt," verbally apologize, or add criticism or correction when you apologize? Or do you avoid apologizing altogether?

5. Do your apologies seem to contribute toward relational restoration or make things worse?

6. What is your mindset about making mistakes?

7. What is God asking you to do in response to any new self-awareness gained from reading this chapter?

TWO

WHY WE FEEL STUCK

MOST OF US PICK UP A BOOK like this because we are either in a relationship that is falling apart and the methods we have tried so far to mend it aren't working, or we have hit a wall regarding how to help others in conflict. Conflict situations can cause us to feel stuck, even helpless. This chapter uncovers some typically hidden layers related to our unique understandings of conflict, our cultural backgrounds, and our personal contexts that can contribute to individuals feeling relationally stuck. While far from exhaustive, this content provides a starting place for you to talk with the Lord and gain insight into your own situation.

UNDERSTANDING THE SOURCE AND NATURE OF CONFLICT

When the Bible talks about fights and quarrels, it emphasizes that conflict starts in the heart. James 4:1–3 further uncovers this root cause of conflicts:

What causes fights and quarrels among you? Don't they come from your desires that battle within you? You desire but do not have, so you kill. You covet but you cannot get what you want, so you quarrel and fight. You do not have because you do not ask God. When you ask, you do not receive, because you ask with wrong motives, that you may spend what you get on your pleasures.

Desires that battle within the heart, internal conflicts, are at the root of external conflict.[20] As a result of not having what we want, we quarrel, fight, and even kill. We don't talk to God about our desires, and when we do, we ask with wrong motives.

> Desires that battle within the heart, internal conflicts, are at the root of external conflict.

Interestingly, Proverbs 19:2 (NRSVue) states, "Desire without knowledge is not good, and one who moves too hurriedly misses the way." When we have strong desires (and opinions), we often look only at what we consider to be wrong instead of first quieting ourselves and looking to the Holy Spirit for what we should do next. In her YouTube video on shifting focus and perspective, Dr. Bertice Berry gives helpful advice: "If you only look at what's wrong, you will begin to dismantle some of what's right."[21] And I would add, if we only look at what's outwardly wrong, our focus may also be too narrow. Through God's enabling and guidance, we need to internally examine our own hearts.

The prophet Jeremiah aptly described the human heart in the Old Testament: "The heart is deceitful above all things and beyond cure. Who can understand it?" (Jer 17:9–10). Without the Holy Spirit's help, we have a difficult time understanding our own hearts—our deep desires, needs, and struggles. And while we like to think we know what's going on in other people's hearts, we are even less likely to understand that without help from the other person! Our lack of personal heart-awareness can contribute to our feeling stuck in conflict.

Our Experience of Conflict

Bernard Mayer, an internationally recognized mediator and scholar, describes three dimensions—perceptions, feelings, and actions—that will all be present at some point when conflict exists.[22] When our hearts are churning, Mayer's first two dimensions of conflict are internally present. We consciously or unconsciously perceive that one of three things is happening: (1) our interests, needs, or values have been ignored or are incompatible with another's, (2) we have to fight over resources, or (3) our goals are being blocked.[23]

This perception causes us to feel angry, resentful, sad, fearful, anxious, helpless, treated unjustly, etc. Sometimes we ignore these feelings because we don't want to acknowledge that we are internally in conflict with someone, especially if we believe it is shameful to be in outward, active conflict with others. Yet, sooner or later, the internal conflict leaks out in some form of action (Mayer's third dimension) and an externally expressed struggle now begins.[24]

"I Don't Have Conflict with Others"

Surprisingly, during my years in China, numerous people said to me, "I don't have conflict with others." The comment puzzled me. I have long agreed with Bernard Mayer, who says "a conflict exists if at least one person thinks that there is a conflict."[25] Even if we keep our anger, disappointment, disagreement, etc., well hidden, the heart distance between us and that other person is still present, thus conflict exists. Because of my understanding of conflict, when people told me they didn't experience conflict, I wondered, *How is it possible to never have conflict with others? Don't we all have conflicts?*

One day, when meeting up with a group of students to discuss conflict and peacemaking, I had an *aha moment*. A student described conflict as an explosion between two people ("冲突爆发了") that results in a shameful breakdown of relationship. I immediately thought, *If this is what people think conflict is, then the assertion that some people don't have conflict with others now makes sense to me!* This understanding of conflict restricts conflict to only existing when it manifests through actions—an external, interpersonal conflict.

Li Jie confirmed this description when he told me what *reconciliation* typically means in Chinese culture:

> Reconciliation refers to no longer having explosive conflict; everyone seems to be at peace with each other, but the problem hasn't been resolved. Lots of problems haven't been resolved; rather they have simply been left there, concealed. One never knows when it will explode again. There is a great likelihood for that to happen.

I soon learned that this understanding, while not the only Chinese view of conflict, has its roots in Confucianism. We'll get to those roots in a moment.

Conflict Definitions in Mandarin

According to Xuejian Yu's research, *maodun* (矛盾, conflict) is the first term that most mainland Chinese people associate with conflict.[26] The term *maodun* closely resembles the meaning of Stella Ting-Toomey's definition of the English word *conflict*:

> A form of intense interpersonal and/or intrapersonal dissonance (tension or antagonism) between two or more interdependent parties based on incompatible goals, needs, desires, values, beliefs, and/or attitudes.[27]

This definition is broader than the understanding of *conflict* that my students held; it includes both the internal (intrapersonal) struggle of conflict as well as the external (interpersonal) struggle. Regardless, *maodun* (conflict) is typically perceived as something negative and destructive that should be minimized or dealt with through an avoidant or evasive non-confrontational manner in order to prevent face loss or any experience of shame for all involved. This begs the question: why is avoidance the go-to choice for dealing with conflict?

The Roots of a Chinese View of Conflict

Both concepts—that conflict only refers to outward actions and that one should avoid dealing with conflict—have their roots in Confucianism. According to the I'Ching, which has deeply influenced Confucianism, conflict can always be avoided. The reasoning is as follows:

- Conflict "can always be avoided *if one strives to conform with nature* by cultivating one's understanding and adjusting one's action in a proper way with respect to a propitious time."[28] This means that if we adjust our actions to conform with nature, seeking to live in accord with natural laws rather than against them, we will avoid conflict.

- Since it is theoretically possible to always avoid conflict, if a person experiences visible conflict with someone, this then reflects badly on that person: "Any conflict that one experiences in society is basically that between the self-interest of petty persons and the good virtues of the superior man."[29]

- To be in conflict, therefore, is "indicative of the weakness of an individual or a community of individuals in their failure to appreciate the intricacies of change and consequently to control or discipline themselves for making conformity to nature possible."[30] In other words, only weak, petty, self-interested people experience conflict, which is due to their failure to control or discipline themselves.

Therefore, since no one wants to be seen as weak, petty, selfish, and undisciplined, people subconsciously tell themselves they shouldn't be in conflict with others. Thus they tend to avoid referring to relational problems as conflict and also steer clear of outward demonstrations of conflict.

This is a big deal. Culturally speaking, one of the implicitly understood differences between a morally superior and inferior person is whether one engages in visible conflict with others.[31] Practically speaking, this means that, when in a Chinese cultural context, if I openly get into conflict or acknowledge that conflict exists between me and another person, everyone implicitly understands this to be inappropriate, negative, and morally inferior, even shameful behavior. This fundamental understanding of the results of experiencing visible conflict with someone may partially explain the conflict-avoidance tendency of many Chinese people.

CULTURAL NORMS

Few people are consciously aware that they view conflict with a Confucian lens or with any lens at all. What we believe about conflict has been so internalized that most people simply label it as just the way things are. We all approach conflict with internalized beliefs and narratives that affect how we engage with the world around us. The question we must ask ourselves is *What is influencing our approach to conflict?*

One influencing factor is our internalized beliefs and narratives from generationally passed down *cultural norms*: "shared, sanctioned, and integrated systems of beliefs and practices that characterize a cultural group."[32] Cultural norms have far more impact than we might realize. Since talking about norms isn't something we do every day, bear with me as I explain.

Cultural norms guide us in our everyday living, prescribing what is correct and moral behavior. They provide meaning and structure, giving us a feeling of belonging, safety, and integrity, enabling us to make sense of life. Definitions can be a bit abstract, so let's look at four specific examples of Chinese cultural norms related to conflict. In everyday life, these norms hinder people from moving toward reconciliation:

1. Externally, we must preserve face at all costs.

2. Admitting mistakes or sin causes internal face loss.

3. Superiors forgive and subordinates apologize, not the other way around.

4. Apologizing puts individuals in a morally inferior position.[33]

If you come from a different cultural background, you may discover that your own culture shares similar norms.

As we explore these four conflict-related, cultural norms, take time to reflect on the following questions:

- How do I see this cultural norm impacting people around me?
- How strongly, if at all, do I adhere to this cultural norm in my life?
- How strongly, if at all, do those around me adhere to this cultural norm?
- What does the Bible say about this cultural norm?

External Preservation of Face at All Costs

Quoting a common Chinese saying, Li Jun described face to me as an essential element in Confucian culture: "树活一张皮，人活一张脸," [translated as "A tree lives because of its skin; without skin, it is naked. It's the same for a person: a person cannot live without face."] For many in a Chinese context, preserving face at all costs is imperative. As a result, some people say that face can impact the start of a conflict or keep a conflict from being resolved.

Liu Haifeng expressed the intense emotion associated with a loss of face that comes through an external challenge of a mistake or sin:

> Everyone longs to be respected. When I was about 20 or 21 years old, I had to fill out and file a very important form with the government. The government needed to write back to me in response. But I made a mistake on my address, so the government sent their response to a different place. That letter was very important to me.
>
> My dad said, "How is it that you've written even your home address incorrectly? You can't even do this right."

Actually, I really did make a mistake in this matter; I didn't do it right. But even though internally I knew I had messed up, you could beat me to death before I would admit that it was my mistake. It was obvious I had made a mistake, but I didn't want to admit the mistake because, if I admitted my mistake, the loss of face would be even worse. At that time, I fought as if my life depended on it. It felt like someone wanted to tear away my clothes and that I must do everything I can to keep my clothes on. I stopped thinking rationally.

For Liu Haifeng, admitting this mistake would have felt as bad as having his clothes torn away and being left naked. He felt that he simply must preserve face at all costs.

Su Lijuan explained the sensitive face challenges that occur if a fault is pointed out when someone else is present:

If there are only two of us, I might more readily accept you pointing out my fault. But when a third party is added to the dynamic, I definitely will counterattack for the sake of my face. Even if I clearly know that what you said is right, I won't admit it and will even strike back. You might feel baffled thinking, "I was doing this for your benefit. Why have you responded like this?" The conflict then develops. Actually, the root cause of the conflict has to do with face.

Even as a Christian, the pull to preserve face is very strong for Zhou Na:

China has a saying, "死要面子活受罪" [translated as "One will go through hell for the sake of keeping up face" or "One will puff oneself up at one's own cost"], meaning, for the sake of face, a person will commit a lot of sin, or bring a whole lot of trouble on oneself. Truly, sometimes I just can't set face aside.

With such an obstacle blocking the way, reconciliation becomes nearly impossible to achieve. Yet God directs believers, "If it is possible, as far as it depends on you, live at peace with everyone" (Rom 12:18), so Christians must grapple with face and its impact on our relationships. There is no way around this issue.

> Christians must grapple with face and its impact on our relationships. There is no way around this issue.

Internally Admitting Mistakes or Sin Causes Face Loss

The Romans 12:8 statement, "As far as it depends on you," emphasizes the second problem to saving face: internal honesty. As illustrated above by Liu Haifeng, the act of internally acknowledging a small mistake, not to mention confessing sin, can cause face loss and bring a sense of shame. Zhang Yong automatically associated internally admitting a mistake with loss of face. He said that when a person prioritizes face, they cannot see their own personal shortcomings. The logic goes something like this:

1. If I admit my mistake, this will cause me to lose face.
2. If I care about my face, I will not be willing to apologize.
3. If I care too much about face, it is very difficult to see my shortcomings, my weaknesses.
4. If I don't see my shortcomings and weaknesses and think that I don't make mistakes, then apologizing is impossible.

Because of the deep-seated belief that acknowledging a mistake causes face loss, prioritizing preserving one's own face sometimes blinds people from seeing their shortcomings or mistakes.

In a similar vein, Zhang Wei described how difficult it still is for him and his wife to admit being wrong, despite being Christians:

> Even though we both are believers, it seems that in our subconscious we can't allow ourselves to be wrong. If I'm wrong, then there is something inside that involves face. In reality, if you're wrong, you're wrong; it doesn't matter. But to be wrong, especially in front of someone you don't know, this is a big deal. It's not easy, and you end up burying a seed of grudge; you set yourself up for a future problem, a storm.

Whether an individual personally acknowledges a mistake or someone else points out the error, both behaviors are culturally understood to cause face loss.

Superiors Forgive; Subordinates Apologize

Li Qiang described to me how, even today, the traditional Confucian way of viewing relationships sets the unspoken cultural guidelines for how two people should relate to each other when in conflict:

> Chinese people rarely relate to each other as equals. In Chinese traditional relationships, there is a superiority order: a father is superior to his son, a ruler is superior to his ministers, a husband is superior to his wife, and an older brother is superior to the younger brother. So, before Chinese people establish a relationship with a stranger, they first establish their position in relation to one another.

The older (or superior) is always right and the younger (or subordinate) needs to obey or behave in a certain way toward the older (or higher ranked). If you are above me, I am expected to respect you, and you are expected to look after me. So, because of this cultural background, it is natural for Chinese people to take time to figure out who is relationally higher and lower when they first meet.[34]

This social ordering obviously affects how, consciously or subconsciously, Chinese people approach reconciliation in relationships. Rather than basing reactions on personal responsibility, a typical Western response, the instinct is to respond according to relationship-order norms.

In discussing this idea, Chen Meizhen explained that people often reconcile when a relationship is with a superior and thus, based on societal norms, they do not feel like they have any other choice:

If reconciling is for the sake of face, it might not be a genuine reconciliation; maybe it is fake. "Forget about it! I'll give you face;" "You are older than me;" or "You are the boss." But the heart hasn't truly reconciled.

Unfortunately this motivation and response tends to only contribute to surface-level reconciliation.[35]

Depending on one individual's relative position to another, certain expectations regarding apologizing and forgiving exist. The need to preserve face requires an individual to act according to the cultural norms for their position: If a superior or elder person apologizes to a subordinate or younger individual, they will lose face and forfeit their elder status. However, a superior or older person is expected to forgive a subordinate or younger person. It is difficult for an older person to apologize to someone younger. It is more acceptable for someone younger to apologize to someone older.

Huang Jingjing illustrates the superior/subordinate apology expectations by describing her own growing-up experiences:

> In China, a lot of parents rarely apologize to their kids. When I was young, my dad frequently said, "Your elder is always right." Parents are always right. He was also quite strict, never giving us the opportunity to explain. So from the time I was young, I never learned about apologizing.

If the elder is always right, then the elder never needs to apologize! But in real life, it's not possible for a person to be right one hundred percent of the time. Thus the tension.

The Apology Bind

Li Qiang was once placed in a bind based on the Confucian ordering and expectations of relationships. After a conflict erupted between him and someone else, he knew that God expected him to apologize. Yet apologizing was the opposite of the cultural norm and could have quite negative ramifications. This was his dilemma:

> I am the leader of my Bible study group. According to the Chinese way of thinking, as the small group leader, I am now, to some degree, an "elder person." And in fact, according to age, I am slightly older than the others. The age difference predisposes me, according to how this culture has established face, to be seen as having more wisdom and as being smarter. I should also be treated with more respect.

So if I behave like someone younger than me, that is, if I apologize, then the previous relationship of "I am higher than you, you are lower than me" changes. In this case, they are now above me and have a certain authority to criticize me. Now they can say, "Look, even though he is older than me, and even though he is a small group leader, he did something wrong here."

Should Li Qiang behave according to the cultural norm and not apologize? Or should he obey the Bible, confess his sin, and face whatever possible negative repercussions may come? What would you do?

Being a Good Elder Person (Forgiveness Expectations)

Li Qiang also said that, while a subordinate is culturally expected to apologize and the superior is not, the superior or older person is expected to forgive the subordinate or younger person:

> For the elder to apologize to the younger is very difficult. But for the younger to apologize to the elder is much easier. And the possibility of being forgiven is also greater. According to this culture . . . face includes the concept of "The elder should forgive."

> China has a sentence that says, "大人不记小人过" [translated as "A person of great moral stature does not remember the offenses committed by one of low moral stature."] As the elder person, one should overlook the younger person's errors or faults. This is how a good elder person behaves. In this way, he gives the impression of being a very tolerant, magnanimous, generous, and forgiving person. An older person is required to be tolerant and find it easier to forgive others.

In short, culturally, an elder is to be magnanimous while a subordinate is to be humble.

The challenge with this expectation of elder forgiveness is that sometimes the elder's offer of forgiveness, like the subordinate's so-called apology or reconciliation with a superior, is not given genuinely from the heart. The forgiveness that is offered may be duty-driven, only expressed externally. Thus one person continues to hold something against the other person rather than truly letting go of the issue. Reconciliation hasn't taken place.

Apologizing Puts One in the Morally Inferior Position

Culturally, not only does apologizing risk face and status loss, acknowledging one's shortcomings may result in an individual being lectured at or criticized by others. As demonstrated by Li Qiang in his experience at the Bible study, one general view is that sharing a personal shortcoming or apologizing lowers a person socially and even morally.

Li Qiang described how apologizing impacts one's position and identity relative to others:

> First, when a person apologizes, identity-wise they will feel that "I am a level lower than you." To be lower than someone else means that I am now in a situation where I can be controlled.

> In Chinese culture, the person who apologizes has placed themselves lower than the other person. "You have rights over me: I can't hurt you, but you can hurt me."

> If I am going to apologize, first I must accept that I am lower than you. Face, however, says that I cannot be lower than others, thus there's a tension.

Chinese people view apologizing as a weakness. One who apologizes admits his mistake, right? So if you compare someone who has made a mistake with someone who has not made a mistake, the first will be lower, right?

Chinese culture has moralized everything. So, someone who makes a mistake is flawed, has shortcomings, is deficient. A person who morally has not made mistakes is higher. They can then comment on and criticize, be critical of, the one who has made a mistake.

Making a mistake, or rather, apologizing for making a mistake, has high stakes associated with it. It's as if choosing to apologize is the equivalent of voluntarily exposing oneself to danger or harm.

Supporting Li Qiang's perspective, Liu Yang described some people's tendency to lecture or advise in response to hearing others share their problems. After Liu Yang vulnerably laid bare a weakness, her small group lectured her. Her gut response was to completely resist all they had to say: "I didn't need their lecture."

Liu Haifeng similarly expressed how, "Apologizing was already very difficult, but then others would lecture me, saying things that I didn't want to hear. So I resolutely did not apologize." In all of these experiences, the person who apologizes places themselves in a vulnerable position which others may instinctively use to further their own status by belittling them.

A NEW APPRECIATION

As a Westerner, this idea that, after an apology, you are now considered lower than the other person was new to me. This awareness fundamentally changed my understanding of the internal conflict processes of the

Chinese individuals with whom I was interacting. I grew up in a cultural environment where owning up to sin or a mistake by apologizing, while uncomfortable and potentially humiliating, was strongly encouraged as an aspect of living in integrity: it is the honest and right thing to do. Apologizing was seen as a relational benefit, honoring God and resulting in deeper trust. As a white American who grew up in a Christian home, the assumption that apologizing means I become inferior to the other person has been absent from my framework. So I perked up my ears and tuned in further when I realized that the Chinese people I was talking with were describing something outside of my experience. I needed to lean in further to better understand what else made apologizing so difficult.

Once I tuned in to this linking of apologizing to a lowering in personal status, I began to see this understanding imbedded in people's comments. Zhang Jing said,

> I think that apologizing is a humbling of yourself. Apologizing is another way to say that we are *putting ourselves lower in rank or are inferior to the other person*, right? First, you must give up your right, your demand to be respected [emphasis added].

And Zhang Min's description of her previous perception of apologizing also had this understanding:

> If I didn't believe in the Lord, if I didn't have this faith, I probably would not set aside face. I would rather let go of the friendship.

> I don't lack friends. So, with the average friend *I wouldn't set aside my social status* and go to another person to say sorry because if I do this, *I will be looked down on*, "You are weak; you are . . ."

But after believing in Jesus, the situation changed. To be a channel of love you should apologize first. This is how faith changed me [emphasis added].

As I heard these comments, I gained a whole new appreciation for the Chinese Christians I knew who had courageously chosen to apologize despite the potential criticism, lecturing, shame, loss of face, and loss of social status that they might experience. Apologizing is not easy for anyone, but I have gained a better understanding of why it can be even harder for those who face the social judgement of being considered morally inferior as a result.

This book focuses primarily on the ways that certain cultural norms shape us. Whether we like it or not, all of us have ways of thinking and personal communication styles shaped in part by the cultures in which we grew up. We each learned to follow certain behavioral protocols in relationships and power structures. Our values and ways of handling emotions have been deeply shaped by the family, school, ethnic, and dominant social and political cultures of our environment and context.[36] All this cultural shaping happened unbeknown to us while we were growing up and just trying to feel safe, known, valued, and loved in this world.

These four cultural norms—externally preserving face as an act of integrity; internally acknowledging mistakes causes face loss; the behavioral expectations of apologizing and forgiving between superiors and subordinates; and the understanding that the act of apologizing itself can place an individual in a morally inferior position—are powerful forces which shape how people respond after making a mistake, sinning, or experiencing conflict with someone. Having an awareness of these cultural norms and their effect further fills out our understanding of why people, perhaps even you, choose to avoid dealing with conflict, and as a result, continue to feel stuck relationally.

INTERNAL FACTORS

Cultural norms are by no means the only factors to impact why someone might feel stuck in conflict. There are a large number of personal, internal factors that should also be considered:

1. Personal pride. Humans tend to overvalue or undervalue ourselves and are excessively self-focused. We often lack humility, awareness, honesty, and preference for others above ourselves (Phil 2:3–4, 21). Our pride stems from a lack of faith and mistrust of God; we rely on our own solutions rather than on God's.[37]

2. Self-reflection skills. We have not learned how to pinpoint and address our root issues, the desires and needs, behind a conflict.

3. Communication skills. We have not learned how to openly discuss our own desires or needs in a constructive, transparent way with self-awareness of our motives. We have not learned to communicate in a way that expresses our consideration of others.

4. Handling emotions. We have little practice regulating our strong emotions or managing them in constructive instead of destructive ways.

A myriad of other internal factors such as personality, emotions, values, personal histories, past trauma, personal communication styles, and how we handle information also influence our thinking and the decisions we make about how to engage conflict and relate to others.[38] Yet when conflict unfolds, we are often unaware of our own and other's internal factors which prompted or enflamed the conflict.

ENVIRONMENTAL FACTORS

Environmental factors and circumstances, which are sometimes but not always linked to culture, also shape and influence us. Zhou Na told me, "I don't know what it's like overseas, but according to our environment in China, from the time we were young, none of us, including our parents, have learned how to properly restore a relationship after having made a mistake." Examples of environmental factors that can complicate conflict situations include:

1. Not having family or social circles that model a proactive way of dealing with conflict. Rarely (if ever) seeing heart-level reconciliation, open communication, sincere apologies, or true forgiveness demonstrated.

2. Economic stress, work/family/housing instability, or adjustment stress due to moving.

3. Power imbalances. The power structures in which we find ourselves dictate certain behavioral protocols. If individuals are not invited to discuss needs and desires openly or to openly disagree, they may believe there is no way out.

4. Power dynamics in relationships which are threatening and cause individuals to feel like they could lose everything if they try to address issues.

5. Authority figures who exhibit manipulative, narcissistic, or other abusive behaviors.

We are frequently heedless of how factors outside of ourselves shape conflict responses. Yet because these and other commonly experienced external factors deeply affect us, it's important for us to take note of them.

We are complex people with many layers of experiences influencing how we respond to situations. For example, trauma affects the majority of us, and therefore affects conflict resolution, but most of us are not familiar with its impact on us or others. The impact that trauma, as well as abuse, have on our conflict responses are important topics that deserve our full attention but are beyond the scope of this book. Some resources for further study are listed in Appendix D and on my website, www.jolenekinser.com.

The shortcoming of looking primarily at the impact of only certain cultural norms is that in actual life, this impact does not take place in a vacuum. The various external circumstances and internal factors, including whether trauma or abuse were part of the conflict situation, all interface with each other.

OUR PERSONAL CONTEXT

In what kind of context did you grow up? I grew up in northern California in a white American, middle-class, Christian family living in a medium-sized town with predominantly white and Latino populations. Many relatives lived nearby, and I was the only daughter sandwiched between two brothers. My family wholeheartedly loved Jesus, was involved in our church community and neighborhood, and regularly interacted with people of other ethnicities through sponsoring refugee families and hosting international students. As a result, I developed a deep interest in and love for other cultures, peoples, and perspectives.

At the same time, I was mostly ignorant and uninformed about many race and injustice issues both locally and internationally. I learned a certain way to exist in the world: how to communicate, handle conflict, and show respect. I also absorbed a set of expectations regarding how superiors and subordinates are to behave toward one another. One could unpack a lot of family and social cultural influences from what I described in this paragraph, yet what I have written just scratches the surface!

As a result of getting an MA in intercultural studies, a PhD in intercultural education, living in another country for fifteen years, and meeting regularly with a coach, I can see some of the ways I have been shaped, for better and for worse, over the years. I'm immensely grateful for the opportunity I had to be immersed in and learn from another culture while overseas which slowly resulted in a better understanding of my own cultural and personal background. Even so, I will be on a lifelong journey of discovering the many ways in which my family, ethnicity, church, and social cultures have and do shape me.

How about you? What family and social contexts did you grow up in? What faith, work, or education has shaped you over the years?

CHAPTER WRAP-UP

Thick books and numerous articles have been written describing the different contributing factors that influence how we think about and respond to conflict.[39] We can impact some of these factors, but some we can't. And after reading this book, you may discover that some factors that you thought you couldn't influence, in Christ, you can!

Considering the various culturally shaped views and norms we all have about conflict, the pride in our own hearts, and all the other internal and external factors impacting us, I have often reflected, *It's no wonder we feel stuck in conflict situations, not knowing how to move forward.* Perhaps you have also thought, with a sigh of resignation, *If so-and-so only expects surface-level reconciliation from me, maybe that's all I should hope for in this relationship, too. It's safer that way.* I hear you.

God has a reconciling Kingdom-culture for us to live within, providing new ways of viewing ourselves, others, and our relationships.

Thankfully the shaping that started when we were young continues throughout life as various beliefs get reinforced or challenged. It is precisely because the shaping continues that we have hope! You and I are not stuck wherever we are. We do not have to live resigned to the status quo. God has a reconciling Kingdom-culture for us to live within, providing new ways of viewing ourselves, others, and our relationships. We come to know and experience God's reconciling Kingdom-culture as we live by faith in Jesus Christ, moment by moment submitting ourselves to Him. Christ in us continues our shaping, giving us great hope (Gal 2:20).

A PRAYER

Lord, I see a little more clearly how so many factors, including my culture, have shaped me over the years, impacting how I respond to conflict. Thank you for your Kingdom-culture that is now shaping me as I submit my life to You.

Please shine a revealing light on my relationship with [insert the name of someone you have conflict with]. *Show me what has kept me stuck in this conflict, unable or unwilling to pursue peacemaking: Fear? Pride? A lack of love? Hindering beliefs about conflict? Wanting to preserve my face and not acknowledge mistakes? Behavioral expectations based on my age or status that restrict me? Power structures?*

I declare Proverbs 3:5–6 today: "I will trust in the LORD with all my heart and lean not on my own understanding; in all my ways I submit to You, and You will make my paths straight." Thank you, Lord. Show me the way forward in my relationship with [insert name of person] *and empower me to take the next step with You and in Your timing. Your divine power has given me everything I need to live a godly life through You (2 Peter 1:3). In Jesus' name I pray, amen.*

REFLECTION QUESTIONS

1. How do you view conflict? (Good, productive, scary, shameful, bad, etc.)?

2. What beliefs have contributed to you feeling stuck in a conflict?

3. Have the cultural norms described here shaped you in any way?

4. What internal and/or external factors have contributed to your feeling stuck in a conflict?

    a. Internal examples: pride; personality; lack of practice looking inside; lack of humility, awareness, honesty, or preference for others above yourself; lack of practice managing strong emotions.

    b. External examples: no family or social role models; power structures dictate behavioral protocols, threatening relational power dynamics.

5. Write a paragraph or make a list describing the cultural environment(s) that shaped you growing up (consider family, social, school, cultural, race, economic, and religious factors).

6. What expectations are present in your family, church, or work in regard to giving and saving face? What about in regard to apologizing and forgiving?

7. In these settings, are you allowed to openly disagree or discuss the real issues of a conflict or would that cause face loss?

THREE

CAN WE LIVE DIFFERENTLY?

MANY PEOPLE LIVE IN A CHURCH, family, or organizational context in which they are socially expected to refrain from expressing personal feelings and opinions in order to keep unity and maintain harmony. Zhang Jing described the fallout associated with only maintaining this type of outward unity:

> In our environment, we really stress the importance of harmony. The mother church that I grew up in really values peace and living harmoniously with one another. So when there was conflict, we would seem to make peace; however, some people chose to leave. Some people had bitterness and weren't able to speak to one another, and then, in the end, left.

When no space exists for hard conversations about differing interests, positions, and ways to meet needs, people often leave a community. As Christ followers, should we resign ourselves to relationships that look fine on the surface but underneath are characterized by intense friction, mistrust, distance, and resentment? Dare we hope for genuine harmony, heart-level reconciliation, and a different way to live in relationship with others?

Thankfully the answer can be a resounding, "Yes!" Those I interviewed described barriers to reconciliation but also the surprising impact of living contrary to cultural norms. When they relied on the Holy Spirit and replaced familiar cultural norms with beliefs and practices consistent with God's Kingdom-culture, they experienced personal and relational change.

The rest of this book goes into detail concerning spiritual and relational insights and practices that have helped many people *change normal* and live differently. However, first, it is vitally important to turn our attention to understanding what makes living out those practices possible:

- God's initiation of reconciliation with us
- God's forgiveness of us
- The impact of becoming a Christian on identity and relationships
- God's provision—His family
- God's call to forgive others

To begin, let's get on the same page regarding what we mean by the word *reconciliation*.

DEFINING RECONCILIATION

The word *reconciliation* is particularly complicated. Because of having been used in many different spheres (religious, political, interpersonal, and community), the term itself is a bit slippery and ambiguous.[40]

Part of the definition challenge for English speakers is that *reconciliation* can be used to describe *an event* (i.e., the colleagues were reconciled yesterday), *a process* (i.e., their marriage relationship is being reconciled), and even *a goal* (i.e., they hope to fully reconcile someday).[41]

Defining reconciliation is challenging to nail down in one culture but even more so in cross-cultural or multi-cultural situations. When conducting my research in China, I discovered that reconciliation, like conflict, is conceptualized slightly differently around the world.[42] My ears perked up as I heard people like Zhang Jing say, "The Chinese type of reconciliation is a surface-level reconciliation. Or it's the parent style of reconciliation. . . . this person is a leader so whatever they say goes. It's that kind of reconciliation." As I specifically listened for how people described interpersonal reconciliation, I realized that those I interviewed used the term in two different ways. Sometimes they talked about surface-level reconciliation, and at other times, they described a much deeper, or truer, heart-level reconciliation.

Surface-Level Reconciliation

Simply put, surface-level reconciliation is a superficial restoration of a relationship.[43] After a conflict, both people behave politely toward one another, cooperating again, but beneath the surface, at the heart level, their relationship remains distant or broken. When some people think about reconciliation, they only consider surface-level reconciliation: "Reconciliation refers to no longer having explosive conflict; everyone seems to be at peace with each other, but the problem hasn't been resolved."[44] Outwardly everyone is polite and things look deceptively fine.[45] Sadly the true relational state is that the conflict issue remains unaddressed and unresolved.

Heart-Level Reconciliation

Strikingly different, heart-level reconciliation not only looks like an improvement in a previously divided relationship, but genuine harmony is also being cultivated or present.[46] Genuine harmony looks like two people being willing to give each other the benefit of the doubt, holding "positive perceptions of each other," and interacting "in a sincere, trustful, active, supportive, accepting, and natural manner."[47] A heart change has happened, and both people are moving in the direction of having an open posture toward each other. Issues are being dealt with. Differences are being discussed and settled when possible. Trust is being restored.[48]

> Heart-level reconciliation not only looks like an improvement in a previously divided relationship, but genuine harmony is also being cultivated or present.

Biblical Reconciliation

In the New Testament, the Greek meaning of the root word for reconciliation (αλλασσο *allasso*) is "to change" or "exchange." *Allasso* is used to describe the exchange of hostility for friendship, the restoration of a friendship after a dispute, and even the establishment of good relations between former enemies. Specifically, the term is used to describe the restoration of a person's relationship with God and others.[49] In the Bible, God uses actions and stories to show what reconciliation looks like—like the vivid demonstration of Joseph's reconciliation with his brothers (Gen 37–50) and the Prodigal Son story (Luke 15:11–32).[50]

Having a clear mental picture of biblical reconciliation is important, but having an experiential understanding of God's heart-level reconciliation with us is critical. Without personally experiencing God's reconciliation, we have no way of knowing whether or not our way of pursuing reconciliation with others imitates God's reconciliation. If you have been a Christian for a while, you might already feel like an expert in biblical reconciliation and be inclined to skip this next section. I invite you to instead read even more slowly and savor, once again, what God has done for us.

GOD INITIATES RECONCILIATION

The Bible details our dire situation and broken relationship with God that has existed since Adam and Eve first stepped away from Him. We are relationally estranged, ungodly, sinners, God's enemy, disconnected from Him, doers of evil deeds, mentally hostile to God, dead in our sins and in the uncircumcision of our flesh (Rom 5:6–10; Col 1:21; 2:11–13).[51] Yet prior to us changing one bit, "God demonstrates his own love for us in this: While we were still sinners, Christ died for us" (Rom 5:8). God acted before any of us ever acknowledged our sins.

God Acted First

At the heart of God's reconciliation with us is a payment for every person's sin. While we were unrepentant and powerless to save ourselves (Rom 5:6), Jesus served us, gave His life as our ransom, and died for us (Matt 20:28). Because of Christ's obedience (Phil 6:8), God "*canceled* the charge of our legal indebtedness, which stood against us and condemned us; He *has taken it away*, nailing it to the cross" (Col 2:14, emphasis added). We were declared no longer guilty and restored to good standing in God's eyes (Rom 5:9, 19). No longer estranged! No longer enemies! All before we took any reconciliatory steps toward God.

"God was reconciling the world to himself in Christ, *not counting people's sins against them,*" (2 Cor 5:19), declaring us *"holy in His sight, without blemish and free from accusation—if you continue in your faith"* (Col 1:22–23a, emphasis added). Whenever I read these two passages, pausing to let them sink in, I find myself once again in awe of God. God's initiation of reconciliation includes such incredible forgiveness; He counts none of our sins against us, releases us from our obligation to pay our debts, and provides freedom from accusing, condemning voices that say we still owe. At the center of forgiveness is a "generous release of a genuine debt," fully, mercifully, and from the heart.[52]

Even as Jesus hung on the Cross experiencing an unjust, shameful, torturous death, He cried out, "Father, forgive them, for they do not know what they are doing" (Luke 23:34). Jesus asked His Father to forgive those who were crucifying Him *before they had even repented.* Wow. Wow. Wow! We typically want someone to repent before we forgive them and are willing to reconcile, but God forgives us even before we acknowledge our sin. This is God's heart. This is God's love in action. I want to jump up and shout with joy!

Forgiveness: The Heart of God's Reconciliation with Us

Forgiveness is at the heart of the gospel—God's reconciliation with us. In the Prodigal Son parable (Luke 15:11–32), Jesus vividly illustrates forgiveness and reconciliation. In the story, a second son demands his inheritance from his living father. This request was horrifically dishonorable, effectively estranging him from the family. Then, instead of honorably using his inheritance, the son wasted all the money in a place far from home. Eventually, trying to avoid starvation, he took on a humiliating job feeding pigs. The pigs were better off than he was. The son then remembered how the servants in his family's household had daily food and shelter. So he thought to himself: *I'll return home and repent and ask to be a servant. Hopefully my father won't turn his back on me, even though I deserve it. At least I'll still be alive!*

As the son approached home, his father saw him off in the distance and ran to meet him. The father welcomed his son back with open arms, having already forgiven him. How do we know his father had already forgiven him? When the son began to speak saying, "Father, I have sinned against heaven and against you. I am no longer worthy to be called your son" (Luke 15:21), his father didn't even wait for him to finish his confession! The son had also planned to say, "Make me like one of your hired servants" (v.19), but his father interrupted him, calling to the servants to quickly bring out the best robes the family had, a ring, and sandals. He even prepared a celebration feast! All the father's actions declared: I have fully restored my son to this family.

In the same way, God has already forgiven us and is just waiting for us to repent. And like the son, our coming home also restores our identity: beloved child of God, member of God's household, co-heir with Christ (Rom 8:14–17; Gal 4:6–7; Eph 2:19). But we must leave our miserable conditions and come home in order to experience God's embrace!

By returning home, life radically changes for us. In God's reconciling act initiated while we were still dead in sin, God made us alive with Christ (Col 2:13). He rescued us "from the dominion of darkness and brought us into the kingdom of the Son He loves, in whom we have redemption, the forgiveness of sins" (Col 1:13–14). In Christ, we are new creations and that's what counts (2 Cor 5:17; Gal 6:15)!

COMING HOME TO GOD'S EMBRACE

What is the path home to God? Jesus Christ.

Jesus said, "I am the way and the truth and the life. No one comes to the Father except through me" (John 14:6). Specifically, we are to:

- *Listen* to Jesus' words and *believe* Jesus (John 5:24)
- *Look to Jesus* and *believe* in Jesus (John 3:36; 6:28–29; 6:40)
- *Demonstrate faith* (Matt 9:5–6; Luke 5:20; 7:47–50)
- *Rely on faith*, nothing else (Rom 5:1–2; Gal 2:15–16; 3:11, 13–14)
- *Repent, turn to God,* and *be baptized* (Luke 5:32; Acts 2:37–38; 3:19; 5:31)

Once we return home, repentant, we experience God's embrace—His reconciling heart toward us as demonstrated through His extravagant forgiveness.

When the reality of how God loves us sinks into the depth of our being and we experience freedom from the guilt and shame of our sin, as well as from whatever condemnation has been heaped upon us, gratitude overflows. We reflect the same joy that John conveys in 1 John 3:1–3:

> See what great love the Father has lavished on us, that we should be called children of God! And that is what we are! . . . Dear friends, now we are children of God, and what we will be has not yet been made known. But we know that when Christ appears, we shall be like him, for we shall see him as he is. All who have this hope in him purify themselves, just as he is pure.

This kind of experiential, heart-level, spiritual understanding changes our lives.

The Impact of Becoming a Christian

As we follow Jesus, experiencing reconciliation with God, and receiving the Holy Spirit, our lives begin to change. When I asked Li Jie where his strength to apologize comes from, he excitedly said,

> Actually, my real change started from my faith and the change it brought me. When I first started studying biblical peacemaking, I wasn't baptized yet. It wasn't until after I was baptized that I truly *experienced the leading of the Holy Spirit in the faith*, in learning His way of truth. It was only from being in the faith that I was able to truly go deeper in understanding about resolving conflict. So, *my faith is what has led to my transformation*.

These fundamental spiritual shifts in our hearts lay the foundation for an openness to engaging in a reconciliation process with others.

For Su Lijuan, being saved by God played a large role in her improved relationship with her father:

> It was only after I was saved that "my heart of stone was turned into a heart of flesh." I believe that the change in my relationship with my dad is primarily related to this.

> Before I was saved, my attitude toward my dad was one of responsibility and obligation. I didn't have any love for him because he had never given a father's love to me . . . I thought: *He is my father; he raised me. I have a responsibility to take care of him when he is old.* But I truly thank God; after I was saved, I started to have more and more feelings toward my dad. I discovered that I love him.

For many, their personal change first impacts their relationship with immediate family members.

To recap:
God initiated an incredible reconciliation with us.
We can't pay the debt to cancel our own sins; Jesus paid.
Through Jesus' death, God made it possible for our relationship with Him to be fully restored.
And God did not wait for us to repent before forgiving us.
God forgave us first.
God restored our position in His family.
We have much to be grateful for,
but there is still more good news for us!

God Provides Even More

Jesus' death on the Cross accomplished far more than our personal reconciliation. God reconciled all creation to himself (2 Cor 5:18–19). God "was pleased to have all his fullness dwell in [the Son] and through him to reconcile to himself all things, whether things on earth or things in heaven, by making peace through his blood, shed on the cross" (Col 1:19–20). Personally, I have not yet begun to fully comprehend the magnitude and daily impact of what God's reconciliation of *all things* to himself means, but I know this reality is truly awesome.

Paul became more specific in his application of God's reconciling work by describing Jesus *as* our peace. Jesus purposed to create in himself one new humanity out of two previously hostile groups: Jews and Gentiles. In Scripture, *Gentile* refers to any person(s) who is not

Jewish by descent and does not believe in God. Belief in God and being in covenant relationship with Him, following His set of commands and regulations, distinguishes Jews from Gentiles. Gentiles do not have this original covenant relationship with God. Today, all of us who are not Jewish by birth fall into the Gentile category.

Yet Jesus reconciled both groups to God *and to each other* through dying on the cross "by which he put to death their hostility." God "destroyed the barrier, the dividing wall of hostility" between Jews and Gentiles, "by setting aside in his flesh the law with its commands and regulations" (Eph 2:14–16). This was window-rattling, earth-shaking news. All the regulations that Jews followed as part of their covenant relationship with God would *no longer serve as the basis for a covenant relationship* moving forward. God completely removed the distinctions and, with Jesus' shed blood as the covenant's foundation, gave a new covenant open to *all who believe*: Belief. Faith.

All May Come

Jesus's sacrifice not only changed up the steps to covenant relationship with God, it made both Jews and Gentiles *equally able* to be in covenant with Him. All can be God's children—God's chosen people. Paul said that those who are far away from God (referring to the Gentiles) have been brought near to God by the blood of Christ (Eph 2:13). To those of Paul's day, these changes were radical, almost unbelievable. Yet Jesus' statements confirmed that God was serious about His inclusivity:

1. "*No one* can enter the kingdom of God unless they are born of water and the Spirit. Flesh gives birth to flesh, but the Spirit gives birth to spirit" (John 3:5–7). **No one includes** Jews and Gentiles.

2. God loved the *world* so much "that he gave his one and only Son, that whoever believes in him shall not perish but have eternal life" (John 3:16). **The world includes** Jews and Gentiles.

3. "*Whoever* believes in him [Jesus] is not condemned, but whoever does not believe stands condemned already because they have not believed in the name of God's one and only Son" (John 3:18). **Whoever includes anyone:** Jews and Gentiles.

4. "This is my blood of the covenant, which is poured out for *many* for the forgiveness of sins" (Matt 26:28). **Many:** Jesus does not specify or distinguish Jews and Gentiles.

5. Unless you "eat the flesh of the Son of Man [Jesus] and drink his blood, you have no life in you" (John 6:53). *Whoever* eats Jesus' flesh and drinks His blood has eternal life, will be raised up at the last day, remains in Jesus, and Jesus remains in that person (John 6:54–55). **Whoever includes everyone:** Jews and Gentiles.

No matter where we come from or who we are, all who believe in Jesus are now members of one family. In Christ, "we, though many, form one body, and each member belongs to all the others" (Rom 12:5). We are one spiritual family together in Christ, no longer foreigners or strangers to each other (Eph 2:19).

We must no longer treat some people as superior and others as inferior based on being in or out of covenant with God (Jews/Gentiles), their status in society (free/slave), their obedience to religious regulations (circumcised/uncircumcised), or even one's prior degree of foreignness or savageness (citizenship or historical political relations).

Christ is *in all* and *is all* (Col 3:11). *All* who are in Christ are part of God's family and are to be treated as family. Much of the rest of the New Testament teaches us how to live as this spiritual family.

The End of Labeling

Jesus' shed blood on the Cross decisively put an end to labels and social class rules determining who should be treated as God's chosen people. Our citizenship, the groups we belong to, the labels we utilize, our various identities, all mean nothing when it comes to determining who is in and out of God's family. As people hard-wired to prioritize our relationships with immediate, blood-related family members, to expand or change the requirements for who belongs in that circle of immediate family members can be quite challenging.[53] Jesus broadened the circle, and I must admit that it often feels uncomfortable (Matt 12:48–49).

Coming together as one family to worship the Lord can be difficult for us. Sometimes God brings Christians our way whom we don't particularly like, who differ significantly from us, or who come from parts of the country or world where the political views or culture are radically different from ours. Sometimes people even come from places with historical hostilities, including persecution or genocide, to our biological and cultural families. Emotional barriers may exist. There may be times when you or those you lead need to work through past hurt, betrayal, hatred, or other experiences in order to embrace certain people as family members. While not often discussed, such issues need to be sensitively and lovingly addressed and healed.[54]

Let's regularly ask God to show us when we personally or our families, churches, or organizations have been less than genuinely welcoming, loving, and caring for all brothers and sisters in Christ whom God brings our way. May the Holy Spirit show us when our thoughts or unconscious behaviors are judgmental or demeaning, when we make assumptions about others based on where they come from rather than viewing them as fellow image-bearers of God's image and new creations in Christ. Together we are on a lifelong, grace-filled, journey of growing in Christ. When we see that our thinking or behavior falls short of loving others as family, we need to repent, come back to Scripture to learn, and, relying on the Holy Spirit, implement what being family looks like.

RESPONDING TO THE CALL TO FORGIVE

Any conflict bumps us up against a thorny question: are we only supposed to be peacemakers and pursue reconciliation when we are in the wrong, or are we also supposed to be peacemakers when someone else has wronged us? In Romans 12:18 (ESV), my go-to peacemaking answer, Paul states: "If it is possible, so far as it depends on you, live peaceably with all." The context here is a situation where someone has been wronged. Instead of seeking revenge, we are to "overcome evil with good" (Rom 12:21). Much easier said than done, right?

Scripture also instructs us, "Be kind and compassionate to one another, forgiving each other, just as in Christ God forgave you" (Eph 4:32). As God's beloved, chosen by Him, we are to "put on a heart of compassion, kindness, humility, gentleness, and patience; bearing with one another, and forgiving each other, whoever has a complaint against anyone; just as the Lord forgave you, so also should you" (Col 3:12–13, NASB). In practice, however, we often find forgiving others to be extremely difficult, especially before they have repented.

Coming to deeply know that we are loved and forgiven by God, despite our sin, can enable us to finally obey God and fully forgive someone else, whether the other person has repented or not. Wang Min described what led to a forgiveness breakthrough in a relationship that had been estranged for nine years:

> This person was a church leader who had discipled me, resulting in a very close, personal relationship. Yet when conflict erupted between this leader and another church leader, I felt caught in the middle. And when, in the discipling relationship, I opened up my heart and shared some of my personal weaknesses with this church leader, the leader rejected what I had shared and did not respond. For many years, I felt deeply hurt and unable to forgive her. The church leader moved away, but in the past two to three years . . . I found myself face to face with the opportunity to deal with my own feelings and the relationship.
>
> Forgiving has been a difficult lesson to learn in my life. In the past, I found it very challenging to say I was able to forgive someone. My recent change is because I have experienced God's forgiveness.
>
> Every week my husband and I take communion together. This year God has used the process of taking communion to soften my heart. God let me see His sacrificial love for me. I have believed in the Lord for over ten years and knew this truth, but only recently did God do this deep work in my heart, and I truly understood God's forgiveness. Realizing that we all sin, we're all the same, suddenly enabled me to let go of the hurt caused by this leader.

Although there are many facets to Wang Min's story, experiencing a deeper understanding of Jesus' sacrifice, forgiveness, and love for her was the tipping point which led her to completely release her hurt and forgive the other person.

Shifting Focus

Peter asked Jesus how often he should forgive someone who sins against him—is seven times enough? Peter seemed to think that surely there would be a time when it's okay to not forgive. Jesus responded saying, "Not seven times, but seventy-seven times" (Matt 18:22). Jesus then told a story illustrating that Peter's question about how many times to forgive is not even the most important point on which to focus.

In Jesus' story, a servant owed his master, the king, more than a lifetime's worth of money. When the king discovered the amount of money this man owed him, he ordered that the servant and his family be sold to repay the debt. Upon hearing this news, the servant fell to his knees before the king and begged, "Have patience with me and I will pay back everything" (Matt 18:26, BRB).

I had previously interpreted the servant's begging as repentance, but a friend recently pointed out to me that the servant did not indicate any remorse for having amassed such a huge debt. Remorse and repentance might have sounded like, "I messed up. I am so sorry for accruing so much debt. It was irresponsible and unacceptable. I know there is no way that I can pay it all back, but I will change my ways so that it won't happen again. Please, oh please, forgive me." Instead, the servant focused on how he would pay the debt back—his effort to do the impossible.

Even though the servant did not express repentance, the king generously wiped clean the entire debt in response to the servant's begging. Everyone listening to Jesus' story knew the servant could not possibly do what he promised and pay back everything. So when the king mercifully forgave the entire debt, freeing the servant from his obligation, everyone knew the king went above and beyond what his servant had asked for. At this point in the story, Jesus focuses on the king's incredibly merciful and generous response and not so much on the state of the servant's heart when he made his request.

However, that's not the end of the story. The servant then turned around and denied a fellow servant forgiveness of a much smaller debt.

> When that servant [who had been forgiven] went out, he found one of his fellow servants who owed him a hundred denarii [a small amount of money]. He grabbed him and began to choke him, saying, "Pay back what you owe me!"
>
> So his fellow servant fell down and begged him, "Have patience with me, and I will pay you back."
>
> But he refused. Instead he went and had the man thrown into prison until he could pay his debt.
>
> When his fellow servants saw what had happened, they were greatly distressed, and they went and recounted all of this to their master.
>
> Then the master summoned him and declared, "You wicked servant! I forgave all your debt because you begged me. Shouldn't you have had mercy on your fellow servant, just as I had on you?" In anger his master turned him over to the jailers to be tortured, until he should repay all that he owed.
>
> That is how My heavenly Father will treat each of you unless you forgive your brother from your heart. (Matt 18:28–35, BRB)

Through this story, Jesus shows us where we need to put our focus when we are sinned against. We are not to focus on whether this is the third, fourth, seventh, or seventieth time someone has sinned against us. Rather, we are to take time to remember how mercifully and generously we have been forgiven by God. Then instead of angrily forcing our brother to pay for his sin, we are to show mercy and forgive in the same way God forgave us, generously and from the heart. Perhaps Jesus gave us the Matthew 18 story because God knew we tend to focus on other's sins and what is owed to us. Remembering God's forgiveness of our own sin, when we have been wronged by someone else, can strengthen us to obey and imitate God.

No Excuse

In Luke 17:3–5, Jesus adds that we have no excuse not to forgive in response to someone's repentance: "If your brother or sister sins against you, rebuke them; and if they repent, forgive them. Even if they sin against you seven times in a day and seven times come back to you saying, 'I repent,' you must forgive them" (Luke 17:3–4). The disciples' response, "Increase our faith!" seems to indicate that they thought forgiving, even in response to repentance, was incredibly difficult. I agree. Forgiving is rarely easy, especially in cases of abuse, where there is a victim and perpetrator, and in situations where the other person commits the same sin repeatedly.

Jesus taught us that in our daily life with our brothers and sisters in Christ, we are to forgive, forgive, and forgive yet again. However, forgiveness does not mean we never address the sin issue. Just before telling this story, Jesus gave clear instructions regarding how to deal with sin (Matt 18:15–17). We are to both proactively address sin *and* forgive. Later chapters will give examples of what being proactive can look like.

Choices and Consequences

Jesus also makes it clear that, like the unforgiving servant, we also will experience consequences if we do not forgive from the heart (see Matt 18:21–35). To be honest, I wish Scripture was a bit clearer on what those consequences are. From my studies, I believe there is enough Scriptural evidence for me to confidently say the consequences of our struggle to forgive others is not a return to sinner status and removal from God's family. But perhaps, like Peter's question, we have more important concerns to focus on: Will we imitate and obey God? Will we forgive our brothers or sisters?

We must always remember:

- In the same way that we are unable to pay God for our sin against Him, we also are unable to pay for the sins *we commit against others*.

- Similarly, those who have wronged us are unable to pay for the sins *they have committed against us*.

- None of us are able to make things right by paying. *Jesus paid for all.*

Knowing these truths, we can choose *to humbly confess* and *ask for forgiveness* when we have wronged someone. Knowing these truths, we can choose *to generously forgive* when we have been wronged. God is the one who enables us to imitate himself and pursue peace in broken relationships.

Resistance to Forgiving

Yet our hearts may still cry out, "But God, it really feels impossible to forgive!" We then heap shame and condemnation on ourselves for not obeying God. Though we want to lovingly obey Him, we have no desire to forgive the person. The severity of the sin committed against us has devastatingly impacted our lives. We feel stuck in the mud of unforgiveness.

To begin the process of forgiving, you may need to find a safe person to share the whole story with. Sometimes we feel stuck, angry, fearful, and unable to forgive because we haven't fully processed the extent of what happened. Perhaps out of necessity, you have buried the pain and hurt of an event.

You may find it helpful to think about forgiving as a five stage process of moving through hurt, similar to Dr. Elisabeth Kübler-Ross' five stages of grief. "Since any hurt is a loss that is like a small death, we pass through these same five stages in forgiving a hurt."[55]

1. **Denial:** "It didn't really bother me."

2. **Anger:** "It's their fault that I'm hurt."

3. **Bargaining:** "I'll forgive if they apologize."

4. **Depression:** "It's my fault that I'm hurt."

5. **Acceptance:** "I'm not glad for what happened but I'm glad for the gifts that came out of it."[56]

Dennis Linn, Sheila Fabricant Linn, and Matthew Linn, who conduct retreats and speak around the world, point out that when we share these stages of pain with a significant other, we automatically move through this process which heals emotional and spiritual wounds.

Together with God and a safe person, you can name sin as sin and process how the incident and the pain have impacted you. Telling someone the whole truth of what happened can be a critical step in receiving healing and getting to the place where your heart can forgive. *Forgiveness requires great courage.*

Releasing Someone to God

Personally, I know the struggle to forgive. While I'd like to say that I am always quick to forgive, that's not the case. Occasionally I have needed to talk through a situation with a therapist, coach, or mature Christian friend, multiple times!

Sometimes I will do something tangible to help me, such as drawing a cross on a piece of paper and writing on it, "Jesus died for the forgiveness of [name of person]. He paid the debt they owe me." Next to the cross, I list out all the wrongdoing, sin, and disappointments. I allow myself to feel whatever emotions surface and acknowledge them. When my heart is ready, I then write, "I forgive because Jesus already paid the debt for these things. I will let go of what is owed to me." Accepting that Jesus died for the sin that was committed against me, that He paid this debt too, helps me release and forgive. I know that one day God will either bring that person to repentance or they will face the consequences of their sin (Rom 12:17–21).[57] I can let go. A physical and visual act like this, perhaps completed over a period of time instead of in just one sitting, can help our hearts and bodies more fully forgive.

Unfortunately, in this broken world, not every person is safe to be in relationship with, so sometimes we need to forgive but not pursue reconciliation. Forgiveness and reconciliation are not the same thing:

1. When reconciliation happens, forgiveness is a critical contributing component, but forgiveness, in and of itself, does not reestablish a relationship with another person.

2. Forgiveness can be granted by someone with or without interacting with the other person.

3. Forgiving someone does not obligate you to seek immediate reconciliation with someone who is unrepentant.

In unsafe relationships where physical boundaries are needed, reestablishing an in-person relationship is not advisable. In fact, in certain situations, reconciliation should only be considered when the other person has demonstrated genuine changed behavior.[58]

RECONCILIATION VERSUS PERSONAL PEACEMAKING

In conversation, Liu Haifeng commented, "I think true reconciliation is very difficult. I don't think it's possible to say that in one's whole life, all relationships will be reconciled." It's true that sometimes we live out Romans 12:18, doing our best to pursue peace with someone, but do not end up reconciled. Since not all relationships will be reconciled, we need to understand that there is a difference between personal peacemaking and reconciliation. The following personal story illustrates this distinction.

In one season of working in China, a woman began slandering my team and I to local Chinese church leaders. At first, I was angry, fearful, and avoided seeing her. I felt I couldn't look her in the eye, and I didn't know what to do. Besides feeling deeply hurt, I wondered, should I defend myself to the church leaders or ignore it?

At that time, God arranged for me to attend a biblical peacemaking training in Hong Kong. Through the training, I came to realize that whether or not the woman who had slandered me was willing to apologize, I still had to choose how to think and feel about her in my heart.

I still had to come to terms with the question: What does it mean to live peaceably with her, as far as it depends on me, according to God's modeling? That was my moment to learn that God was calling me to forgive her in the same way that He had forgiven me—before I had confessed anything.

> When our forgiveness of another is not dependent on their confession, we are no longer bound to the other person with their choices dictating ours.

By forgiving her prior to her confessing her wrongdoing, I could shift to having an open posture in my heart toward her. My heart was ready to reconcile if she was willing. For me, the game changer was realizing that I must make my own independent choices no matter what choices the other person makes. When our forgiveness of another is not dependent on their confession, we are no longer bound to the other person with their choices dictating ours. Guided by and relying on the Holy Spirit, we do our best to live peaceably with others.

This story demonstrates personal peacemaking. As far as it depended on me, with God's help, I did my best to live peaceably with her by

1. Recognizing and acknowledging before God how she had hurt me and sinned against me;

2. Searching my own heart to see if or how I had contributed to or exacerbated the problem;

3. Attempting to talk with her;

4. Forgiving her even though she never admitted wrong.

Though I reached out to her, unfortunately, to date, she has not been willing to meet and reconcile. Through Jesus' death, God made my reconciliation with anyone possible, but for reconciliation to be actualized, just like in our relationship with God, confession and forgiveness must be given and received.

Reconciliation happens when both parties engage in personal peacemaking, often beginning when one party humbly initiates and the other softens in response. If one of the parties is unresponsive or unwilling to pursue peace, reconciliation doesn't happen. Confessing sin, acknowledging harm, making reparations for damage done, and changing one's behavior, together with granting and receiving forgiveness, are critical aspects that enable genuine reconciliation to happen.

RECONCILIATION RESULTS

When sharing their stories with me, people often sighed when describing surface-level reconciliation with others as the expected norm in their communities. But they got bright eyes and spoke with excitement when describing how their personal experience of God's reconciliation with them made genuine reconciliation with others possible. Reconciliation with others looked like deeper and stronger relationships, new expressions of care, and reengagement with renewed cooperation:

- After a reconciliation, Yang Lin said, "My heart was set free. Even now, when we have some connection with each other, it is all very good."

- Wang Fang explained that, after reconciling, subsequent conflicts with her Christian colleague were not as large: "For the next three years, I saw that we were able to complement each other very well."

- Describing her reconciled relationship, Wu Chunhua said, "I feel more secure, safer, now. I can speak openly, and she will listen; she can speak, and I will listen."

- In another relationship, she said, "After reconciling, I feel comfortable, at ease; the atmosphere is very relaxed and happy."

- Li Ailing described her husband as "no longer blaming me, no longer complaining. Now he respects me, he supports me going to church and doing church activities."

- After reconciling in her marriage, Chen Dandan said, "I no longer hold a grudge against him or avoid him."

- Chen Dandan also expressed that "after conflict, I especially treasure our differences and feel that both the differences as well as the person who is different from me have many strengths."

Wu Chunhua described a reconciled relationship as being more beautiful than a harmonious relationship that has had little conflict:

> Two people in a harmonious relationship look like a very pretty glass, which is good. However, in a reconciled relationship, the glass has been broken to pieces. But God will glue those pieces back together again in a beautiful way, maybe using gold. It will be a beautiful glass, even more beautiful, more artistic than the original.

A reconciled relationship can be even deeper and more beautiful because of having worked through something difficult together.

CHAPTER WRAP-UP

In China, I frequently witnessed that as people become Christians, they are changed. After experiencing the joy of being reconciled with God, many experienced breakthroughs in how they viewed conflict, apologizing, face, and forgiveness as they went through a peacemaking study. Yet it is still easy for us to keep following old ways of thinking and relying on our own solutions for relational issues. It is easy to stick to the safety of avoiding conflict and accepting surface-level reconciliation instead of relying on the Holy Spirit to courageously live out personal peacemaking and prayerfully seek heart-level reconciliation.

Although pursuing heart-level reconciliation may feel dangerous, like driving the wrong way against traffic, we are far more likely to get where we want to be with someone when we pursue it. To drive against the flow of traffic like this requires a new source of power and focus. Driving with the flow of traffic, chasing surface-level reconciliation, can seem easier and more comfortable, but it won't get you to the relational place you desire.

As I read through Ephesians and Colossians, I notice a loose pattern. Toward the beginning of each letter, through a prayer of praise or declaration, Paul says (my paraphrase), "Look at how awesome God is! Here's what He did and how He reconciled us! Look at *all* that God has given us in Christ! Here's how He changed us and changes us!"[59]

Paul also explains that he fervently prays for the believers. He prays they will receive a Spirit of wisdom and revelation to know Christ and God's will; have the eyes of their hearts opened to the hope, inheritance, and power that are theirs; and be strengthened in faith and rooted and established in love, able to endure, be patient, and joyfully give thanks.

Paul also prays the believers experientially know and grasp the vastness of the love of Christ so they can be filled to the measure of all the fullness of God and bear fruit in every good work (Eph 1:15–23; 3:14–21; Col 1:9–10).

Only after he shares these things does Paul give detailed instructions on how to live together as a family. We first need to taste God's goodness, experience His reconciliation and forgiveness, and recognize that which is now ours in Jesus Christ. We need to deeply understand that all these gifts are ours because of faith, not because of something we have done or will do (Eph 2:4–10). I think Paul knew that if we weren't clear on where the power comes from to live a life "against the flow of traffic," we would rely on our own striving, thinking we could somehow do it on our own.

Only as we are in Christ and God fills us with knowledge of His will are we able to live a life worthy of the Lord (Col 1:9–10; 2 Thess 1:11). We need to focus on believing and being in Christ! Then God enables us to gain a new understanding of face (see chapter four), live by the Spirit (see chapter eight), and proactively communicate when conflict happens (see chapter nine).

A PRAYER

Lord, living differently is impossible unless You make the change in me. Please do what You need to do in me! I ask for the yearning to have an open heart, to receive all of Your love, and to be released from desires and habits that keep me from knowing and walking in Your ways.

Your act of reconciling with me was one in which You chose not to hold my sins against me (2 Cor 5:19). You proved Your love for me by Christ dying for me even while I was still a sinner (Rom 5:8). You offered forgiveness before I had even an inkling of what I had done and would do—before I understood my sin (Luke 23:24). You made a way for me to come home. And the way to come home, to enter into this reconciliation, is to listen to Jesus, believe in Him and His words, confess, repent, and act in faith. I believe. Thank You for welcoming me home.

You tell me that if I claim to be in the light but hate my brother or sister in Christ, I am still in the darkness (1 John 2:9). Though You have forgiven me, when I claim to be in a close relationship with You but have bitterness, resentment, and hatred toward someone in my life, the reality is that I am still in darkness. Help me, Lord. How can I live out the type of reconciling forgiveness that You modeled? How can I have the strength to loosen my grip, to not hold [insert name of the person you are in conflict with] *sins against him/her when he/she hasn't acknowledged the damage?*

God, expand my own heart. Tear down the walls that are there. I acknowledge my fear, hesitancy, and desire to not be hurt or taken advantage of if I treat all Christians as family. Some places inside me need healing and help. Please teach me what it means to be in Christ together as one family. My own thoughts are surely influenced by my past experiences and culture.

I acknowledge that my ways of relating to the difficult people in my life have left me feeling [frustrated, self-righteous, angry, hopeless, detached, etc.]. *I come to You to learn Your ways today, to walk with You, and to learn Your pace. I submit my whole self to You for Your renewing of my thoughts and perspectives* (Rom 12:2). *Thank You for being gentle and patient with me. I open myself up to Your spirit of humility and gentleness today, receiving the rest for my soul that You offer me* (Matt 11:28–30). *In Jesus' name I pray, amen.*

REFLECTION QUESTIONS

1. What actions, behaviors, and heart attitude did God's reconciliation with us include?

2. What are the key characteristics of God's forgiveness?

3. What do you need to do to begin to prepare your heart for personal peacemaking or a potential reconciliation with a person who is on your mind right now?

4. In what ways do the stories shared here give you hope?

5. In what ways is a current conflict challenging you?

6. In what ways might church life look differently if God's big family in Christ related to each other as "in Christ" rather than as labeled by race, citizenship, marital status, job status, etc.?

7. Who do you struggle to love in the same way that God loves you?

PART 2

THE COMPLICATIONS

AS YOU LEARN ABOUT GOD'S KINGDOM-CULTURE and more deeply understand your identity as a child of God, part of one spiritual family in Christ, you may find yourself emboldened, challenged, or both. Part of the challenge is that our transformed identity does not come through our own efforts to become better versions of ourselves or through beating ourselves up with condemnation, hoping to motivate change. Our transformation comes as we are crucified with Christ, He lives in us, and the Holy Spirit empowers our inner being (Eph 3:16–17). In Jesus Christ, we are not only given hope for the possibility of changing what has been normal, but we are genuinely transformed!

> Galatians 2:20 "I have been crucified with Christ and I no longer live, but Christ lives in me. The life I now live in the body, I live by faith in the Son of God, who loved me and gave himself for me."

Discovering that our understanding of who we are and how to relate to others is different from God's understanding can be incredibly freeing, but it can also create internal distress, particularly as it relates to face. Whether we realize it or not, face is an integral part of all of us but has been marred by the Fall. How we relate to our own face and the face of others often dictates our conflict responses as well as our peacemaking steps. In transforming our identity, God also transforms our face. But this transformation may start with a painful stripping away.

Allow me to encourage you with an image to carry with you on this journey through inner turmoil. A computer needs regular updates, debugging, and rebooting to stay healthy, right? Like a computer, we also want our "hard drive," which holds our understanding of ourselves—our identity, purpose, and value— to be healthy. Just as a computer unknowingly downloads bugs and viruses into its system, we also unknowingly download the values and norms of culture and society into our "system." Many of these values and norms are good, but mixed in are some bugs and viruses.

We need constant virus-protection and updates. Spending time reading God's Word and abiding in Christ debugs and updates our ways of thinking, attitudes, and perspectives. For many of us, this debugging and updating has not yet touched our internal software related to face, status, power, looking out for the interests of others, or apologizing. The bugs and viruses related to face issues are particularly damaging and need to be discovered and removed.

Following the debugging and updates, a computer must be rebooted in order to effectively function again. Similarly, as you read this chapter and see ways of thinking that need updating or debugging, remember to pause and take time with God in prayer to receive the update, virus removal, and rebooting your hard drive needs to function optimally.

FOUR

FACE MATTERS

TO BEGIN THE DEBUGGING PROCESS, let's start with the challenging subject of face. As people share with me about their struggles with face, many questions surface:

- Who and what currently determines my identity, value, worth, and acceptance in society and in life?

- Is face bad? Should we try to get rid of face?

- As Christians, what should our approach to face be?

As I mentioned in the introduction, *face* in the Chinese context refers to each individual's perception or awareness of their own reputation in the eyes of others which then forms the basis for their personal sense of integrity, honor, shame, prestige, and dignity.[60] Chris Flanders, researcher and missionary, describes face at its core: "Face is about the pervasive human attempt to establish a sense of worth and meaning ('esteem') and to find acceptance (esteem that is 'social')."[61] Simply put, a person feels they possess face when they perceive that their reputation is intact, they feel solid and respected in their identity, and they feel accepted and socially affirmed as having value to others and their community.

Many Christians consider face to be a negative and significant hindrance to living the Christian life. Wang Lei said, "In my heart I know that face is something that *only hurts us*; the more you care about face, the more you hurt yourself."

Li Jie explained, "The concept of face is a very important fact *hindering* us from apologizing."

Likewise, Wang Min emphasized that

> Face doesn't help reconciliation at all. If no one else is present to mediate and a person has been shamed in a group, they will not reconcile because they feel like they have lost face. Even if they were clearly wrong, they won't admit it.

> When a person is paying attention to face, they would rather die before reconciling. Or they reconcile at the surface-level, only reconciling in response to the pressure of someone else being present.

In light of such issues, these Christians view paying attention to face as an obstruction to any kind of genuine reconciliation.

Like many others, I have also viewed face as hurting and hindering, akin to pride, so I was excited when I learned that a different perspective on face is available to us. Chris Flanders presents the idea that face, in and of itself, is not bad, negative, or a hindrance. In fact, the existence of face—where face is described as one's sense of worth, meaning, and acceptance based on our good reputation—is part of God's plan for humanity. God instilled in the human heart the longing for acceptance and affirmation of value which are the roots of face.

Our face-problems stem from looking in the wrong places for our face-needs to be met. We constantly look to those around us to give us face or determine our face, but the only source of lasting face is God's Face, mediated to us through the face of Christ (which is intended to be experienced in Christian community *in Christ* as well). But I'm getting ahead of myself. First, let's briefly explore some aspects of Flanders' theology of face.[62]

A FACE-GIVING GOD

Flanders argues that the concept of face was not a result of sin entering the world at the Fall but was present in a positive way pre-Fall. God created us in His image (Gen 1:26–27), which is by nature relational (Father, Son, and Holy Spirit).[63] As God exists in relationship, we too exist in relationship. Thus, we are hardwired to desire being in peaceful, joyful, and harmonious relationship with others in community. Face is "a natural product of relationality," and a gift from God that structures our identity and relationality at a basic level.[64] God intended that we would sense acceptance, affirmation, worth, meaning, and esteem in our relationship with Him and others. Giving and receiving acceptance and affirmation of value through the mechanism of face establishes harmony in community which *is how God intended things to be*. Thus, at this basic level, Flanders suggests "we can offer a qualified acceptance of face."[65]

From the beginning, God was relationally involved with Adam and Eve and met their face-needs for acceptance, esteem, and affirmation of value. Prior to humanity's fall, as recorded in Genesis, open and transparent communication and harmony occurred on all levels between God, humankind, and the world. Though physically naked, Adam and Eve felt no fear; they had nothing to hide from God (Gen 2:25). In face terms, Adam and Eve perceived that their reputation was intact, their identity was secure, and their value was affirmed.

Only when Adam and Eve disobeyed God did they feel afraid and view their nakedness as something shameful to be hidden (Gen 3:7). Instead of coming to God, confessing their sin, and seeing what God would do, they hid, no longer connecting or getting their face-needs met through the Face of God. From that point on, people have used negative face-saving strategies— such as hiding and denial—to respond to situations in which they feel shame, embarrassment, and loss of face.[66] Being afraid, experiencing shame, and hiding from God and others *did not exist prior to sin*.

The Importance of Face Connection

Flanders describes how a biblical mention of the literal face of a person metaphorically represents their presence. "To know someone's face is thus to know the person. To seek the face of someone is to seek the person."[67] Psalm 24:6 refers to "the generation of those who seek him, who seek *your face*, God of Jacob." The psalmist of Psalm 67:1 prays, "May God be gracious to us and bless us and make *his face* shine on us." Job talks of how a person "will see *God's face* and shout for joy; [God] will restore them to full well-being" (33:26) after praying to and finding favor with God. In Deuteronomy 31:18, God talks about *hiding His face* because of the Israelites' wickedness. Thus, the Bible connects seeking, seeing, and experiencing God's face with God himself.

Flanders also describes the significance of connecting with a person's physical face for healthy development. In childhood, our early formative experiences of face are typically with our mother or significant caregiver. As a child, when we see our caregiver's expressive and engaging face, we experience their comforting presence and love. Flanders notes that "our earliest experience with relationality, acceptance, and esteem grows out of this connection."[68] Our sense of well-being—acceptance and affirmation—is initially rooted in this physical face connection.

We experience comfort and love through seeing our caregiver's face, and sometimes when our caregiver is absent, we experience anxiety. In response, a yearning for continuous acceptance and affirmation develops and roots in the very nature of our being. We then seek this security in various human relationships, striving to have our face-needs met through others. But people always leave. They are unable to be sensitively and responsively present every time we want them to be, so we feel anxious.[69]

Relationship with God is the only answer to this affirmation anxiety:

> The Face of God, which meets us in the face of Christ, establishes, in no uncertain terms, that God accepts us in full and esteems us as possessing incalculable value. Unlike both the mother's face and all subsequent face experiences in life, this Face is a continuous and perfectly consistent one."[70]

Only God will never leave us nor forsake us; there is no human being truly capable of this. Through a deep connection with the Face of God, our face-needs can be fulfilled!

> The Face of God in the face of Christ is one that is completely true, completely loving, and completely for us.

> It is in the experience of being faced by the Face of God that we gain a new and true face. We come to be esteemed and accepted by God and, by extension, his worldwide people. God then, is the ultimate giver of face, yet such is always a true face. Indeed, from this perspective, the acceptance and esteem that come from God forms the only proper source for human face. . . . . [God] faces us with a face of grace and ratifies our innate human face needs to be esteemed (honor) and accepted (community). It is in these ways that the Face of God can function to orient a Christian account of face.[71]

Based on this understanding of the origin of face and its relational purpose, as Christians we don't need to get beyond face or get rid of face; rather, we need to look to God instead of people to meet our fundamental face-needs for love, affirmation of value, esteem, honor, and acceptance. Instead of basing our face on our perception of our reputation in the eyes of others, we should base our face on the knowledge of our reputation in the eyes of God.

Face Fragility

Marred by the Fall, our current face-condition—apart from Christ—is quite fragile. Our face is easily impacted by others when we measure it based on our own perception of our reputation in the eyes of others, not in the eyes of God. What we say or don't say, do or don't do, all have the potential to impact our face. We can gain or lose face at any moment and feel the need to preserve it. When people disagree with us, raise concerns, or point out our mistakes or sin, we unconsciously sense that our reputation is in jeopardy because we feel a loss of face or shame. We get defensive and angry, feeling the need to prove our position or protect ourselves.

And the challenge of living in this fallen world is that our reputation in the eyes of others, particularly those in power, can profoundly impact our daily lives. Bosses give respect or promotions and express trust or support when they look favorably on us. Therefore, like Adam and Eve, we hide from God and others out of fear of our nakedness (sin, disobedience, mistakes, failures) being exposed. And, when we are exposed, we also respond like Adam and Eve: Adam blamed Eve. Eve blamed the serpent. We blame others for causing our behavior rather than taking responsibility for our own actions (Gen 3:11–13).

At a gut level, we believe exposure of our mistakes or sin will ruin our reputation in the eyes of others. Thus, we experience a deep, visceral need to protect our reputation like Liu Haifeng felt in being willing to fight to "keep his clothes on" rather than admit a genuine mistake (see chapter two). How might things have been different for Adam and Eve if, once they realized their nakedness, they openly confessed their disobedience to God and took responsibility for their own actions?

How might things be different if my face-needs are already met by God, and I am grounded in the knowledge that who I am already has God's approval, affirmation, and validation?

When someone points out a mistake or concern with some aspect of my work, my unconscious, gut response is to defend: "Oh no, (my nakedness is showing)! They think I'm not good enough. I better explain myself to demonstrate (to them and to myself) that I really am capable." Alternatively, my instinct is to shut down: "Something about me isn't good enough. I better quit. It's better not to try than to make mistakes and appear incompetent." It's easy to respond defensively, feeling like my face is in danger so I must prove myself or hide.

How might things be different if my face-needs are already met by God, and I am grounded in the knowledge that who I am already has God's approval, affirmation, and validation? Remembering that the state of my reputation in God's eyes never changes can bring steadiness, calm, humility, and confidence. When we are rooted in the love of God, if someone points out a mistake or concern, we might have the same immediate response as before, but we can follow up differently.

From my own experience, I can now speak to that part of myself that just had my worst fears confirmed (I made a mistake; I won't measure up; I let people down). I can separate my value as a person from my mistakes or sin, reminding myself:

This issue does not define who I am.
How well I do at this does not determine my value, God does.
I make mistakes.
"My nakedness shows."
I am vulnerable.
I won't get everything right.
People will disagree with me.
My mistakes might impact my reputation in the eyes of others,
but God's view of me doesn't change because of mistakes or sin.
God's view is the most important.

From this rooted place, I can take a deep breath and then ask the person to tell me more. When I have made a mistake, I can acknowledge it: "Oh, I did miss that detail! Let's fix it." I don't have to cover up my nakedness and protect my face by brushing off their comments, defending myself, getting angry, and devaluing the other person in the process.

When a mistake has bigger ramifications, I can acknowledge it and express genuine sorrow over having caused so many problems for others.

The same goes for sin. We don't have to beat ourselves up or hide like Adam and Eve did. Instead, we can humble ourselves, admit our nakedness, seek God's Face, be reminded of our true face from God, learn from the situation, deal with the consequences, and thank God for the opportunity to grow. We may need to regain the trust of others, but our God-given value and identity is not shaken.

Possessing face matters. In this world, our foundation for face is shaky and fickle; face is easily lost. Thus, being unable to lose the face that God gives us is incredibly good news!

SET ASIDE FACE?

Based on this understanding of face, do we, at times, need to set face aside? In one sense, definitely. We need to set aside the marred, I-rely-on-others'-opinion-of-me face. Sensitivity to a loss of face and a lack of dying to self keeps us stuck in conflict. To move out of conflict, setting aside this marred face, is necessary.

Li Jun's experience of deep conflict in his marriage forced him to further die to self and go to new places with God. After four years of trying to salvage his marriage through his old practices, he knew he was not going to be successful. God then directed him, saying, "You must *set aside* all your past training, theology, experiences, everything, and return to my Word alone." Li Jun described this experience as a reformatting of his internal hard drive. All that he had previously learned was of no use and had to be erased.

I said to God, "Can you leave a small crack for me to take a thumb drive to save some of it and not have to reformat everything?"

"No, definitely not," God said.

So, I asked God, "If I really give myself over to this reformatting process, will I truly live through it?"

Seriously yet joyfully, Li Jun told me,

It's a kind of death, you know. Furthermore, it is a very terrifying thing. God was merciful. He saved my marriage. I returned to His Word alone. In this way God led me to walk from death to life, confess my sin, and put to death my old self.

When we die to self, we shift away from relying on others or ourselves for face preservation to relying on God, our source of true face. Like Paul, we say, "I have been crucified with Christ and I no longer live, but Christ lives in me. The life I now live in the body, I live by faith in the Son of God, who loved me and gave himself for me" (Gal 2:20). We are now God's beloved children and nothing can separate us from God's love (Rom 8:31–39).

Dying to self also shifts us away from saving or protecting our own face. When speaking about apologizing to one of his younger Bible study group members, Li Qiang explained:

My identity before God is the most important; it is of chief importance. My relationship with others is secondary. If he now views himself as better than me because I chose to *set aside my face* and apologize after doing something wrong, I won't pay attention to this. No matter how he feels about me, how God views me is most important.

By apologizing to his younger Bible study group member, Li Qiang prioritized honoring and loving God over saving and protecting his own face. How God viewed him was of primary importance to Li Qiang, more important than whether someone else looked down on him because he apologized. Using Flanders' framework: Because Li Qiang has already received face from God, gaining or losing face from others does not shake his sense of being valued, accepted, and loved.

A Changed Perspective on Face

Chen Meizhen discovered that, after apologizing, her face was not impacted the way she had feared it would be:

> I originally thought that if I, the leader, apologize, I might become lower than my co-worker. I would worry and wonder: *Will she look down on me*? But after I truly apologized, she didn't look down on me! She still respected me! Apologizing doesn't impact face. So often we assume, "If I go apologize, I'll lose face." In fact, it's not this way.

Su Lijuan went so far as to say that genuinely apologizing restores one's own face:

> What I knew to be true has been turned upside down. Previously, I thought that any time you apologize, the result will be a loss of face. However, if you can sincerely apologize, you actually restore your own face, your own dignity and honor.
>
> Now I teach my daughter that any time you do something wrong, if you can lower your head and humble yourself, you are actually raising yourself up. I have had this transformed perspective.

Her story reminded me of James 4 where we are instructed to humble ourselves before the Lord. God will lift us up.

James 4:7–10: "Submit yourselves, then, to God. Resist the devil, and he will flee from you. Come near to God and he will come near to you. Wash your hands, you sinners, and purify your hearts, you double-minded. Grieve, mourn, and wail. Change your laughter to mourning and your joy to gloom.

"Humble yourselves before the Lord, and he will lift you up."

Li Jie explained how being his true self, instead of exhibiting a fake shell, actually builds closer relationships:

Today, when I express this new life from God, I live out my true self. For example, if I don't have any money, I don't have any money. If my finances are in trouble, I am in trouble. I won't intentionally pretend to live as if I have money. Even in these circumstances, I can be joyful. In this way, I open up my true self, my healthy, joyful self. This is more compelling than something fake—a mask.

So, I got rid of my old views about face. But to completely be rid of them is a process, a very difficult process because we still have our vanity. But we do our best to replace vanity with a life that is true and joyful.

Sometimes we are afraid of other people knowing us, right? But in fact, when I truly open up, people are even more willing to accept me. I'll give an example. We have never bought a car. On one hand, I have felt that if you buy a car, you have to take care of it, and the financial pressure would be high. Public transportation is well developed, so I'll just use it. But sometimes an activity requires a car, so I'll borrow a car from a friend.

I have analyzed this before. If I borrow a car from my friend, will this have a negative impact? I decided that no, it does not, so I started to occasionally borrow a car from my university classmate.

We have a great relationship, but in recent years, we haven't connected as much. But we will connect at least once a year when I need to borrow his car. Every time I borrow his car, he is very happy. Why? I think it's because we have increased our connection, our mutual trust, and reliance on each other. True care is being expressed.

Li Jie discovered that, contrary to general perception, being one's true self can be received and accepted by others.

Each of these people have learned to no longer look to others as their ultimate source of face. Just as Chris Flanders describes, when our face needs are met in the Face of God, we can adjust how we interact with others. Though we may feel an initial sting of loss of face in certain experiences, we can recover and respond in God-honoring ways, remembering from where our true face (identity, worth, meaning, and acceptance) comes.

A FACE-SAFE COMMUNITY: HONESTY

Christian community, be it church, family, or organization, should be a place where people can be honest with one another. Liu Yang, Li Jie's wife, told me of a time when she vulnerably shared their marital problems at a Bible study for couples. Surprised by her transparency, one of the husbands in the group asked her, "Sister Liu Yang, don't you feel uncomfortable when you talk about this?" She explained to me:

> What he meant was, don't you feel uncomfortable face-wise? Li Jie responded to this man on my behalf in a wonderful way. He said, "No. On one hand, we are all brothers and sisters. We are talking about this problem as brothers and sisters. On another hand, I am willing for our experiences to become a blessing to others. So, we don't have the problem of face."

They both felt they had a safe place because the relationships were church relationships.

Christian community should be a place where admitting mistakes and confessing sin is commonplace, where there is no fear of losing face because of an admission. First, we don't fear losing face because our identity is rooted in Christ not in the eyes of others. Second, we don't fear losing face because our community has become a face-safe place.

Chris Flanders described Christian community in this way:

> The Christian community is a laboratory where the Face of God is distilled into real-life attitudes and practices. It is a place where legitimate face needs are protected. It is a sanctuary where people may escape the often brutal face-denigrating world. In a word, the church becomes a "face-safe place."[72]

Christian community is meant to be a place in which we can acknowledge that every person has legitimate face-needs—the need for acceptance, honor (esteem), validation (worth; value), and a secure identity. In Christian community, we can point each other to God to have these fundamental face-needs met first in Him.

As people who have had our face-needs met in God, we can then "image" God's Face to each other. Instead of shaming, scolding, lecturing, or viewing us as lower when we acknowledge a mistake or confess sin, our brothers and sisters in Christ accept, love, forgive, and support us to "go and sin no more" (John 8:11b, NLT). In this way, we not only experience God's acceptance and affirmation of our value directly from Him but also through each other. And even if we do feel a loss of face because those around us fail to imitate Christ as they should, we can forgive them and remind ourselves that our identity and true face rests in God. We are deeply loved.

Since we all mess up in life, often daily, it is imperative that our churches, families, and organizations become face-safe communities where we can give and receive apologies and confessions honestly. You might be thinking, *I know that confessing and apologizing is a characteristic of God's Kingdom-culture, but it sure wasn't characteristic of the culture in which my church members or I grew up. Where do we start?* Keep reading! Specific examples, advice, and application is coming (see chapter seven).

A face-safe Christian community is also a place where sin, grievances, and complaints are not ignored.

A FACE-SAFE COMMUNITY: SIN IS NOT IGNORED

On the surface, what I say next might seem contradictory to the last section: A face-safe Christian community is also a place where sin, grievances, and complaints are not ignored. Jesus emphasized how critical it is that we—as Christ-followers—address sin among us: "If your brother or sister sins, go and point out their fault, just between the two of you. If they listen to you, you have won them over" (Matt 18:15). Jesus tells us to go privately and then bring others if necessary.[73] The Jewish and Roman cultures of Jesus' day were much more like current Chinese culture than Western culture. These cultures had a greater sensitivity to honor and shame, face issues, position, and status. Even so, we see Jesus prioritize addressing sin.[74]

Unfortunately, personally addressing someone else's sin can be hard to do well. Our own pride often gets in the way. Sometimes we carry a self-righteous, judging, condemning manner that is highly unlikely to win anyone over. At other times we do not say anything at all because we are afraid of how the other person will respond. These approaches hinder the development of a face-safe community.

Jesus also teaches that we are to proactively work things out when we know someone else is upset with us:

> You have heard that it was said to the men of old, "You shall not murder," and "Whoever murders shall be guilty before the court." But I say to you that everyone who continues to be angry with his brother *or* harbors malice against him shall be guilty before the court; and whoever speaks [contemptuously and insultingly] to his brother, "Raca (You empty-headed idiot)!" shall be guilty before the supreme court (Sanhedrin); and whoever says, "You fool!" shall be in danger of the fiery hell.[75]

> So if you are presenting your offering at the altar, and while there you remember that your brother has something [such as a grievance or legitimate complaint] against you, *leave your offering there at the*

altar and go. First make peace with your brother, and then come and present your offering (Matt 5:22–24, AMP, *sic*).

Our Christian communities would look very different if we developed the regular practices of (1) apology and confession, and (2) proactively talking with those who we know are upset with us.[76] Our communities would not only appear to be, but would truly be, face-safe communities.

To help you develop these types of face-safe communities, much of the remainder of this book fleshes out what these two practices look like.

GIVING FACE TO OTHERS

One important aspect of Chinese culture is giving face to others. Giving face is valued and seen as an appropriate action to take when conflict surfaces. We are expected to avoid saying or doing something that would embarrass or shame another person in front of others. This is a good thing.

But with my American cultural lens, there appeared to be a negative side to giving face. I viewed giving face as a surface-level cover-up, keeping people from being honest and dealing with issues. Internally, I rhetorically questioned: *When conflict happens, should we just give face, say nothing, and go on with life as if no disagreement or difference exists, no mistakes made, or sins committed? (Of course not.)* It seemed to me that giving face could not possibly contribute to creating a genuine face-safe community. Thankfully, I realized I was wrong. Chinese Christians helped me see how God-honoring giving face can be.

For Zhang Jing, giving face is the equivalent of giving respect, so from her perspective, giving face is a positive and appropriate action when responding to conflict. However, she also commented, "Chinese people can take giving face a little too far. They expand the meaning of 'giving face,' but giving face in and of itself is good and has its place." So my question changed from *Is giving face a good thing?* to *What should we do after giving someone face?* Before answering that question, let's look at the benefits of giving face.

Benefits of Giving Face

The act of giving face when in conflict has a number of benefits. First, giving face may keep a conflict from worsening. As Wu Chunhua explained: "If you give a person face, that person will slowly relax and won't be as confrontational and resistant in the relationship. So the conflict will ease up. It won't continue to get bigger." In short, giving face can diffuse a relational explosion.

Second, giving face may keep a relationship from completely breaking down. Sometimes a younger person gives face by apologizing to an elder person just to keep a relationship from breaking. Even if this apology is only an outward behavior and insincere, and even if the resulting forgiveness is because of face requirements and not from the heart, the action has benefits because it can keep the relationship from completely ending.[77] Though not ideal, the relationship has at least been maintained at a surface level, leaving room for the possibility of heart-level reconciliation in the future.

Third, giving face can provide safety in a relationship, creating space to speak more vulnerably. Liu Haifeng gave a beautiful description of how giving face can provide a face-safe place in Christian community:

Everyone has a deep desire to be respected. When we give someone face during a conflict, we are helping to protect that person. . . . For example, when I feel that I am the only person who can protect myself, I will do so at all costs. But when a person gives me face, I will first feel that they didn't hurt me.

Since they didn't hurt me, I don't have to protect myself. Since they helped me protect myself, I know that they are for me.

When I know that the person is for me, I am then willing to bring up my mistake and share it with them. I'll listen to their advice because now I know that they are not in opposition to me. Furthermore, they are standing on my side. I feel this is very important.

Creating this kind of space for more open and honest communication may take the form of offering the other person "a step down." Offering a *step down* to someone means to give that person a way out, a method to avoid embarrassment. Zhao Cheng described how offering a step down in a conflict can help:

Because their reputation suffered less damage and they don't feel so ashamed, it is easier to be more open with the other person. Once they engage in a more honest conversation, then it is easier for the parties to find a solution that works for both, and it is easier for them to forgive and reconcile.

Giving face eases the stress on relationships, keeping doors from slamming shut that might otherwise open wider given time and patience.

There are at least three benefits to giving face in a conflict situation or a potential conflict:

1. Giving face in the moment *can keep a conflict from escalating* and *can allow a relationship to continue, at least at a surface level, instead of breaking down.*

2. Giving face by not immediately, verbally disagreeing, especially if in public, *can be a helpful and appropriate expression of respect.*

3. Giving face instead of immediately pointing out a fault or mistake, especially if in public, *can be considered a compassionate act, one that minimizes embarrassment or awkwardness for the other person.*

This type of face-giving sounds a lot like offering compassion and grace.

More Is Needed

While giving face does have these various benefits, Wu Chunhua described how giving face is a good start but does not go far enough:

> Giving face is a very surface level thing. If you truly want to reconcile with someone, it's not a matter of just giving him face; it's both parties continuing to move forward together. Giving someone face may be a good start, but to reach reconciliation, there is still a distance that one must travel.

At this point, it is important to take our cues from God regarding what to do next. How does God relate to us? God doesn't just give us face, affirming and accepting us at the surface level while ignoring the issues. He doesn't pretend everything is fine relationally when it is not. God genuinely loves, values, and forgives us, *and* He addresses issues, pointing out specific areas such as fear and calling us to acknowledge our sin (see Ps 32:1–11; 103:8–14; Matt 10:31; and John 8:10–12). God purposefully addresses issues with us so we can be transformed (see Rom 12:2 and 2 Cor 3:18).

In order to address root conflicts and live with integrity before God and others, there are times when it is necessary for a private conversation to follow up giving face in public. But there are also times when a conflict issue doesn't need to be addressed.

Choosing to Overlook and Forgive

When conflict happens, sometimes we just need to remind ourselves of Proverbs 19:11, "A person's wisdom yields patience; it is to one's glory to overlook an offense," and choose to forgive and let the offense go. In these situations, you might decide that the issue isn't important enough to bring up. You are able to work through the offense with God which enables you to forgive the other person sincerely and fully from the heart. You are able to let things be. Your forgiveness is reflected in how you continue to have a generous, non-judgmental attitude toward that person. All is still well for you relationally, on both the surface and heart-levels.

> Your forgiveness is reflected in how you continue to have a generous, non-judgmental attitude toward that person

Private Conversation Follow Up

At other times, however, it is imperative to address an issue by having a follow up conversation. For example, if you see someone's sin continuing to harm that person or others, having a private conversation is crucial. Or when disagreement festers in your heart and you find yourself replaying an offensive conversation repeatedly, you first need to deal with God with what's going on in your own heart, but you may also need to have a conversation with the other person. Those thoughts and emotions can easily become lodged as critical judgment or resentment coloring your future relationship.

After studying biblical peacemaking, Li Jie changed his communication style from criticizing people in front of others to giving face, even to someone younger, by talking about issues in private in a non-condemning way:

> In the past, if I was the older person, including being the teacher, I would criticize and find fault with students in front of others without considering the location or their situation. Usually I criticized students in front of others and didn't care about whether or not that mattered. I would say what I felt I wanted to say.
>
> Now, as the older person, including among our church co-workers, when someone does something that isn't right, I will always talk privately to that person to point out the issue. I will share what to do, and if they aren't clear, I will share how they should do it.
>
> Sometimes they should already know how to do it. In that case, I share how I would have handled the situation if I was in their shoes. I won't directly tell them what they should do. This method has had

a much better effect. I especially work hard to talk privately. In this way, we don't experience conflict in our relationship.

So those who serve as elders at our church all have a great relationship; we all go directly and privately to talk to each other when there is conflict. When I haven't done something well, they also remind me. I am still learning and growing in this area.

Li Jie and other church workers have formed excellent relationships with one another: "Everyone is very united. Even though our personalities are different, and our ways of handling issues are different, the unity that we have as a group is very, very, very good." Creating a face-safe community is possible but requires some courageous, grace-filled actions on our part.

Speak Truthfully and Build Each Other Up

In Ephesians 4:25, Paul teaches that each of us "must put off falsehood and speak truthfully to [our] neighbor, for we are all members of one body." In this verse, being truthful is contrasted with lying. Only a few verses later, we are also instructed, "Do not let any unwholesome talk come out of your mouths, but only what is helpful for building others up according to their needs, that it may benefit those who listen" (Eph 4:29). Ephesians tells us to speak truthfully *and* respectfully to others in ways that build them up.

In Christian community, we can recognize and openly acknowledge that none of us are perfect. We are all, like Adam and Eve, naked. While I might need you to restore me today, you will most likely need me to restore you tomorrow. When we see sin in others, we are to show grace and compassion, addressing the sin gently: "Brothers and sisters, if someone is caught in a sin, you who live by the Spirit should restore that person gently. But watch yourselves, or you also may be tempted" (Gal 6:1). When there is trust, humility, and a willingness to give and receive corrective feedback (no fear of causing face loss) in a respectful way, individuals may be more willing to openly share with one another. It forms a positive cycle: because they are united, they are willing to share; and because they are willing to share and humbly receive the sharing from others, they become more united.

CHAPTER WRAP-UP

This chapter offers much to prayerfully ponder regarding face and face-needs. Living in a world marred by the Fall, we have grown up with fragile faces, relying on the acceptance and affirmation of others to determine our value and worth. We have been conditioned to cover up and hide our nakedness—our disobedience, sins, mistakes, and failures. But we are now members of God's family, citizens in His Kingdom, blessed with a new understanding of face! Here's how these two versions of face compare:

The Marred-by-the-Fall and Reliant-on-Others View of Face

In this view, *face* refers to our individual perception or awareness of our own reputation in the eyes of others. Our face increases or diminishes and can even be lost based on what we say and do or based on what others say about or do to us, especially when a third party is present. Giving, saving, and protecting face is about our attempts to find acceptance and establish a sense of worth, value, honor, and esteem.

God's Kingdom-Culture View of Face

In God's Kingdom-culture, *face* first and foremost refers to the reality of our own reputation in God's eyes. Our true, God-given face does not increase or diminish and can't be lost based on what we say and do or what others say about or do to us, no matter who is present.

Giving, saving, and protecting face is about reflecting God's Face to each other as we seek to live in harmonious community. The worth, value, honor, esteem, and acceptance that God has already given us, we also give to one another.

This Kingdom-reality of having received God-given face can embolden us to acknowledge our nakedness to others and help others acknowledge their nakedness as well. By the empowering of the Holy Spirit, we can recognize, repent of, and set aside our reliance on the validation and acceptance of others as our primary source of identity and value and receive our true face from God instead.

Romans 8:14–17 emboldens us to wholeheartedly believe in and accept the face God bestows on us:

> For those who are led by the Spirit of God are the children of God. The Spirit you received does not make you slaves, so that you live in fear again; rather, the Spirit you received brought about your adoption to sonship. And by him we cry, *"Abba,* Father."

> The Spirit himself testifies with our spirit that we are God's children. Now if we are children, then we are heirs—heirs of God and co-heirs with Christ, if indeed we share in his sufferings in order that we may also share in his glory.

I invite you, beloved child of God, to consider making the following prayer a part of your weekly and monthly prayer-life to regularly remind yourself of your source of true face.

A PRAYER

Lord, I believe I am your beloved child and declare these truths today:

- God loves and accepts me, affirming my value.
- In all relationships, I can live out of my identity in God and not live behind a fake mask.
- I can, therefore, humble myself to apologize or confess sin when I need to.
- I can, therefore, humbly and gently address sin in others.
- I do not lose true face based on what others do or say to me or about me.
- I do not lose true face based on what I have said or done.
- I do not lose true face when I acknowledge to another person my mistakes or sin.

Lord, when I begin to feel loss of face or shame because of what someone else has done or said to or about me, I will:

- Acknowledge my feelings without condemning them (hurt, fear, anger, disappointment, embarrassment, sadness, etc.)[78]
- Ask God to help me become aware of my unmet need(s) and my longings and desires (for respect, power, understanding, competence, dignity, communication, participation, etc.)[79]
- Tenderly hold my unmet needs before God
- Turn my mind to God, remember who I am in Christ, and rest in God's love
- Acknowledge to myself and to God that I am deeply impacted by people's words and actions

- Repent of over-valuing the opinions and words of others (or whatever the Holy Spirit reveals to me)
- Remember that I am fully loved by God
- Receive restored confidence that comes from Christ
- Delight in the reality that my true face is intact

Thank you, Lord, for this new Kingdom-culture. You make this transformation in me possible!

In Jesus' name I pray, amen.

REFLECTION QUESTIONS

1. Considering what you have learned in this chapter, in what ways, if any, has your view of face changed?

2. Who and what do you often rely on to give you face?

3. Who or what do you often rely on to protect your face?

4. As Christians, what should our approach to face be?

5. In light of God being a face-giving God, what does it mean for Christians to give face to one another?

6. To what degree does your church, ministry team, or family currently reflect the kind of face-safe community that Chris Flanders describes?

FIVE

STATUS, POWER, AND CULTURAL EXPECTATIONS

IN ADDITION TO FACE ISSUES, status and power differentials are often mentioned as significant barriers to resolving conflict. When I asked Zhang Wei if he would respond in the same way to conflict with someone of an older generation as he would a peer, he replied that he is far more passive with the older generation. For example,

> Suppose my mother-in-law and I get into a conflict. She's not happy with me about something and, in the moment, I don't respond well.
>
> Afterwards, at first I can't say much; I need to calm down. Then I need to deal with my own emotions because I definitely will have feelings of having been treated unjustly. After dealing with those feelings, the next time we are together, I seek peace by choosing to help her with something [shopping, cooking, etc.] ... But if I want to talk about the original conflict issue, that's not very easy to do.

As soon as I attempt to talk about it, she naturally moves into a condescending teaching mode. At this point, it is very difficult. I really have no options. Sometimes, in this type of situation it is impossible to talk about these things. Instead, I just say to myself, "Forget it, we just won't talk about it. I'll just let that thing pass." Whether or not she forgives, I don't know, but for me, I forgive. That's all I can do.

In his example, Zhang Wei describes only using "getting the salt" types of actions, not words, to express his desire for peace because he feels that the way his mother-in-law approaches conflict makes it impossible to dialogue about issues. Yet this approach results in issues not being addressed.

Do you find yourself relating to anyone in your life in this way? While this chapter won't present all the answers you might be looking for regarding situations like Zhang Wei's, it will provide some different questions to ask yourself when conflict happens. As you read, prayerfully consider how power, status, and culture might be affecting communication dynamics in your relationships.

HIGHER AND LOWER STATUS

Over time, all of us find ourselves in a lower position in some relationships and a higher position in others. By the time we become adults, none of us are exempt from being in both positions. Position often determines status.

Take a moment to consider those relationships in your life in which you hold the higher status. You might be the grandparent, parent, aunt, or older brother. You might be the pastor, elder, a church ministry leader, or an "auntie" or "uncle" at your church. Perhaps you are a team leader, coach, manager, or executive director in an organization. Note how many relationships you have in which you hold a higher status than the other person.

Now think about those relationships in your life in which you are the person of lower status. You might be the thirty or forty-year-old child of your parents, the adult grandchild, niece, or younger brother. At your church, you might be a member of a ministry team, of the younger generation, or a pastor under the board. Perhaps you are an employee or middle-level manager in an organization. Note how many relationships you have in which you hold a lower status than the other person.

Being aware of our own status in relationships can help us recognize what we need to pay closer attention to for more meaningful and constructive interactions with others.

TYPES OF POWER

Regardless of our position or status, we all hold some degree of power. And we all have more power than we think we do. Don't resist that statement. It's true. In English, the word *power* means "having the capacity to do something, to act or produce an effect, to influence people or events, or to have authority."[80] Diane Langberg states, "Power is inherent in being human. Even the most vulnerable among us have power. How we use it or withhold it determines our impact on others."[81] Based on Genesis 1:26–28, she explains:

> God created us to multiply his image and likeness in everything we do. God created humans in his own image, in his likeness. Power was given to humans, who reflected the God who made them. And what do we know about this God? He is good; he is faithful; he is a

refuge; he is truth; he is love. So, God gave human beings power in order that they might bear God's character in the world.[82]

God also gave human beings power to be fruitful and multiply; to fill, subdue, and rule the earth; and to do this together, not pitted against one another. As Christians, it is essential to recognize that any power we have originates with God.

When considering the idea of power, most people think of positional power. We see positional power displayed in an interaction between Pilate and Jesus when Pilate said, "Don't you realize I have power either to free you or to crucify you?" (John 19:10).

Jesus responded saying, "You would have no power over me if it were not given to you from above" (19:11). Jesus knew the Scriptures: "Power belongs to you God, and with you, Lord, is unfailing love" (Ps 62:11b–12a). Jesus' response made it clear that Pilate's positional power was given to him by God, and Pilate was tasked with using that power wisely and justly.

While we primarily associate power with position, people possess many other types of power as well:

- verbal (use of words to manage or control situations)
- intellectual (education, skills)
- emotional (the capacity to express, read, and process emotions)
- spiritual (knowledge of Scripture, relationship with God)
- relational (trust-based relational credibility, perceived power, *guanxi*—who you know and can access)[83]
- physical (strength, physical characteristics, gender, sexual identity)
- cultural (age, race, gender, ethnicity)
- resource-related (money, time, material goods)[84]

Recognizing these various types of power is important if we want to actively improve our relationship dynamics.

The relationship between a baby and grown-ups illustrates how even the most vulnerable have power. In the middle of the night, the four-day old infant, Sarah, cries.[85] The adults get up from bed and sleepily respond with either attention and care or anger and neglect. Even though baby Sarah is extremely vulnerable and the adults are in the more powerful position, her cry influences the adults. The adults' response also impacts baby Sarah. "The power of the vulnerable infant to express her needs exposes the hearts of the more powerful adults. Our responses to the vulnerable expose who we are. This is an important principle to keep in mind as we consider the use—and misuse—of power."[86] Regardless of status, we should strive to be self-aware of how we are wielding the power we do hold.

My Personal Power

I distinctly remember having my understanding of my own personal power turned upside-down after reading Eric Law's book, *The Wolf Shall Dwell with the Lamb*.[87] Prior to that, I was oblivious to the reality that some people ascribed certain power to me simply because I was white and my family was upper-middle class. I didn't understand that the society I grew up in conditioned me regarding ascribed power. When I learned this, I was angry and frustrated. I didn't want it to be true. I realized my naiveté; I had much more to learn about power dynamics. Part of my learning journey needed to involve recognizing when power has been ascribed to me. Even though I didn't like the reason for being given power, I had to acknowledge it and decide how to use the power I had been given.

After this revelatory moment in my life, I prayed about what to do. I learned that I can begin to change this dynamic by using the power ascribed to me by others in ways that empower them as well. I can advocate for and resource others. In group discussions or meetings, I can ask questions inviting others to lead the conversation instead of prioritizing my own voice and thoughts. I can follow up anything that I say with a question seeking to draw out what others think and then listen well. Or, when there is awkward silence, I can choose to not say what I think first but wait patiently for others to speak up. Or choose to not speak at all. I began to see that I need to put myself in other people's shoes more often.

Use of Power

Daniel Teater, president of Live at Peace Ministries, once asked a heart-probing question in a workshop, "Are the people you are serving flourishing because of your use of power?"[88] Based on his inquiry, I ask you to consider:

- To what degree are your family members, church members, colleagues, and employees flourishing because of your service to them from your place of higher status?

- To what degree are your family members, church leaders, colleagues, and employer flourishing because of your service to them from your place of lower status?

- When you use the various types of power that others have given or ascribed to you, to what degree do others flourish?

God intends for us to wisely steward the power He has given us. Don't shrink away from it. In his book, *The Power Paradox*, Dacher Keltner says that the purpose of power is to make a difference in the world and to change other people's lives for the good.[89] Certain practices increase personal power:

- expressing empathy for others
- giving
- showing gratitude and respect
- uniting others through story

Yet the paradox of power is that once our power increases, we tend to stop following the very practices that caused others to ascribe that power to us.

Research shows that these practices (skills) get corrupted when we experience increased feelings of power or have unchallenged power. Increased power impacts us in several alarming ways:

- We lose our focus on others; our attention shifts to our own interests and desires and diminishes our:
  - capacity to listen carefully
  - capacity to engage in and understand what others think and feel (empathy)
  - ability to read others' emotions effectively
  - ability to shift our perspective from our own view and look from another person's perspective
  - concern for others' suffering (compassion)
  - reverence for what others give (gratitude)
  - inspiration coming from appreciating others' goodness (healthy elevation of others)
- We act in self-serving, self-gratifying, and impulsive ways
- We pay less attention to how our actions affect others
- We begin to communicate more disrespectfully and rudely

- We are more likely to impose our requests
- Our declarations are more direct
- Our comments, criticisms, and feedback may be too sharp-edged
- We rationalize and justify unethical decisions based on our elevated rank or wealth
- We feel we are above the law and become blind to our own moral missteps while at the same time express outrage at the missteps of others
- We tell stories that divide and demean[90]

Pause and let the impact of increased power sink in. Personally I find it sobering to realize the different types of power I have and the likelihood of being influenced negatively by that power, even though power is meant for good. This negative influence is even more likely to occur when I am in positions of absolute power.

We all need honest, face-safe community around us, people who will gently and compassionately make us aware of when we're being influenced negatively by our own power so we can humble ourselves and actively counter it. We also need to proactively and intentionally invite feedback from others; otherwise, we most likely won't get the feedback we need in a helpful, constructive way. Instead it will leak out sideways from people in forms like complaints, criticism, lack of participation, gossip, distancing, abandonment, or even more extreme behavior.

UNSAFE OR ABUSIVE RELATIONSHIPS

All of us need to seek increased sensitivity and respond in repentance to the Holy Spirit making us aware of when we use our power in self-serving ways. Tragically, some people misuse power through self-service in harmful ways. As a result, it's not always possible in this broken world to have the conflict resolution or peacemaking conversations we desire. For a variety of reasons, including abuse, some people are not safe enough for us to have these types of conversations with. When a person misuses their power and is abusive, it is often necessary to change our communication and conflict resolution approach with that person.

We need to work toward recognizing when we are addressing everyday conflict versus conflict that has escalated to abuse. The South Dakota Coalition Ending Domestic and Sexual Violence writes:

> Conflict can be good and it can be bad. It is good when conflict motivates us to think, grow or do things another way. In healthy relationships, there is no fear when conflicts happen. For those raised in violent homes where a person is out to "win," rather than resolve their differences through talking and compromise, the conflict can move from a disagreement to abuse or violence.[91]

Many words and behaviors experienced in a conflict may seriously hurt or offend, but there is an intentionality to abuse that differentiates it from non-abusive words or behaviors: "Abuse occurs when power is misused in relationship to another image bearer of God to exploit, manipulate, or control the vulnerability of another for their own ends."[92] In other words, abuse involves individuals using control, manipulation, or humiliation tactics that violate or take advantage of another's personhood or body in order to satisfy themselves with no consideration for the other's well-being.

For example, let's consider an intimate partner relationship such as marriage. Typical couples may experience conflict and disagree or argue about many things like household chores, spending, grooming, in-laws, children, and family members or friends. When arguments regularly occur, the relationship might be considered difficult but not necessarily abusive.[93] The chart below outlines similar-looking behaviors in an intimate partnership, differentiating between abusive and non-abusive. Note the purpose or intention of the abuser.[94]

Abusive Behavior	Non-abusive, Normal Behavior
Berating repeatedly or verbally attacking a partner. Verbal attacks are attempts to humiliate or make the partner feel as if something is intrinsically wrong with him or her.	**Raising your voice during an argument.** A raised voice may not be ideal, but it can be a normal reaction to a stressful situation under some circumstances.
Putting down something that is very important to a partner. Putting down something that matters to a partner is an indirect attack on the partner or an attempt to isolate the partner from the person or thing. It's meant to either make the other person feel bad or to control him or her.	**Disagreeing with a partner's opinion or idea.** Respectful disagreement on various opinions is healthy and expected.
Refusing to talk about something that is a problem in the relationship. Refusing to talk about an issue is stonewalling and communicates a message of inequality to the partner that his or her concerns are unimportant.	**Asking for a break from a conversation to cool off.** It's healthy to ask for a break to cool off when feeling that a discussion is no longer productive.
Gossiping or spreading lies or rumors about a partner. Some abusers try to manipulate a partner into staying silent about abuse by claiming the partner is "gossiping" if they tell an outsider. Some abusers may also actually lie and gossip about their partner to keep others from suspecting that they are abusive.	**Talking to a friend or therapist to gain support or let off steam.** It's not gossip if you need to talk about what's happening to gain support.

If you see in yourself any of the actions, purposes, and intentions described under the abusive behaviors column, now is the time to face it and seek help. God delights in us coming to Him in our brokenness.

If you are in a relationship in which you think the conflicts have shifted from disagreement to abuse, do not attempt to have a one-on-one conversation about the conflict issue with that person.[95] It is not safe for someone experiencing abuse to address conflict issues alone with an abuser. It is important to *use the power that you do have* to seek out a safe person to help you navigate the situation, set appropriate boundaries, and get somewhere safe if needed. Using the power you do have to get help is God-honoring and vastly different from the "self-serving" use of power previously referenced. If you don't have someone nearby that you can reach out to, see the resource list in Appendix D for some organizations that provide help.

HELPING OTHERS

Unfortunately, most of us have not had training in how to respond when someone is seeking help from an abusive or unsafe situation. I have done conflict coaching and some mediation work for more than a decade, and only in the past few years have I started to receive more specific training in this area. We need to learn to respond differently to people who come to us for help when their conflict includes abusive dynamics. We also need to pay attention to power imbalances present in relationships and determine if a different approach is needed as a result of those dynamics. Those from a Western cultural background often assume that power dynamics among parties are relatively equal, sharing mutual responsibility, but this is not necessarily the case.[96]

Y. Joon Choi conducts trainings for Korean pastors on how to assist and not harm someone who, when seeking help, describes an abusive situation. In her training, Choi says the best thing for pastors to do is to be present for the person: to listen and believe them. People inevitably ask, "But what if they aren't telling the truth?" *Please give them the benefit of the doubt first.*[97] Proverbs 18:13 says, "If one gives an answer before hearing, it is folly and shame," yet we often give advice, brush things to the side, or move to praying with people too quickly without fully understanding the situation. Instead of just praying with the person and sending them back to an unsafe environment, we need to listen and connect them to the help they need.[98]

In his training for Christian conciliators and pastors, Daniel Teater emphasizes that when a person who comes for help starts describing abusive dynamics, the mention of abuse should be a game changer for how you help them. While your first instinct might be to bring the two parties together to try to work through the issues and reconcile, it is imperative that you slow things down, investigate further, and meet separately with each party as you move forward.[99]

Mariam Ibraheem, the co-founder of the Tahrir Alnisa Foundation, a small nonprofit that assists women facing domestic abuse, says, "Christian leaders often feel they need to investigate allegations of abuse before they can act. That can send a message to survivors that they are not trustworthy." She instructs, "You don't need to hear two sides of the story when someone comes and tells you, 'I'm abused and suffering.'"[100] Leaders simply need to respond by first getting the person to a safe place and then following up on the conflict issues.

In the case of domestic abuse in marriage, many pastors mistakenly try to bring survivors and abusers together for counseling, focusing more on keeping the marriage together than on the safety of the one being abused. As a result, many individuals stay in unsafe situations, viewing staying in the relationship as an act of faith. While both people need counseling, Holcomb says that this should be done separately: "Survivors need safety, hope and healing. Abusers need to learn how to stop their abusive behavior and to take responsibility for their actions."[101] They are each valued and loved by God, but change doesn't always happen instantly. Each person has a difficult path to walk and not necessarily together.

Instead of just praying with the person and sending them back to an unsafe environment, we need to listen and connect them to the help they need.

If you bring an abuser and survivor together for mediation or counseling but the abusive dynamics in the relationship have not yet been addressed, the survivor can easily be retraumatized and revictimized by the help you are trying to provide. Only when two conditions are met should the pastor or conciliator bring the abuser and survivor into the same room together: (1) the abuser is repentant, shows the fruit of that repentance, and is seeking restitution (to make things right), and (2) the survivor is ready and/or has reached a certain place of healing.

To better enable those involved in discipling, counseling, or coaching others in any context to minister in healing ways and to know when to seek help from other professionals, I strongly encourage seeking out learning opportunities related to understanding and supporting survivors of abuse. These resources include but are not limited to teaching on different types of abuse, the impact of trauma, the use of storytelling, and relating to high conflict individuals.[102]

NAVIGATING OTHER POWER DYNAMICS: WHEN TO SEEK HELP

Perhaps you're thinking: I'm not in an abusive relationship, but the power dynamic of the relationship is such that I don't feel able or comfortable to have a one-on-one conversation with the person to discuss the conflict issue. This person has no desire to know what I think or care about.

Time and again people have told me that some of the hardest conflicts to navigate are those with people who are older than them or are positionally superior to them, be it a mother-in-law, parent, church leader, or boss.[103] Many people feel it is personally or culturally impossible to bring up any issue with that superior, even small contradicting opinions or oversights, not to mention bigger issues of significant differences, mistakes, or sin. Even though Jesus taught us to address issues with all people (Matt 5:24; 18:15), internally some of us feel it is impossible. If you are in such a situation, I encourage you to prayerfully get help from someone who will seek God's counsel together with you and can help you process how to respond to the conflict. The person might even be able to facilitate or mediate a conversation(s); however, not everyone is good at doing this. See chapter ten for more on what a helpful companion looks like.

I have facilitated conversations between individuals who, alone, would get upset or stuck and give up before discovering the root interests or misunderstanding that led to the conflict. I have also experienced someone else facilitating a conversation between me and another person of higher status because I couldn't have the conversation on my own. Having someone else guide the conversation can sometimes facilitate breakthrough that might not otherwise happen.[104]

SELF-ADVOCACY IN THE FACE OF INACCURATE ASSUMPTIONS

In some circumstances, we may need help; at other times, God enables us to advocate for ourselves. In 1 Samuel 1:9–18, we meet Hannah, a woman desperate to bear a child. In Hannah we see an example of personal advocacy in the face of significant misunderstanding by the revered priest, Eli. Hannah had been praying in the Tabernacle when Eli noticed her unusual behavior. She was praying in her heart and moving her lips, but no sound could be heard. Eli did what we all naturally do: he drew a conclusion about Hannah based on his observation. He thought, *she must be drunk*.

But instead of checking his assumption and asking Hannah what she was doing, Eli said to her, "How long are you going to stay drunk? Put away your wine" (1 Sam 1:14). Ouch! If I was in Hannah's shoes, I might be tempted to immediately take offense and respond by defending myself and returning an accusation: "I am NOT drunk. How could you think that of me?" Then I might shut down the conversation because of my anger, sadness, and embarrassment over my outburst.

Hannah chose a different response. As a marginalized woman speaking to a person in a position of power—a male religious leader who had misunderstood her—Hannah did the unexpected: she courageously and vulnerably advocated for herself. Speaking with great sincerity and openness regarding her grief, Hannah responds with a plea saying, "Not so, my lord. I am a woman who is deeply troubled. I have not been drinking wine or beer; I was pouring out my soul to the LORD. Do not take your servant for a wicked woman; I have been praying here out of my great anguish and grief" (1 Sam 1:15–16). Hannah speaks at potentially great cost to herself due to her lower status.

Eli believed Hannah and blessed her in response: "Go in peace, and may the God of Israel grant you what you have asked of him" (1 Sam 1:17). Though he initially misinterpreted the situation and inaccurately judged Hannah, Eli changed his response.

Hannah's Self-Advocacy

Hannah demonstrates a positive example of self-advocacy when facing misunderstanding and accusation from someone above her who had not previously abused her or made her feel unsafe (as far as we know). In Hannah we see the following modeled:

1. Be sincere, open, honest, respectful, non-judgmental, non-defensive, and non-accusatory.

2. Speak up when stated assumptions are incorrect and clarify / explain your behavior.

3. Be honest about your emotions.

4. If needed, make a request, asking the other person to change their view of you.

Sometimes, when encountering misunderstanding and injustice where there is a status difference, like Hannah, we also need to advocate for ourselves courageously and vulnerably.

Standing in Eli's Shoes

Eli gives us a good model of what *not to do or say* when standing in his shoes. When we respond with a non-judgmental tone and a desire to better understand the situation, instead of accusation and commands, we can create a safe environment where others (our children, church members, teammates, employees) do not need to advocate for themselves because we have done the work on our end. The specifics of how to proceed depends on the already established dynamics of your relationship, but here are some options to consider:

1. **Hold conclusions lightly:** When you have observed behavior in someone that you interpret negatively, hold your conclusions lightly. Eli's immediate reprimand of Hannah based on his conclusions reflects poorly on him, but his quick change of perspective when presented with Hannah's self-advocacy demonstrates that he was willing to hold those conclusions lightly and change his mind.

2. **Observe rather than accuse:** State what you observe *in a calm, non-judgmental tone* instead of reprimanding or making a condemning accusation. "I noticed you stayed on your phone past our agreed upon time/I noticed you were an hour late."

3. **Regulate your emotions:** Do not let anger control either the tone of your voice or timing of your response. Breathe deeply before speaking; wisely choose a time to respond. Sometimes waiting to address something you've observed can be extremely beneficial to a productive conversation.

4. **Be curious and compassionate:** Ask non-judgmental questions; seek to understand the reasons behind the person's behavior instead of immediately criticizing them. "Can you help me understand what happened?" Pause and listen.

5. **Give the benefit of the doubt:** Practice thinking the best instead of the worst about the person. "Did something happen that kept you on your phone/kept you from getting here on time? Is everything okay?"

6. **Check assumptions:** Check your negative conclusions by gathering more information about the situation through asking questions: "I tend to interpret this kind of behavior as intentionally disrespectful/disobedient. I then feel angry and hurt. Is that your intention or is something else going on?"

7. **Apologize:** When you recognize that your initial response is critical, accusatory, or based on your assumptions, apologize to the person for your behavior. For more on apologizing, see chapter seven.

Choosing such responses lays a foundation of trust and safety for our interactions with others.

CULTURAL VERSUS BIBLICAL EXPECTATIONS

When it comes to a subordinate raising an issue with a superior in a Christian context, does the Bible or one's culture have the greater influence on the power dynamics and communication expectations? The answer is not as straightforward as one might think. Most of us are not consciously aware of who or what influences our responses to conflict.

Benjamin Shin and Sheryl Silzer put it this way:

> When Christians do things in the same way over a period of time, they tend to interpret their preferred way of doing things as the right and biblical way to do things, even though their actions do not always lead to or result in godly behavior. That is, their responses do not produce the fruit of the Spirit, God's *shalom*, or the proper functioning of the body of Christ in their lives or in the lives of those around them.[105]

The reality is that all of us unknowingly interpret the Bible with culturally tinted glasses. In every culture, we all must face and respond to this reality.

Confucian Expectations

The roots of some current Chinese cultural expectations regarding whether a subordinate can or should address an issue with a superior come from the Confucian way of structuring relationships. Confucius taught that the proper structuring of five key relationships regulates all interpersonal relationships: father and son, sovereign and subordinate, husband and wife, elder brother and younger brother, friend and friend.[106] This relational order determines who has positional power, seniority, and authority: "The hierarchical structure of particularistic relationships ascribes the ruler (supervisor), father, husband, and older brother with authority to receive more power or control over their counterparts."[107] These roles are governed by strict ethical expectations as seen in the chart below. Those in the superior role should make decisions following certain principles when relating to their subordinate (i.e., father treats son with kindness), while those in the subordinate role should relate to their superior's instructions in certain prescribed ways (son responds with filial duty).[108]

Superior Role	Father	Elder Brother	Husband	Elders	Ruler (Sovereign)
Make decisions following principles of:	Kindness	Gentleness	Righteousness	Kindness	benevolence
Relate to superior's instructions in the following way:	Filial duty	Obedience	Submission	Deference	Loyalty and obedience
Subordinate Role	Son	Younger Brother	Wife	Juniors	Minister (Officials)

Within these structured relationships, a person's hierarchical status determines their role and the expectations regarding how that person will contribute when in group settings. For example,

> In official settings in China, deference is shown in one direction, from the lower to the higher level of the power hierarchy.... Nobody should behave counter to expectation. This Chinese demeanor stems from Confucius' idea that maintenance of social order depends on every member of society staying in his/her own place in the hierarchy.[109]

It is generally understood that, in life, the subordinate is to obey and defer to the superior and, in conflict, to stay silent and submit.[110] How do these expectations, or any set of culturally influenced relationship protocols, impact one's interpretation of biblical teaching and behavioral expectations?[111]

Interpreting Biblical Expectations

In 1 Timothy 5:19–20, Paul instructs Timothy to publicly reprove elders in the church who sin, "Do not entertain an accusation against an elder unless it is brought by two or three witnesses. But those elders who are sinning you are to reprove before everyone, so that the others may take warning." The public nature of this instruction seems to violate Confucian relationship protocols. Yet as believers, we can't avoid the reality that the Bible clearly states church leaders must not be exempt from having their sin addressed. How should we apply this teaching? Does "reproving before everyone" mean that an elder who sins should be publicly chastised at a Sunday morning service? How much should be said? Who should say it? Which sins should be addressed in a public way? Unconsciously, we often rely on our culture to be our primary guide regarding how to respond to such practical questions.

In Titus 1:6–9, Paul says that an elder, among other things, must not be overbearing, quick-tempered, given to drunkenness, or violent. How does one decide what is violent versus acceptable behavior? When does scolding become harsh or overbearing? Is it ever okay to hit someone? What defines drunkenness? One glass of wine? A bottle? How would you answer these questions? What is your source for answers?

One final scenario comes from Ephesians 6:1–4 where Paul teaches children to obey their parents in the Lord and to honor their fathers and mothers. Since obedience and honor are expressed differently from culture to culture, the degree to which a grown adult does everything their parent asks would be answered quite differently in Chinese and American cultures. In this passage, Paul also teaches fathers to not exasperate their children but, instead, bring them up in the training and instruction of the Lord. What characterizes training up a child? What methods should parents use to discipline their children? Our cultural lenses usually guide us in our responses.

These types of questions related to the practical living out of biblical principles and instructions happen to be where a lot of conflicts surface. Confucian relationship protocols unconsciously serve as a guide or function as the lens through which individuals in some Asian cultural contexts see and respond to these questions. People living in other cultural contexts have different philosophies and values that also serve as their lens and guide. After living in cross-cultural and intercultural contexts, I have come to recognize that some of my understanding of what is "correct" biblical behavior has, unbeknown to me, been significantly influenced by the lens (norms) of my own culture and context.

RECOGNIZING CULTURAL INFLUENCES

Not only is our practical application of Scripture impacted by our cultural lenses, our ethics and interpretation of other people's behavior are also significantly impacted. In LuLu Wang's movie, *The Farewell,* a Chinese American woman named Billi immigrates to the United States with her parents when she is six years old.[112] As a young adult, Billi discovers that her beloved grandma (奶奶 *nai nai*) has been diagnosed with terminal lung cancer, but the family has withheld the news from her grandma. Billi's entire extended family fakes a wedding for her cousin as an excuse to bring everyone together in China to say farewell. Only Billi's grandma doesn't know the real reason for their gathering. While it is common to withhold this type of information in some places in Chinese culture, it is not common in American culture.

The Chinese title of the movie, 《别告诉她》 (*Don't Tell Her*), indicates one of the main conflict issues in the movie: Under what circumstances is it right to tell someone important information that might negatively impact them emotionally? The director does a wonderful job illustrating the intense emotional struggle that Billi experiences because of growing up with American ethical values and not understanding the Chinese ethics that guide her family's communication.

Is not telling someone they are terminally ill the ethical thing to do? What about not telling someone their grandfather has died because they live far away and can't come home for the funeral? Or what about making a life-changing decision on a child's behalf without talking with them? You may discover you have strong feelings one way or the other. Our initial feelings regarding ethics are at least in part influenced by our culture. When multiple cultures rub shoulders, which is unavoidable in our increasingly globally connected world, we discover that not everything is as black and white as we thought!

Misunderstanding Motives

At one point in *The Farewell*, Billi releases to her mom her pent-up feelings about leaving China as a child and about how her parents have communicated to her over the years. When her mom says that she knows it was hard for Billi to leave and that it was hard for them, too, Billi emotionally bursts out:

> But you chose to leave. You were adults and you understood why. I was just a kid. Nobody ever asked me what I wanted or how I felt. I just had to trust you. You told me it was a good thing to leave, but it didn't feel like a good thing when you and Dad fought all the time because we didn't have money and I was the weird Chinese girl in school who didn't speak English and had no friends or anyone to talk to. I wanted to believe that it was a good thing, but all I saw was the fear in your eyes. I was confused and scared constantly because you guys never told me what was going on.

Billi continues her diatribe, saying, "And then *Yeye* [her grandpa] died and you didn't even tell me he was sick, so it felt like he just vanished suddenly. And you didn't even let me go to his funeral!"

Billi's mom's reply is key to recognizing the root of their conflict: "You were in school. We didn't want you to miss school. We did what we thought was best for you." Billi's parent's primary influencing motivation (among others) was care and concern for Billi and her education. But Billi's experience of her parents' actions and words was to feel neglected, unheard, ignored, and uncared for.

This story illustrates how we hear people's words and see their actions yet often mistake or misunderstand their motivations and intentions. When there is a lack of verbal communication, good motivations and intentions are frequently misunderstood as bad. When cultural differences are involved like this, it is even harder to guess correctly or understand the intentions and motivations of other people.[113]

Misunderstanding Generational Differences

As illustrated in the aforementioned conversation, generational differences between those of higher and lower status can further complicate matters. Sometimes individuals from older generations believe that sacrificially providing in practical ways is the best way to express love and care for their children or younger church leaders. This sacrifice often comes with the expectation that it is their role to offer advice, scold, direct the subordinate's actions, and be protective.

The problem is that the younger generation often feels stifled and controlled by their elder's words and loving care. And when they bring up concerns, they frequently feel discouraged, ignored, or even rejected. The younger generation's view of love looks more like the meeting of physical needs plus dialogue, autonomy, words of affirmation, safety in vulnerability, and physical touch. They may express their dissatisfaction or disappointment in hurtful ways: complaining, challenging, withdrawing, or resisting. Deep misunderstanding can wreak havoc in relationships when we are unaware of each other's implicit, unstated, and sometimes cultural or generational expectations regarding what communication, respect, and love should look like.

I have experienced the benefits of multi-cultural and multi-generational engagement as described by Shin and Silzer: "When believers interact more regularly with people from other cultures, they more easily recognize their own cultural interpretation of doing things and are more willing to make changes in order to further the Kingdom of God on earth."[114] Even if we have studied the biblical languages of Hebrew and Greek and the cultural contexts in which the Bible was written, we need to keep a humble heart, knowing that our own cultural lens, be it influenced by Confucian thought or any other value system, will still influence our interpretations of both the Bible and people's behaviors.

CHAPTER WRAP-UP

Being consciously aware of our societal position—with the associated culturally-conditioned expectations regarding deference, submission, communication, and obedience—can help us broaden our conflict response choices. The next time conflict surfaces, or perhaps the next time you notice conflict is just beneath the surface, pause and consider what choosing to "Do to others as you would have them do to you" (Luke 6:31) could look like in that situation.

When you are the superior or person of higher status, this might look like experimenting with putting yourself in the shoes of the other person and recalling what you feel when you are in the lower position. Take time to remember the frustration, constriction, perhaps even the apathy or sense of powerlessness that you feel in those situations. Try to recall the ways you would like your parent, boss, or pastor to relate to you when you try to raise or address an issue from your lower position. Then try to be the person you wish your superiors would be with you. Attempt to use the power that has been ascribed to you in better ways.

Conversely, as the subordinate or person of lower status, when conflict happens, consider taking time to step back from your frustration and, instead of focusing solely on your concerns, seek to understand and empathize with the challenges the person above you may be facing. Taking this step can be perspective-changing and help you approach communication from a more balanced place.

There may be some relationships in which, like Zhang Wei and his mother-in-law, due to power dynamics or the other person's unwillingness or inability to engage in healthy ways, you can only go as far as personal peacemaking. Keep praying. Prayer is critical. Get godly help. Seek personal healing. Stay sensitive to God opening reconciliation opportunities. Keep growing in Christ. God is the only one who can change hearts.

A PRAYER

Lord, as I reflect on the power and status that I have in different relationships, show me new ways to serve others and to have accountability. Remind me to put myself in others' shoes and help me see when I use the power that I do have in self-serving or selfish ways instead of for the good of others, particularly when conflict happens.

In my relationships with superiors or those of higher status, give me humility, wisdom to see the bigger picture, insight to know when to speak, the ability to listen well, and courage to advocate for myself and seek help when that is needed. In my relationships with subordinates or those of lower status, I also ask for humility, wisdom to understand them and know when to speak, the ability to listen well, courage to dialogue, and discernment regarding how to use my positional power.

In my relationship with [insert name here], *I am beginning to see how differing cultural or generational expectations may be impacting our approach to issues and even our interpretation and application of Scripture. With these differences in mind, help me determine whether we need to create a new kind of conversation space so we can better understand one another. Show me the way forward. I open myself up to the discomfort of changing normal for the sake of learning to express love and respect in ways that honor You and are meaningful to* [insert name here], *not only in the ways in which I have been culturally conditioned to express love and respect. In Jesus' name I pray, amen.*

REFLECTION QUESTIONS

1. In which conflicted relationships do you have the higher status and would be considered the superior (due to age, position, rank, experience)?

2. In which conflicted relationships do you have the lower status and would be considered the subordinate (due to age, position, rank, experience)?

3. Which types of power do you currently have?

    a. positional

    b. verbal (use of words to manage or control situations)

    c. intellectual (education, skills)

    d. emotional (the capacity to express, read, and process emotions)

    e. spiritual (knowledge of Scripture, relationship with God)

    f. relational (trust-based relational credibility, *guanxi*—who you know and can access, perceived power)

    g. physical (strength, physical characteristics, gender, sexual identity)

    h. cultural (age, race, gender, ethnicity)

    i. resource (money, time, material goods)

4. How can you create accountability in your life so that your use of power helps others flourish rather than negatively impacts them?

5. In what ways should your conflict responses look different when abuse is involved?

6. When helping someone who is in a conflict situation that has abusive dynamics, what should help look like?

7. What lessons do you take away from Hannah and Eli's encounter in 1 Samuel 1:9–18?

8. When you feel like you have no status or power in a relationship, do you often feel unable to bring up issues? What would you like to do to address this situation?

9. When addressing conflict issues, what degree of impact has the traditional Confucian relationship structure had on your own approach and/or the approach of those in your family, church, or work context?

SIX

LOOKING OUT FOR INTERESTS

IN CLOSE RELATIONSHIPS or as the older/higher status person in a relationship, it is easy to think, *I'm already looking out for their interests. I know what they need.* Parents, spouses, and leaders, beware! In reality, we often are looking out for the interests that *we assume they have or think they should have.* Sometimes, unbeknownst to us, the interests that we think they should have are actually based on our own interests (for example, to protect or give us face) and not on Christ's interests or their heart-level interests.

In his letter to the Philippians, Paul comments about Timothy, his co-worker and son in the faith, saying, "I have no one else like him, who will show genuine concern for your welfare. For *everyone looks out for their own interests*, not those of Jesus Christ" (Phil 2:20–21, emphasis added). Timothy's genuine concern for the Philippian church members' wellbeing was not because of some personal interest or *guanxi* benefit. Timothy's concern came from having a heart that cared about the people Jesus Christ cares about.

A few verses earlier, Paul first mentions this idea of *interests* and the importance of looking out for other's interests—not just our own. Believing, internalizing, and obeying Philippians 2:3–4 (ESV) can be relationship-changing: "In humility count others more significant than yourselves. Let each of you *look not only to his own interests*, but also to *the interests of others*" (emphasis added). I like how the Amplified Bible states it: "With [an attitude of] humility [being neither arrogant nor self-righteous], regard others *as more important than yourselves*. Do not merely look out for your own personal interests, but also for the interests of others" (*sic*). *Interests* here refers to a person's needs, concerns, desires, fears, limitations, values, or preferences. Interests are the motivating reason(s) behind someone's position or stance on an issue.

No matter our status in a relationship, when in conflict, our focus invariably gets stuck on ourselves and what we want to see happen; though, sometimes this self-focus gets masked by or mixed in with concern for the community or the other person. But how do we look after each other's interests? First, we have to know what each other's interests are.

DISCOVERING INTERESTS

When in conflict, our ears tend to filter out everything but the other person's opposing position, or defense thereof, and their demanding or judging words toward us. We often have no idea how to listen for the other person's core interests (their needs, concerns, desires, fears, limitations, values, or preferences). We also might bump up against the challenge that we only have a vague idea of what our own core interests are. Or, if we know, we struggle for clear articulation. In our disagreements, when no one's heart-level interests have been voiced or acknowledged, we remain stuck at the surface level and keep arguing or avoiding.

Here's an example of how this conflict dynamic could play out.

Gao says to his wife Mei: "Honey, I want to get a dog." (He states his position.)

Mei responds: "I don't want a dog. What are you thinking?" (She states her position and adds a critique.)

Gao begins to explain his position but moves into defense mode: "A dog would protect our home, provide more joy, and be good for our kids."

Mei also defends her position and adds on an accusation/judgment: "Dogs are smelly, make a mess, take time to care for, and cost money that we don't have. How could you think of spending money on a dog when you won't even get the new car that we need?"

Gao does not respond to the car-need but speaks with judgment, accusations, and another attempt at defending his position: "You only care about your own convenience, but what about our kids? Why can't you see how good this will be for them? Besides, our home will be much safer with a dog."

Mei ends the argument for now while adding a few demands: "Fine. If you want a dog, then get a dog. But you better tell me when we're going to get that car that we need. And don't expect me to be happy about the dog or to take care of it!"

They pick up the argument again on a later day, recycling a similar conversation with no resolution.

BREAKING THE CYCLE

When we disagree on something, our behavior often follows this downward spiral pattern:

- State your position; hear the opposing position
- Defend your position
- Push for or demand agreement with your position
- Judge the other person for holding their position and not agreeing with yours
- Keep arguing or avoiding each other
- Communication breaks down

Taking the time to understand interests, both yours and the other person's, can help break this cycle.

Depending on how you are wired, understanding your own interests can be done through personal reflection or talking with someone. Personally, by the time I get to a communication breakdown, I am usually so annoyed or angry that I need to vent in my journal as my first step to recovering and understanding my own heart.[115] I might even need to go for a walk before or after journaling to help my body calm down from the emotional flooding and anxiety I experience in response to what I perceive to be a clash of interests.[116] I need to take some quiet time to try to understand what my own interests are. Some people process thoughts and feelings better through talking and need to find a trusted individual who won't gossip or unquestioningly support their opinion. Both are good options.

My Interests

If you choose to journal, here are some ideas for the types of things you might explore as you seek to discover your core interests. I often journal my thoughts in the form of a prayer, "Lord, I feel so angry! . . . "

1. Write out your feelings and acknowledge them without condemnation.[117] (Feelings are neutral, neither good nor bad. They are like flags that our body waves, signaling that something about this issue matters to you, and it would be good to pay attention to that.)

   - *I'm so angry!*
   - *I feel so disappointed and sad.*

2. Pour out, uncensored, all the judgements and accusations you have toward the other person.

   - *She is impossible to work with!*
   - *He is so selfish.*

3. Write out all the ways you perceive the other person is being unfair, inconsiderate, misunderstanding, demeaning, disrespectful, etc.

   - *I feel like he doesn't value or see the effort that is required to plan an event.*
   - *She never asks for my input.*

4. List out, as specifically as possible, what you want from the other person—your unmet desires.

   - *I want him to listen to me without interrupting (the desire or need: to be listened to).*

- *I want to be able to trust that she has done her best, but right now I keep doubting (the desire or need: peace of mind or stability).*

5. List out what they don't seem to care about, but you do.

    - *She doesn't seem to care about how having a dog will make me happy.*
    - *He doesn't seem to care about how distressed I will be by having a dog.*

6. Look at all your prayer notes (mine are usually messy and unorganized) and ask God, "Lord, what is it that, at my core, I really want or feel I need when I judge [insert name] in this way? What deeper desire or need is going unmet?" Make a list of all the heart-level core needs, desires, and longings that surface.[118]

    - *I long to be understood, for security in our relationship, for consideration, and trust.*

Gao's journaling might look something like this:

- *Lord, I'm so angry and frustrated! Why can't Mei see how much safer our home will be with a dog? Why won't she acknowledge how good this will be for our kids? I feel so disconnected from her. It just irritates me that all she can think about is how much of a mess a dog makes. Now that I think about it, I'm sad, too. I always wanted a dog and was never allowed to have one as a kid. She should see the value of getting a dog and all that it will mean to me and the kids.*

- *Lord, when I judge her by saying that she cares only about her own convenience, what's behind that? What do I really want? Hmm, I think I'm really wanting her understanding and partnership. Yeah, that's it. I want her partnership in life. I want her understanding. I also want her to trust me that getting a dog will be a good thing for us. I feel like she doesn't trust me in this.*
- *Jesus, I hold these desires before you with open hands. Help me find a way to talk about these core desires with Mei. Our last conversation derailed so badly.*

Their Interests

After you have sorted out what your interests are, jot down or talk through the following points with a trusted person in order to take some initial steps toward understanding the other person's interests. Let's continue exploring Gao's journaling.

1. Note what you observed about the other person's emotions. (Those emotions signal that something about this issue is important to them and it would be wise to seek understanding.)

    - *Mei seemed frustrated, too, and worried, overwhelmed, and even disgusted by the idea of having a dog.*

2. Write out the judgments and accusations the other person made about you.

    - *Mei accused me of being insensitive, uncaring, and unable to handle money wisely.*

3. Ask yourself and God, "What do these judgments and accusations reveal about what [insert the other person's name] cares about?"

    - *Mei seems to need to be understood and to be shown care. She also seems to care and even worry about how we spend our money. There's something about money that concerns her. Maybe I should try to understand that better.*

4. Pray and ask God for the insight and ability to look after the other person's interests, not only your own.

    - *Lord, I need Your insight and help to look after Mei's interests. I don't even know if my observations and guesses are correct. I need to find out what she is concerned about. I want to express my care to her in a way that she can receive, to understand more about her concerns about money, and to see what we can do to help in this area. I still want the dog, but I need help to know how to love her well as my higher priority.*

A Summary of Gao and Mei's Disagreement

The Conflict Issue: Should we get a dog or not?		
	Gao	Mei
Their Positions	I want to get a dog.	I don't want to get a dog.
Their Surface-Level Interests	A dog would provide protection, bring joy to the home, and be good for the kids.	Dogs are smelly, make a mess, take time to care for, and cost money that we don't have.
Their Demanding and Judging Thoughts	Why can't she see how much safer the home will be with a dog? She only cares about her own convenience, but what about the kids? Why can't she see how good this will be for them?	How can he be so insensitive and uncaring? Can't he see how burdensome this will be for me? How could he think of spending money on a dog when he won't even get the new car that we need?
Their Emotions and Feelings	Irritation, indignation, anger, sadness, disappointment, unhappiness, disconnection	Frustration, fear, worry, distress, being overwhelmed, disgust
Their Heart-Level Interests/Needs	Security, safety, trust, understanding, pleasure, joy, partnership	Security, ease, understanding, trust, consideration, care, awareness

Did you notice how digging down deeper reveals the many heart-level interests/needs that Gao and Mei have in common? While they both desire security, understanding, and trust, their strategies differ for meeting these needs.

Strategies Conflict, Not Needs

I was once told that core human needs are never in conflict with each another. Rather, our priorities and strategies for how to meet our core needs may conflict. I'm still pondering this statement but can see the potential for this to be true. Choosing to shift from having a "He/she is opposing me" perspective to a "Let's get to the bottom of what our actual interests/needs are and then see how to prioritize them" perspective moves us from viewing our needs as conflicting to viewing our strategies for meeting those needs as the source of conflict.

For example, in the above scenario, the husband's strategy for meeting some of his heart-level interests/needs was to get a dog. The wife's strategy to meet her heart-level interests/needs that surfaced in response to her husband's plan was to refuse to get a dog. But is getting a dog the only way to meet his heart-level needs? Is refusing to get a dog the only way to meet her heart-level needs? No. There are multiple strategies available that could be considered once they both understand what each person's deeper, heart-level interests/needs are. Will you take the time to pursue this kind of deeper understanding in your relationships?

"BUT I'M RIGHT!"

Proverbs 18:2 (ESV) explicitly states: "A fool takes no pleasure in understanding, but only in expressing his opinion." Yet many of us have situations in which we tend to present our position on a topic in a very decided way without taking time to understand the interests of others. For example, if we feel passionately about our position on something, we may present our ideas quite forcefully and talk as if there is no room for any other position. Others may feel equally as passionate, but they don't know how to share their different position because (1) culturally they aren't expected to speak up based on their lower status, (2) they have been shut down in the past, or (3) they feel there is no space to be heard.

Several years ago, on separate occasions, a couple of Chinese team members told me that they were intimidated by me. They reassured me this wasn't a bad thing, but even so, to hear them make this comment was sobering. I realized that as the team leader and boss, I needed to change my communication if I wanted to have a different type of impact. I could still be passionate, direct, and have high expectations, but I also needed to let others know that I am willing to understand their perspectives. When I heard myself passionately making definitive statements in conversations, I began catching myself and following up with an invitation for others to share their perspectives: "There may be other options I haven't considered. What are your thoughts?"

When you are the person in a higher position of power, you need to ask yourself if others should be given the opportunity to be heard. If you have been shaped by a culture with a Confucian-relationship structure, making a decision without asking for input from those of lower status is completely normal, so you may have never considered such an idea. If you believe others should be given the opportunity to be heard, I invite you to consider the following questions:

- When am I stubborn?
- What am I focused on in such moments?
- What does my stubbornness communicate to others?
- When I choose to end a discussion, for what reasons do I end it and insist on my own way?

- Would I be willing to pause, listen, ask more questions to understand the interests of others, and search for multiple options rather than only present and hold to my position? What might that look like?

You might not yet have answers, but now that you are aware, you can begin to observe when your stubbornness rears its head. At such times, take a few moments to reflect on these questions. And when you notice someone else's stubbornness, let that serve as a prompt for you to take a deep breath and gently, calmly, and inquisitively, avoiding a judgmental tone, ask questions to try to understand the deeper interests of the other person (their needs, concerns, desires, fears, limitations, values, or preferences).

God calls us to prioritize loving one another and having God-honoring relationships over being right or getting our way, even if we believe that our way is the biblical way. If a relationship has been broken in the process of us getting our way, we likely have sinned to get there. We need to take responsibility and address the broken relationship even if it is with someone of lower status or age (this challenge is addressed in the next chapter). To start, let's explore examples of differentiating between surface problems and deeper heart-level needs.

"YOU LOVE YOUR PETS MORE THAN ME!"

Liu Haifeng and his wife, Su Lijuan, had a serious conflict over having animals in their home. Well, at least that is how the problem appeared on the surface. Liu Haifeng's stubbornly held position was he must keep his pets. His wife's position, which turned into an ultimatum, was get rid of the pets. As you read this story as told from Liu Haifeng's perspective, think about what each of their core interests/needs might be. Notice the misunderstanding that was present. Observe the ways in which they adjusted their thinking and approach to each other and the impact this had on their relationship.

> I have always had various unique pets in my home. After getting married, I continued having pets. While my wife doesn't despise them, neither does she like them. When the two of us first got together, she thought it was okay. But I spent more and more time on the animals. After arriving home from work and greeting my wife every day, I would immediately check on the animals to see if they needed anything. I intentionally spent my energy on the animals; I enjoyed it.
>
> In my mind, life is pretty simple. If we have food and clothing and are happy, that's enough. But my wife spends a lot of time thinking about many things: the rent, needing to take care of our parents, issues related to schooling for our child.
>
> My wife began to think that the animals were controlling me. She concluded that raising these pets took up far too much of my energy, and if I didn't have these animals, I would take time to focus on these other issues she felt I should be thinking about.
>
> Fed up, she finally gave me an ultimatum: you can't raise these animals. When she said this, I couldn't take it. As a result, we argued a lot about this issue.
>
> The reality was that I simply didn't consider the issues she thought about constantly as sufficiently important enough to stress about. I preferred to make time to go out and enjoy nature, to enjoy life, to have pets. Isn't that a good thing? My main desire was that she would understand my way of thinking and see me as I saw myself.

After studying biblical peacemaking, I shifted our conversations from focusing first on being understood to first listening to her views. Then, after she finished speaking, I would understand what she was concerned about and respond with a focused explanation.

But even after I gave my explanations, she didn't feel what I said was believable. By this time, I had thought about these things a bit more. If comparing who is more important, the animals or my wife, of course my wife is. I decided to make some changes. I sold all my animals. For quite a while after that, I didn't have any pets.

From this action, my wife saw that I truly cared about her feelings. However, after selling the animals, I was dejected for a period of time. My wife saw this and said, "Maybe you should go ahead and buy another one?"

Through this experience, I was moved to see that we were both able to give according to the needs and feelings of the other and that she really cared about my feelings, too. I have found that there is nothing that can make a person happier than feeling loved by someone else.

Emphasizing again the importance of love, Liu Haifeng went on to say that first understanding the other person's feelings (what they cared about) enabled them to sit down together and discuss a suitable, effective, long-term solution to the problem that had surfaced.

Let's take a look at the dynamics of this story. What interests and misunderstanding surfaced? The chart below lists my analysis based on having heard only Liu Haifeng's side of the story.

	The Surface-Level Conflict Issue: Should Liu Haifeng get rid of his animals or keep them?	
	Liu Haifeng	Su Lijuan
Their Positions	Keep my pets.	Ged rid of your pets.
Their Surface-Level Interests	To enjoy life, which included raising pets; to not stress about other things	To take care of worrying family matters; for Liu Haifeng to spend what she considered to be an appropriate amount of time on family matters
Their Heart-Level Interests/Needs	Ease; relaxation; space; consideration; acknowledgement; understanding of his way of thinking, approach to life, and feelings	Care; partnership; dependability; consideration; acknowledgement; understanding of her way of thinking, approach to life, and feelings

Liu Haifeng realized his wife misunderstood him. She thought he would spend more time on family matters that she considered important if he didn't have pets. He began to see that the main problem was *their differing about what they considered important to spend time on.* This was significant. He also noticed that even after changing his approach to listening first, his explanations didn't change her belief that he cared more about the pets than about her. Even though her perception about him in this situation wasn't true, he decided to take action to prove to his wife that he truly cared more about her than his pets.

Putting Christ's interest and his wife's interests before his own, Liu Haifeng chose to sell all his animals. He recognized Christ's interest to be, "As I have loved you, so you must love one another" (John 13:34), and "Husbands ought to love their wives as their own bodies. He who loves his wife loves himself" (Eph 5:28). His sacrificial actions brought reconciliation and moved his wife to greater compassion toward him, setting the stage for them to discuss how to meet both their core needs and accommodate their differing values. This story is a great example of recognizing differences, moving toward one another in empathy, and discovering one another's interests. In choosing to love each other well, they also were looking after Christ's interests.

"THE FONT IS TOO BIG!"

This next example focuses on the approach to the conversation and the types of questions one can ask to discover interests. As you put yourself in this scenario, you may want to use different questions or ways of phrasing things. Feel free to modify the questions to better suit your situation and personality. Our conversation goal is to get to an accurate understanding of the other person's interests, not to use a certain set of questions.

Imagine you are the leader of the worship team at your church. Determining the PowerPoint (PPT) format for the songs is your responsibility. Several months ago, you determined the slides' font size based on feedback from members of the church. One day you hear that a team member has been complaining about the font being too big. At first you feel annoyed and start to have some critical thoughts. You even consider simply declaring at the next worship team practice, "I'm the leader; I call the shots, and the font size is staying as is." But as you journal and pray, you realize that this wouldn't be a God-honoring or loving approach.

After praying, *you decide to talk privately* with the complaining team member to *learn what she is thinking*. You find a quiet, non-chaotic time and ask in an inviting, friendly tone, "Xiao Zhou, can we talk for a few minutes? I'm grateful for your contribution to the worship team! You have a beautiful voice. I heard recently that you think our PPT font size is too big. I'd like to hear more about your concerns." Or perhaps you say, "Can you help me understand why having smaller font is important to you? I'm interested in hearing your concerns." Or simply, "What concerns do you have about using this font size?"

You listen while she energetically tells you that a song verse should not be split between two slides because it is too confusing for the audio-visual (A/V) volunteer to follow.

You refrain from interrupting and listen carefully to what she has to say. You take notes when possible to catch the details.

Then, *to clarify, you repeat back to her what you heard her say*, "I heard you say that you are looking out for the A/V volunteer who sometimes struggles to keep up with forwarding the slides. Did I understand correctly? Did I miss anything?" You listen and repeat back again.

Next you follow up with *another question*, "Are there any other reasons why you'd like the font to be smaller?"

You listen as she tells you, "Since I have bad eyesight, I need to have the songs printed on paper. The size of the font doesn't actually impact me personally. I'm concerned about the congregation; they get confused and can't follow the songs. And if they can't follow the songs, this reflects poorly on us."

Once again *you engage with and repeat back to her what you heard her say*: "Ah, I didn't know you had bad eyesight. That helps me better understand why you ask to have the printout of the songs. It sounds like your concern at this time is mainly for the A/V volunteer and for the congregation to be able to follow the songs more easily, is that right? However, you also want to be seen as a competent and thoughtful song leader, correct?"

You acknowledge the problem(s) or perceived problem that she has observed and tell her that you appreciate her concern: "Thank you for so thoughtfully caring about the A/V volunteer and for those singing. I know that sometimes the PPT slides move too slowly which then impacts the congregation's ability to sing. Your suggestion to make the font smaller is one possible solution. There may be some others that we can also consider."

At this time, you transition and ask or tell her: "May I share with you why I chose this font size?" or "I'd like to tell you why I chose this font size so you can understand my viewpoint also. Then, I'd like *to share (or discuss) some possible solutions* that would solve the issue that you raised."

You then tell her about the needs of certain church members which is why you chose the bigger font size. If she is having trouble listening and interrupts, you can kindly ask her to wait to comment until after you have finished. "Xiao Zhou, let me finish first, okay? Also, if you could repeat back to me what you heard me say when I'm done, like I did with you, that would help me know that you have heard me as well."

Following this, you can *tell her the specific action that you will take to address her concerns* saying something like, "Since your concern is about the PPT slides being forwarded correctly and timely, not about the actual font size, I will work with the A/V volunteer to practice and improve on forwarding the slides. I will also have the song leader for that day be sure to review the PPT slide order with the A/V person before the service. If you notice that the same confusion is still happening a month from now, please let me know and I will address the issue again or we can come up with a different solution." Then *thank her* for her contribution to the worship team.

In this example, through taking time to talk with the team member, the worship team leader discovered that the complaint (the font is too big) *was not the main issue.* Instead of getting into a long discussion on font size benefits, they could now discuss the real issue: the need to improve forwarding the PPT slides in a timely manner so that the congregation can follow along and sing. Without the worship team leader initiating the conversation, the team member might have continued to complain to others about the font size or even dropped out of the team in frustration.

By asking good questions and repeating back what we hear, we can discover and clarify what is motivating another person's position on something. We can seek to meet the interests/needs that surface. We may also discover some heart areas that need discipleship, gentle correction, and growth. For example, notice in the worship team scenario, Xiao Zhou's last statement: "When the congregation can't follow the songs, this reflects poorly on us." As a leader follows the Holy Spirit's prompting in the above conversation, they can ask God whether or not this is the time to further explore this comment. It may be a good time to compassionately address any pride, fear, or insecurity issues that are present. Or, it may be best to simply take note and pray about this on the person's behalf.

> By asking good questions and repeating back what we hear, we can discover and clarify what is motivating another person's position on something.

Once again, please remember that what might be a good question for one person or in one relationship might not be a good question in another! If the sample questions given here don't work in your situation, feel free to create different questions that meet the same purpose: to discover and understand interests.

SUMMARY OF PRACTICES TO CONSIDER WHEN BRINGING UP SENSITIVE ISSUES WITH OTHERS:

1. Prayerfully consider what to do.
   - What is the best method for you to gain clarity and understanding of the interests and motivations behind the other person's position, concern, complaint, opinion, or sin?
   - When is an appropriate time to gather this information?
2. Ask an open-ended, non-threatening question.
3. Listen with the goal to learn what the person is thinking and feeling—what are their interests?
   - Refrain from interrupting.
   - Jot down notes as needed to help you stay focused on what the other person is saying and to remember details.
4. Repeat back what you heard to make sure you heard correctly and caught what matters most to the other person.
5. Ask more questions. Seek as much clarity as possible.
6. Listen closely to the answers, engaging and repeating back what you hear.
7. Acknowledge the problem(s) or perceived problems.
8. Be appreciative of the concern—the interests—of the other person.
   - Whether or not you personally view their interest(s) as important is not relevant. Because it matters to them, recognize its importance.
9. Only after you have listened to, demonstrated understanding of, and expressed value for the other person, transition to explaining your perspective.

- Without judging or arguing the words, values, or interests of the other person, briefly explain your perspective.
- Share your ideas about a solution or possible solutions.
- Ask if they have any solutions they would like to share.

10. Consider the following:
    - What specific actions will you take to address their concern?
    - How can they follow up with you if they do not think those actions are working?
    - What length of time would be appropriate for them to allow to pass to see if the solution is working?
    - Let the person know you are available and open to future conversations.

Depending on the type of relationship, the context, and the issues, not every conversation will follow this exact methodology, but the basic ideas of praying, asking questions, listening carefully, sharing, and valuing the other person and their interests will usually be appropriate.

As your family members and those serving with or under you know that their core interests have been listened to and are being considered, there is a much greater potential to come to mutual understanding or agreement. And if your decision as the leader or parent is still, "No," those who disagreed or who aren't getting what they wanted have the potential to be more willing to submit and support the final decision. Why? Because they felt heard, respected, and understood in the process. They have hope that they'll be heard and their interests will be considered in future discussions, too.

CHAPTER WRAP-UP

When I lived with a Chinese family in the heart of China for ten months, I often ate out with them and their friends which gave me a front row seat to learn the local, Chinese toasting etiquette. Over time, I observed a pattern: the host or the older/higher status person would begin the toasting. Toasts would then be liberally given, back and forth around the table, until everyone had been toasted and praised for something, even me. When at a large banquet, it was quite common to see people get up from their table and go toast people at other tables.

In my native, shaping culture, toasting is reserved for special events such as weddings, anniversaries, or retirements. Even then, typically only a handful of toasts are given to the person or couple being celebrated. Everyone raises their glasses and drinks together to honor them. That's the end of the toasting.

The toasting culture I experienced in China felt completely foreign to me. It slowly dawned on me that I should be raising my glass and toasting individuals around the table, too, especially in response to toasts given to me. I should also honor others by proactively initiating toasts. I realized that toasting was infused with meaning and purpose and was so much more than just clinking glasses together in celebration.

For many months I felt like my glass was glued to the table. I would put my hand around my glass to raise it up, but my arm felt heavy, like I just couldn't do it. Toasting in this manner felt so uncomfortable; everything within me resisted it. I could raise my glass to respond to someone's toast, but I couldn't initiate a toast. I was used to praising people whenever something came to mind, not at prescribed times, so it felt unnatural. My fear over saying something wrong or toasting the wrong person first, coupled with the embarrassment I imagined experiencing, also hindered me.

I finally learned what to say in Chinese when toasting someone, and I began initiating toasts even though it felt incredibly awkward and clumsy. I still remember the first time I forced myself to push past the discomfort, raise my glass, and speak out a toast of praise to someone else at the table. Though a small thing, it felt like such an accomplishment! I regularly prayed, asking God to fill me with genuine praise that I could share with others when toasting, and I gradually got used to initiating toasts though it never became entirely comfortable.

Changing the way we handle conflict from our normal way to God's Kingdom-culture way often feels similarly unnatural, awkward, and foreign. Perhaps asking questions to understand interests or creating conversation space for dialogue about ideas or concerns feels as unnatural to you as toasting around a dinner table felt to me. If no one modeled biblical conflict resolution and reconciliation practices in our families or culture growing up, should it surprise us that living this way feels unnatural?

Intentionally working to discover and understand other's interests has been one of the transformative practices for my conflicts. Sometimes it takes asking multiple questions and lots of listening with a non-condemning posture before a person is willing to open up and share what they truly think. Sometimes we have to prove that we are genuinely willing to listen by giving the person time to think. But if the person opens up and shares, we will discover relational gold and will have received an incredible gift.

These kinds of conversations take time, but God-honoring conversations are worth it. Proverbs 19:2 reminds us: "Desire without knowledge is not good, and one who moves too hurriedly misses the way." Let's give the time it takes to understand Christ's interests, others' interests, and our own interests so as to not move too hurriedly and miss our way.

A PRAYER

Lord, I realize that in my natural self, I wish others were just like me and agree with my position on everything. But I know that our differences bless the body of Christ. When we build each other up and seek to look after each other's interests instead of just our own, our relationships are strengthened, and You get the glory!

Increase my awareness of when:

- *I am stubbornly holding on to my position without considering others*

- *I am tearing others down with criticism and judgment, taking offense, and not listening or asking good questions*

- *I act on my assumptions of what other people's interests are or should be instead of taking the time to ask*

In my relationship with [insert name here], *I desire to have the same mindset and humility as Jesus Christ (Phil 2:5–8). I ask for the grace to discover and look after the interests of others. In Jesus' name I pray, amen.*

REFLECTION QUESTIONS

1. How might community and family life look different if leaders, spouses, and parents initiate more conversations seeking to listen and understand the interests/needs of others?

2. Do you have a typical conflict cycle or pattern with someone? If so, what ideas from this chapter would you like to prayerfully consider implementing to help break your contribution to the cycle?

3. What is one thing you can do to help yourself better understand your own interests?

4. What is one thing you can do to help yourself better understand someone else's interests?

5. Do you have any relationships in which you think it might be difficult to ask questions to understand the other person's interests? What are the relationship dynamics that cause the difficulty? How might you change those dynamics in order to open up the relationship to better understanding?

SEVEN

CONFESSION-APOLOGIES

FACE, STATUS, POWER, CULTURAL EXPECTATIONS, and our own interests. The last several chapters have opened up each of these complex topics, increasing our awareness of how they impact us. Left unnoticed and unaddressed, our mindset regarding any one of these has the ability to sabotage our efforts to have better relationships with others. Our mindsets toward apologizing and confessing (see chapters one and two) can also keep us stuck in conflict, but learning God's Kingdom-culture expands our thinking beyond these mindsets, empowering us to humbly address conflict issues. Experiencing something relationally new becomes possible.

AUTHENTICITY MATTERS

There tends to be a lack of authentic apology practices both inside and outside the church. Li Jie said ruefully, "An apology is where you admit you have done something wrong, admit you have hurt the other person, admit your responsibility. It's that simple. But we aren't able to do it. It's so difficult for us to actually do." Li Jun described why he thinks he has experienced authentic apologies with his wife and children but rarely at church:

> On one hand, I think this is related to our spiritual life; on the other hand, I think this is related to our training. Many Chinese people know when they are wrong, but they don't know how to apologize, so they just let the conflict sit there.

Li Jie also expressed that he feels Chinese people have not been taught how to make an authentic apology: "If you look at human nature and the education that we have received from our environment, we basically don't know how to make an authentic apology." Imagine the difference in our churches, families, and organizations if we create face-safe spaces where giving authentic apologies is taught and modeled. Confession-apologies could become commonplace, the new Kingdom-culture norm of our communities.

What is a *confession-apology*? I have used *apology* and *apologizing* and *confession* and *confessing* somewhat interchangeably in the first chapters of this book. Here's the conundrum: the words *apology* and *apologize* are not actually in the Bible but are commonly used in society. *Confession* and *confessing*, on the other hand, are used biblically and in courts of law but not in day-to-day life. Both the Old and New Testaments describe the need to confess sin (e.g. Lev 5:5, 26:40; Num 5:7; Neh 1:6; Ps 32:5; James 5:16; 1 John 1:9). Yet in daily life, we tend to apologize.

When apologizing in Chinese or English, most people tend to say *I'm sorry* (对不起 *dui bu qi*, 我很抱歉 *wo hen bao qian*). In both languages, *I'm sorry* is supposed to reflect a genuine expression of sorrow for the hurt caused by that person's words or actions, yet far too often this statement carries no hint of remorse and regret. Confession of any specific wrongs is also absent from a simple *I'm sorry*.

Biblically speaking, confession means that we agree with what God says about our actions, attitude, or words.[119] If God calls something a sin, we also call it a sin and repent. So what should we do—confess or apologize? I propose that we consider thinking of our apologies as *confession-apologies*. In a confession-apology, a person does not excuse, explain, or defend themselves; the person knows that, to some degree, they sinned or made a mistake; they acknowledge the hurt the other person felt and take responsibility for their own contribution to the conflict. This kind of apology includes honest confession. It is authentic.

WHERE TO START

The starting place for confession is to the Lord (1 John 1:9). Confession to God of commonplace sins might sound like this:

- *Lord, I just (again) interrupted my husband. I thought my words more important than his. I was arrogant. Thank You for forgiving me. Thank You that, once again, You have made me clean.*

Or

- *Lord, I confess my pushiness this morning when I wasn't noticed. I was making room for myself when You say You'll make room for me. Thank You for forgiving me. Thank You that, once again, You have made me clean.*[120]

In both of these examples, there is a recognition of what God sees as sin, there is repentance, and an acceptance of God's gift of forgiveness. But confession doesn't stop there.

The Bible instructs believers to also confess our sins to each other, not just privately to God (James 5:16). A prayer confession can be turned into a verbal confession-apology to the other person:

- *I am sorry for interrupting you again. It's my arrogance coming through. I confess that at times I subconsciously think that my words are more important than yours. I know this is not true. What you have to say is very important to me, and I want to give the time needed to fully listen. I need to grow in this area. Would you forgive me?*

Or

- *I am sorry for being so pushy and disruptive in our meeting this morning. It was rude and disrespectful. I need to be more patient and wait for the appropriate times and places to contribute. Would you forgive me?*

Again, identification of sin, without excuse, and heart-felt repentance with an ask for forgiveness is the basis of this confession-apology.

We are often tempted to just confess to God and skip the confession-apology to the person. This temptation might stem from pride, face, or fear of the other person taking advantage of our apology to attack us. While at times people do respond in hurtful ways when we apologize, I am convinced that Satan wants to deceive us; he wants us to believe that everyone will respond negatively. Yet, particularly for interactions between believers, the Holy Spirit will often move the other person to positively respond to an apology if the giver is sincere and courageous enough to express it.

A VERBAL APOLOGY MATTERS

"We know that confession and apology is important to God and critical for relational health, but is giving a verbal apology really necessary?" I heard this question raised so often at peacemaking trainings in Chinese contexts that I started including a case study for discussion. How would you advise the church co-worker in the following scenario?

> A church leader publicly scolded a church sister in a rather strong voice about being lazy. Afterwards, the sister stopped coming to church. Others went and comforted her and encouraged her to come back. She finally came back, but her relationship with this church leader remained distant.

What do you think this church leader should do to fully restore the relationship with this church sister?

> a) Treat her to a meal
> b) Give her a gift
> c) Sincerely, verbally apologize
> d) A combination of a, b, or c, or something else

While training participants' answers will vary, one response stays consistent: a sincere, verbal apology would make a significant difference in this situation. Participants often suggest coupling the spoken apology with some kind of action (gift, meal, etc.).

The consistent response that a verbal apology is needed fascinates me. How often do we avoid verbally confessing when we have messed up? We choose to bring our spouse tea instead. We go out of our way to help a colleague at work. We intentionally compliment that person at church. It's so much less embarrassing and painful than confessing and apologizing. But when it comes to receiving an apology, we want to hear a verbal apology; an action-only apology doesn't adequately convey the confession—the admission of wrong. Such inconsistency!

A verbal confession-apology often includes some or all of the following components, the Seven A's of Biblical Confession:

1. **A**ddress everyone involved (all those whom you affected)
2. **A**void *if*, *but*, and *maybe* (do not try to excuse your wrongs)
3. **A**dmit specifically (both attitudes and actions)
4. **A**cknowledge the hurt (express sorrow for hurting someone)
5. **A**ccept the consequences (such as making restitution)
6. **A**lter your behavior (change your attitudes and actions)
7. **A**sk for forgiveness (and allow for time)[121]

Not every relationship or situation needs the same type of confession and apology. The severity of the offense plays a part in determining how much needs to be said and done to restore a relationship. Even a verbal confession-apology that minimally includes a genuine, sincere expression of sorrow, remorse, or regret often makes a significant difference.

PRACTICE IS NEEDED

Many I interviewed admitted that giving a genuine, verbal apology was extremely difficult for them and required practice. Huang Jingjing described how she felt when she first started apologizing:

It wasn't natural and didn't feel like it came from my heart. It felt awkward and embarrassing. I wrote out my apologies according to the peacemaking study steps [the seven A's of biblical confession]. I still remember the first time I wrote out my apology, Steps 1, 2, 3, 4, and then apologized to my son.[122]

Chen Yuling also described the need for practice:

I think there is a drilling process involved. People are unable to just immediately open their mouths and apologize. It requires constant practice, constant commitment, constant humility. Only when the Lord is truly first in a person's life are they able to incorporate apologizing into their life and live it out.

Now a habit, Chen Yuling often apologizes to her daughter when she has said something wrong. Her daughter accepts her apologies and forgives her. Recognizing that apologizing is a learned skill can help many of us overcome what may seem like a barrier to living out successful, biblical peacemaking.

Apologizing from Above

When you are the person of higher status and you have made a mistake or sinned, what are *you* going to do? Although the standard cultural practice may be to ignore the issue, the way of God's reconciling Kingdom-culture is to confess, no matter your age or how high your position is. And while apologizing from above can be particularly challenging, being the person of lower status doesn't necessarily make apologizing easier. We all can use more practice in confession-apologies.

Consider the following example. A seventy-year-old church pianist, Zhang Li, had gotten upset at a significantly younger man at church because he had not provided her with a copy of the music score that she needed in the timeframe she needed it. Even though it was a small matter, the situation had the potential to impact their relationship, so she initiated an apology to him. Acknowledging her anger, in her apology Zhang Li said,

> My attitude wasn't very good that day; because you didn't give the music to me, I got angry. But I hope that in the future, if something like this happens again, I mean, if someone needs something urgently like this, that you can get what is needed for the person. I also wasn't right in how I behaved.

At the time, he ignored her apology, but a few days later, he smiled and treated her just as he always had, demonstrating that he had in fact received her apology, and they were reconciled.

While Zhang Li had a sincere and repentant heart, which is key, and her apology was received, her apology included a few components that, while tempting to include in our apologies, I typically encourage people to avoid: explanation and blame. Here's what I would suggest deleting from her apology:

> *My attitude wasn't very good that day; ~~because you didn't give the music to me, I got angry. But I hope that in the future, if something like this happens again, I mean, if someone needs something urgently like this, that you can get what is needed for the person.~~ I also wasn't right in how I behaved.*

Here's how I would suggest revising it:

My attitude wasn't very good that day. I wasn't right in how I behaved toward you. I'm sorry for getting so upset and saying that you don't consider other people's needs when you didn't provide the music within my time frame. You have provided the piano music on time in the past. I know that you care about us.

What do you notice is different between these two versions?

In my apology revision, I left out her explanation of why she got angry and her expressed desire of what she wanted from him in the future. My revision also includes an acknowledgement of his care and corrects her original (implied) accusation. During an apology, it's important to avoid blaming the other person for your behavior. Instead, you need to take full ownership of your behavior.

Later, in a follow up conversation, you can discuss the issue that triggered your anger and explain your behavior and your needs. This also takes vulnerability and practice. Zhang Li could say something like,

Can we take a minute to talk about the timing for giving the music to the pianist? When I got upset, it was because I felt embarrassed to play poorly in front of everyone and I didn't want to be a distraction. Because I don't play very well and need to practice ahead of time, I really need to get the music at least one week in advance. Is that possible? Are there any challenges for you that make it difficult to provide the music a week in advance? [If yes, discuss alternate solutions.]

I still need to grow in setting aside my face and just enjoying the worship together when something keeps you from getting the music to me early enough, but if we can avoid that problem, I would feel a lot more confident. Thanks for all you do.

In this hypothetical follow up conversation, Zhang Li acknowledges some of the deeper core issues behind her original anger and expresses, in specific terms, why she needs to get the music early, as well as a preferred timeframe. She checks to see if he is able to meet that need by asking some questions. And she is prepared to discuss alternate solutions or offer a way to help if he finds it difficult to meet her request.

I deeply respect Zhang Li. In discussing her apology, Zhang Li indirectly referred to the social expectation that someone older should not have to apologize to someone younger:

> What should you do if you are wrong? Don't admit your mistake but instead wait for the other person to admit his mistake and reconcile with you? What if that person hasn't studied a biblical peacemaking course and is younger than you?
>
> In my situation, this church brother is only fifty years old; I am almost twenty years older than him. But you can't say, "Forget it, forget it!" You still need to proactively go reconcile. After studying biblical peacemaking, my heart is so relaxed.

In a cultural context where she is expected not to apologize due to her seniority, she chose to follow God's reconciling Kingdom-culture practice and experienced the resulting peace and joy. She was and is willing to keep learning, stretching, and changing. Our apologizing and follow-up conversation skills are all a work in progress.

A MATURING PROCESS

One aspect of biblical peacemaking is recognizing that our understanding of apologizing, like many areas in a Christian's spiritual growth, will go through a maturation process. I have heard a few people describe their reason to apologize and view of apologizing as maturing through roughly three stages: (1) before faith, (2) after faith, and (3) after learning biblical peacemaking (further faith maturation). Each of us has a unique starting place based on our past experience with apologizing.

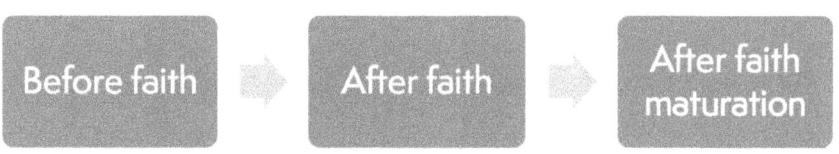

Yang Lin described this maturation process in her life. As you hear Yang Lin's story, consider what phases you have gone through regarding your views on apologizing and what phase you are at currently.

> I grew up spoiled. I was not willing to acknowledge mistakes, and being the youngest child, everyone praised me, so I did not experience any conflicts or criticism until I got married. Then the conflicts began.

> In my first phase, I would apologize when my husband was angry so that the relationship would return to normal. After repeated cycles of this, my husband asked me, "Do you really feel like you have done something wrong?" I realized that I did not think I had done anything wrong but was giving a verbal apology only to get him to stop being angry.

In her first phase, before her relationship with Christ, Yang Lin artificially apologized with no true intent behind her words.

> In the second phase, after becoming a Christian, I would apologize to prove that I was an obedient wife, a good Christian. I felt like I "should" apologize and reconcile since I was a Christian. But when apologizing, I had complaints in my heart. I would think, *Why am I the only one apologizing?* Or, *Why do I apologize so often but you don't?* Bitterness welled up and I would explode sometimes, bringing up all the past things.
>
> My husband would then say, "Were all the past apologies fake then?" and "You are apologizing to prove that you are good." He helped me see the heart of the matter. At first, I didn't want to admit it, but after reflection, I realized that I was apologizing for this reason.

In her second phase, Yang Lin began apologizing more often, desiring to follow Christ's example, but her apologies were oriented toward obedience and proving something; they lacked remorse. Then, four years ago, after leaving their high-paying jobs to work at a low-paying Christian organization, her third phase began.

> We had to start at the bottom again, both financially and in work roles. We argued often. But at that time, we met many international Christians, people who were an example in faith. We interacted with many different churches through which our worldview expanded, maturing us.
>
> Through all the struggles, we grew in humility. Starting our own organization two years ago, we now see how much we have grown and changed.
>
> We still have conflict, but now we can quickly reconcile. I am the type of person who escapes in conflict while my husband is the type

of person who attacks. So in the past, the conflicts were always right there between us. We just didn't talk about them. Now we sit down together and talk about the matter, reconcile, and then start again.

Huge transformation for me has come through more deeply understanding that if I did not have God's love, I wouldn't be able to do anything, and what I do, I would do poorly.

I used to think, from the time I was young, that I always had great relationships with people; I never had conflict. Now I see that those were all superficial relationships; not one was deep.

Yang Lin moved from giving artificial apologies to apologizing because it is the right thing to do as a Christian but without real repentance to finally being broken, growing in humility, and seeing herself more realistically. Together with deeply valuing the love and grace of God, these changes have enabled her to openly talk about issues, sincerely apologize, and truly reconcile. She has moved past only having superficial relationships to having many deep ones.

Apologizing: Yang Lin's Three Stages of Maturing

Stages	Reason to Apologize	State of Heart	View of Apologizing
Before Faith	When husband was angry, to return relationship to normal and stop his anger	No remorse, no regret No sense of having done something wrong	Not needed
After Faith	To prove I was an obedient wife To prove I was a good Christian	Complains (Why am I the only person apologizing?) Bitter Brings up past issues	Something I should do because I'm a Christian
After Faith Maturation	To restore a relationship To reconcile To talk openly To have a deep, sincere relationship	Values God's love and grace Humble Loving Repentant Broken A realistic view of self	I should look at myself first

The quality of Yang Lin's apologies was influenced by the state of her heart, her reason for apologizing, and her view of apologizing. She matured in these three areas over time. However, it is only through maturation in faith that Yang Lin is now able to apologize for the purpose of reconciliation. Apologizing for this reason was something she never considered before. Having matured in faith doesn't mean that she now never apologizes out of a desire to stop her husband's anger or to prove she is a good Christian. Maturing is not static. However, maturing did move her to a new place where something not previously possible is now possible.

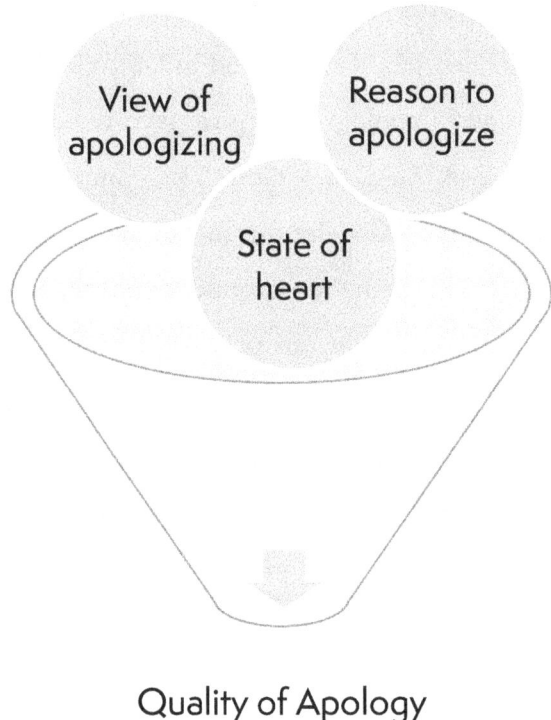

Quality of Apology

Giving confession-apologies requires not only a maturation in skills but also of the heart. While it is possible to practice and become better able to give confession-apologies that can begin to heal another's wounds, if heart maturation doesn't also occur, practiced apologies will be mechanical and fake no matter how good they sound. Heart maturation happens as we draw closer to God, believe His Word, better understand His love for us and others, and recognize that He designed us for deep, intimate relationships, not fake, superficial ones.

Sources of Strength and Courage

Giving authentic apologies is not for the faint of heart. When those I interviewed experienced true face, rooted in God's love, they received strength and courage to apologize, forgive, face rejection, proactively communicate, and love those they didn't like. Many recognized "that true strength comes from God letting me understand myself better, that I am not perfect. This is the most foundational aspect."[123] Knowing ourselves means "we know that our plight is just about the same as everyone else's. You make the same mistakes yourself. If you don't have this awareness, it is easy to deal with things in the same way as others, by taking revenge."[124] Gaining a true view of ourselves is humbling and freeing and can spur us on to own and apologize for our contributions to conflict. But this strength-giving awareness only comes through experiencing a new identity rooted in God's love, the gospel power at work in our hearts, and an expanded view of love.

A New Identity Rooted in God's Love

Gaining a true view of self while embracing a new identity is a powerful strength-giving combination. God first forgave us, loved us, died for us, gave grace, and offered us a place in His family; this is the foundation of our true identity and face. Some I interviewed expressed how knowing God loves them, despite their problems, gives them strength to apologize. Others said that being secure, safe, stable, and valued in God gives them strength.

As one person explained, when God points out our faults, He does so in love; therefore, there is no shame and nothing to fear. Yang Lin described how she has grown to understand that without God's love, she is unable to do anything:

> My strength comes from knowing Christ's sacrificial love. The Lord Jesus Christ died for me. I used to casually think, "Alright, He died for me," but now I feel more that this was a great grace that God has given me. If I have received such a great grace, why do I still treat others the way I do? This greatly impacted my change.

For Zhao Cheng and many others, God's love not only gives strength to apologize but also to forgive:

> Our sin nature is prone toward our internal selfishness, toward battling for revenge. If I've been hurt, I should get revenge. Without this faith, without often thinking on the Lord Jesus' sacrifice for us, the price He paid, every day recalling His grace. . . . If I don't return again every few days to these thoughts, to Father God's love in my life, then it is impossible to forgive.

This rooted identity in God's love provides the security we need to be courageous in our fragile human relationships—to apologize, forgive, proactively communicate, and even face rejection.

Gospel Power at Work in the Heart

With a believer's new identity comes the experience of the changing power of the gospel, the Holy Spirit's work in the heart. Chen Yuling explained, "It is the power of Jesus, the power of the gospel, that enables us to have this strength to dare to [apologize]. It's not something that a person is able to do. I truly know that it is the power of the Holy Spirit in us renewing us." As they sought God through prayer and recognized the need for humility, many of those I interviewed began experiencing Christ as Lord.

Recalling and singing Scripture gave Chen Yuling strength to face rejection and continue visiting her mother-in-law who had hurt her deeply over the years.

> I am divorced . . . but I still needed to maintain a relationship with my mother-in-law. You know, in China, daughters-in-law and their mothers-in-law have a lot of conflicts. At that time, my mother-in-law regularly said hurtful words and rejected me. As a result, I had a lot of inner struggles every time I went to see her. Having to regularly face her rejection was extremely painful.
>
> Before going to visit her, I would sing songs from 1 Corinthians 13:4–8 and Proverbs 15:1 about the true meaning of love and how "a gentle answer turns away wrath, but a harsh word stirs up anger." I had to receive both God's Word and the Holy Spirit's work in my heart giving me strength before going to face her rejection, coldness, and indifference.

The combination of recalling God's Word and receiving the Holy Spirit's work in our hearts can give us the courage and strength we need for difficult relationships.

In Liu Yang's case, God gave her the strength she needed to proactively talk to her mother about her mother's role in exacerbating a conflict pattern with her older sister-in-law:

> I had not been willing to talk to my mother about this issue. For one, I was very tired, and second, I just wanted to avoid it. As a result, conflicts kept happening for several years.

So one day, I prayed. I discovered that I had to exert all my strength in prayer, begging God to give me strength. Only after receiving strength from God was I able to break down my barrier, my unwillingness to communicate. After praying, I acted in accordance with the peacemaking principle of going face to face to talk to someone (Matt 18:15).[125]

God gave Liu Yang the strength to do something completely contrary to her normal way, to obey God's Word and gently confront her mom on an issue. This took a lowering of herself in her own eyes and an admittance of personal weakness and dependency on the Lord's strength. May we all gain such strength and find empowerment through humbly allowing God's Spirit to work in our hearts.

Having an Expanded View of Love

Knowing how deeply God loves us can make a pivotal difference in our loving others. When we understand that God cares more about our relationships than whether we are recognized as being right or wrong, we start to see that a difficult relationship is still worth our investment. For Ma Huan, because she has Jesus and spends daily time with Him, she can now relate to her husband differently: "I no longer feel alone. Every day I have devotions and am immersed in Jesus' love. My ears love to listen to the Lord's words. Then, when my husband scolds me, it's as if I don't hear any of it." The time spent in prayer with Jesus and reading the Bible has also enabled her to care for her husband's interests far more than before, contributing to great improvement in their relationship.

Similarly, God enabled Chen Yuling to love people that she didn't even like:

I lead a spiritual growth, small group at our church. In this group, we have all different types of women. Some of the women truly are not loveable, to the degree that sometimes, frankly speaking, they are annoying. But, when that happens, I remember that Jesus loves this woman just as He loves me. . . . At this time, I talk to the Lord, drawing strength from Him, "Lord, let me exercise patience to bear with her. Lord, I pray for her."

Our relationship with God will expand our understanding of love, and God can give us strength to love even those we previously would have ignored.

Loving someone who is irritating or hard to love is quite difficult. Yet when we have a true view of ourselves combined with gospel power at work in our hearts and the meeting of our ultimate need for love, acceptance, and identity in the Face of God, we gain an expanded view of love. We learn to love in ways we didn't previously think possible, including apologizing, forgiving, and having hard conversations. The Holy Spirit enables us to die to self and take responsibility for our thoughts, words, and actions. An expanded view of love leads to more expansive love in the small yet impactful day to day events of life.

CHAPTER WRAP-UP

Realizing and acknowledging our limitations, sins, mistakes, and contributions to conflicts requires humility and courage. Knowing that God loves us immensely as we are and that our true face comes from the Face of God enables us to take the next step to die to ourselves, set aside our old, marred, rely-on-others'-opinion-of-me-based face, and take responsibility for our sins or mistakes by confessing and apologizing. Being willing to give a confession-apology requires this reorientation of face that comes as we grow in Christ.

As a final note, this chapter has not covered all there is to say about apologizing. Some common complications and questions surface as people begin incorporating confession-apologizes into their lives: Am I apologizing too much? Why do I feel resistant to apologizing? How do I receive an apology? See Appendix C for some thoughts in response to a few of these types of questions.

A PRAYER

Lord, I acknowledge that apologizing is hard for me, especially apologizing to [insert name of person]. *I confess that, at times, I have apologized with self-serving motives rather than from a place of recognizing how I have hurt or wronged* [insert name of person]. *I pray for a truer view of myself, a deeper understanding of Your love, Your gospel to work powerfully in my heart, and for an expanded love for others.*

I need strength and courage to take that step to make a confession-apology when I have sinned or even made a mistake that impacted others. When I need to apologize to someone, help me to remember where my true face comes from and to value the face that You give me over and above the face that others give me. Thank you for Your promise to me that if I confess my sins, You are faithful and just and will forgive me of my sins and purify me from all unrighteousness (1 John 1:9). *Strengthen me to confess my sin to others so that I may be healed* (James 5:16). *In Jesus' name I pray, amen.*

REFLECTION QUESTIONS

1. How frequently do you apologize to others?

2. How have you viewed taking responsibility for your contribution to the problem in a conflict?

3. Do your apologies typically express your sorrow for something you did wrong and for the hurt you caused the other person? Or do you tend to make excuses or point out their part of the problem in your apology?

4. Would you say your apologies are "getting the salt" action-only apologies, confession-apologies, or both?

5. What has given you strength and courage to apologize when needed? To forgive?

6. In this chapter you read about three stages of maturation in understanding what apologizing really is all about. Which of these three stages would you say you are at (or are you at a different stage)? Where would you like to be?

PART 3

WHAT GOD MAKES POSSIBLE

IF YOU HAVE EVER SWUM IN THE OCEAN, you may have discovered that it can be surprisingly tiring. Your body must constantly deal with the pull of the tide. The force of crashing waves can be intense—pushing, pulling, trying to drag you down. When it seems like so many forces are against us in life, we need to swim with someone who can strengthen us to push through the crashing waves of conflict to calmer waters. We need God. But drawing near to God when waves are crashing down on us in the middle of conflict can be unexpectedly hard; our natural tendency is to draw away and try to figure out how to manage on our own.

Generally-speaking, Christians in an active relationship with God are regularly exposed to biblical guidance for relationships through reading the Bible and other materials; taking classes; or through listening to sermons and podcasts. However, because what the Bible teaches rubs against our old habits and ways of thinking, and due to habitual self-reliance, we often fail to apply what we learn.

In John 15:4–9, Jesus says that unless we stay connected to Him, like a branch is connected to a vine, we cannot bear fruit in this life. In fact, He says, "apart from me you can do nothing." We must remain in Jesus—in His love—and allow His words to remain in us. Staying connected to Jesus is vital. From time to time we all find ourselves feeling frustrated in a relationship and wondering what's gone wrong. In these moments, taking time to check our connection with Jesus helps focus us.

These next chapters are full of testimonies—the stories of people just like you and me who have changed as they died to themselves and began abiding in Christ. With the Holy Spirit's counsel, they began to acknowledge mistakes, confess sin, and apologize. Their mindsets shifted and they began to communicate differently. Those I interviewed frequently told me how their tone of voice, word choice, or openness to others all began to change. Specifically, they described growing in self-control, showing empathy, and engaging gently, calmly, and in love rather than speaking harshly or scolding. They were no longer complaining and criticizing. Instead they were listening better, asking questions, recognizing and accepting differences, and putting situations into perspective. In short, they were demonstrating the fruit of the Spirit!

These individuals took communication to a new level. They began initiating conversations, talking directly with others about conflict issues, talking honestly about their feelings, expressing respect, and even setting communication guidelines. Many began taking time to pray with the person they had differences or conflict with. Some began teaching peacemaking to others and courageously cultivating new conversation spaces.

As you read these next few chapters, imagine God enabling you to communicate in similar ways. Pray and ask God to take your communication to a new level not only when in conflict yourself but when coming alongside others seeking your help in their conflict situations. God makes it possible to communicate in new ways, be a helpful conflict companion, and cultivate an environment of peace in our families, churches, and organizations. When mindsets begin to come in line with God's Kingdom-culture, a group's conflict culture can begin to change as well.

EIGHT

BEARING FRUIT

JESUS HOLDS A HIGHER STATUS than anyone, yet He humbled himself by taking on the nature of a servant (Phil 2:5–7). We can grow in Christ's humble mindset when we abide in Him, firmly rooted in our identity as a child of God, knowing we are forgiven and loved unconditionally. Living by the Spirit, our eyes begin to see Christ's interests, not just our own (Phil 2:3–5), and our hearts begin opening up to the interests of others. As we humble ourselves, the fruit of the Spirit has room to grow in us: love, joy, peace, patience (forbearance), kindness, goodness, faithfulness, gentleness, and self-control (Gal 5:22–23). We are strengthened by God to live out Colossians 3:12–15:

> *Therefore, as God's chosen people, holy and dearly loved, clothe yourselves with compassion, kindness, humility, gentleness, and patience. Bear with each other and forgive one another if any of you has a grievance against someone. Forgive as the Lord forgave you.*

And over all these virtues put on love, which binds them all together in perfect unity. Let the peace of Christ rule in your hearts, since as members of one body you were called to peace. And be thankful.

Galatians 5:22–23	Colossians 3:12–15
Love	Love
Joy; Peace	Peace
Forbearance (patience)	Patience; bear with each other
Kindness	Kindness
Goodness	Humility
Faithfulness	Compassion
Gentleness	Gentleness
Self-control	Forgiving

The following stories illustrate how some of the fruit of the Spirit can look in our everyday, conflict struggles and how they can contribute to relational restoration.

Love, Humility, and Joy:
Loving Actions

Living out 1 John 3:18, "Let us not love with words or speech but with actions and in truth," can significantly impact our relationships. This spiritual fruit of love in action takes various forms but has only one source, the Holy Spirit.

Ma Huan was filled with anger after an incident left her feeling wronged by her invalid mother, so she stepped out of the room to compose herself. After reading her Bible for a while, the anger in her heart subsided and was replaced with joy. With this joy, she chose love and went back to speak to her mother, asking, "Are you still angry?" Her mother did not reply. Ma Huan then said, "I'm not angry," but still her mother did not speak. Finally she asked, "Do you need me to rub your back or do something for you?" In response, her mother looked at her and said, "This late? You should go to bed; it's not necessary. We can talk about it in the morning." Ma Huan's Holy Spirit prompted, joy-inspired love led her to keep reaching out to her mom despite the silence. Offering to physically serve her mother by rubbing her back then broke down the wall between them and paved the way for future communication and true relationship reconciliation and growth.

After years of opposition and relational rejection from her in-laws, Yang Lin's loving actions resulted in both reconciliation and their salvation.

> Last year my father-in-law became ill. . . . I was the only person available to help. So I set aside my work and went to their city to take care of him. I took care of everything for them from finding a doctor to arrangements for the hospital stay.

My mother-in-law's heart was weak at that time, so I couldn't let her stay with my father-in-law at night. I spent the nights with him instead. Sometimes I returned home during the day to teach, making for long days. . . . In the end, he was unable to move and just lay on the bed, so I would bathe his body, including taking care of his waste.

Then my husband's father, deeply moved, said to me, "I never expected that you would take care of us like this. After the way we treated you . . . I am so sorry."

He was later baptized in his hospital bed, and I said to him, "We are one family in the Lord now; I am so thankful!"

Before he passed away last year, he [again] apologized to me. My heart was released, and I felt all these years of effort were not in vain.

[The relationship with] my husband's mother also suddenly and completely changed. She affirmed me and apologized to me . . . for treating me poorly. Additionally, she also came to believe in the Lord!

The relationship changed from one in which they completely ignored me to tolerance and them being kind to me on a surface level. But in the end, when others asked them if I was their daughter (a daughter-in-law would never take care of in-laws like that), they would say, "Yes, she's my girl, my daughter." I was so happy. I finally felt affirmed.

Yang Lin's humble and sacrificial care, despite years of hurt, resulted in her being fully received as a daughter. Here are two individuals who might never have come to a relationship with Jesus without the sacrificial, Spirit-prompted fruit of loving actions from one who could easily have chosen to stay in relational conflict.

PEACE: PUTTING THE SITUATION IN PERSPECTIVE

As the Holy Spirit enables us to put situations into perspective by focusing on the bigger picture, we can experience peace of heart and mind. This focus can play a role in being willing to reconcile with others. But gaining this new perspective doesn't necessarily come easily.

Chen Dandan described a time of conflict which resulted in a communication break with a church leader. The resulting pressure hung uneasily over her for years:

> At the time of the conflict . . . I got up every day at 4 or 5 am to pray. I couldn't talk to anyone else about the conflict since it was a church conflict, so I just prayed by myself. After a month of prayer, I felt like I had sorted things out. I went ahead and let the situation go, but I still didn't feel able to talk to the church leader about the way he handled the conflict. I was not truly at peace.
>
> Two years later, God suddenly helped me to clearly see things from the church leader's perspective. I realized that he had not made his decisions based on his own perspective or that of the particular individuals involved in the conflict. Rather, he had been looking at the situation from the church's perspective. The purpose of his decision was to protect our church as a whole. . . .
>
> Finally I thought: *How the church leader dealt with the situation doesn't matter. He was considering the matter from the church's point of view; whereas, I have been looking at it from a personal perspective. His perspective was broader than mine, so I should not appraise him according to this personal frame of mind. I need to believe that he was acting in the interest of the church.*

And maybe, as he was thinking about the benefit of the church as a whole, he was unable to fully take every person's thoughts and needs into consideration.

To mistakenly overlook something is normal; the pastor's perspective was normal. As a result of this broadened perspective of my own, I was able to be fully at peace in my heart with him. Since then I have had no further thoughts about this situation even though we never talked about the situation.

Gaining a Spirit-given perspective of the conflict and coming to an understanding that the church leader had been operating from his own broader church perspective rather than a personal perspective made the difference for Chen Dandan. She was finally able to be fully at peace in her heart with this leader.

PATIENCE, FAITHFULNESS, AND BEARING WITH: RECOGNIZING AND ACCEPTING DIFFERENCES

1 Corinthians 12:12 reminds us: "Just as a body, though one, has many parts, but all its many parts form one body, so it is with Christ." One expression of faithfulness in Christ's body is recognizing and accepting the differences between our "many parts" and patiently bearing with them instead of relationally giving up when our differences clash.[126]

When I asked Li Min to describe a typical conflict scenario with her husband, she told me, "None of our conflict situations are about big things just daily life things." For example, once Li Min received a text message from their child's teacher, reminding them to pay class tuition. For Li Min, this text indicated that her husband had not yet paid the tuition as he had committed to doing. This left her feeling quite angry.

As she prepared to forward the message from the teacher to him, she drafted an additional text:

> I reminded you to pay on the nineteenth. I reminded you again on the twentieth. I originally wanted to remind you last night, too, but I thought, *I'm afraid he'll get angry and think that I'm always asking him like this.* So I didn't remind you. But look. You still forgot. GO PAY ASAP![127]

Realizing that this complaining, critical, judgmental draft would just add gasoline to the fire of conflict, she deleted it.

In its place, she sent the following message to her husband: "The teacher reminded me to pay tuition. I feel some pressure from it." Notice that she shifted from focusing on what he didn't do to expressing how she felt upon receiving the text from the teacher.

He quickly texted back saying, "Okay. I'm sorry. I forgot."[128]

She then deliberately reminded herself, *You need to forget about it; let it go.* Li Min said to me, "I regularly remind myself that my husband is not the person I imagine him to be. I am learning to acknowledge that maybe our personalities really are different and it's okay." Learning to bear with one another can bring peace to our hearts and relationships.

Wang Fang's reflection upon what contributed to her willingness to reconcile with her older, male, Christian colleague demonstrates a similar growth of spiritual fruit in her life:

> I started to think to myself: *He has worked by himself for all this time, just him. Then I suddenly showed up, trespassing in his safe space. I came too close. Furthermore, my personality is very different from his. In many situations, I was probably too anxious for results, and in the process, I didn't respect him, so he felt violated.*

His work habits. Her value of results. Very different personalities. These were all differences that Wang Fang found difficult, so she disrespected her colleague in her heart and actions. After gaining new awareness, perspective, and compassion, Wang Fang initiated peacemaking by inviting her colleague to a meal where she patiently looked for the right opportunity to be able to give her apology. "He talked for two and a half hours. I can't remember any of what he said. I just know that, as he talked, I was looking for the time when I could say, 'I'm sorry' to him." When a phone call interrupted his monologue, she seized the opportunity and apologized. Their relationship was restored.

Bearing with the other person, practicing patience, and seeking ways to be faithful to reconciling relationships—these are all spiritual fruit that grow as we live by the Spirit in the love of God.

KINDNESS, GOODNESS, AND COMPASSION: NO LONGER CRITICIZING, BLAMING, OR CONDEMNING

Jesus teaches us "Do not judge and criticize and condemn [others unfairly with an attitude of self-righteous superiority as though assuming the office of a judge], so that you will not be judged [unfairly]" (Matt 7:1, AMP, *sic*). Peter reiterates this, declaring, "Do not complain against one another, believers, so that you will not be judged [for it]" (1 Peter 4:9a, AMP, *sic*). And Paul also reminds us in Ephesians 4:22–32 that believers are to put off their old selves, and "be made new in the attitude of your minds" (v. 23). God's Spirit enables us to put off our old criticizing, blaming, condemning, lying, bitter, stealing, slandering, and argumentative self. As we put on our new self, abiding in Christ, God adjusts the attitudes of our mind, enabling us to bear new spiritual fruit:

choosing to speak words that build up and to extend kindness, compassion, and forgiveness.

As we put on our new self, abiding in Christ, God adjusts the attitudes of our mind, enabling us to bear new spiritual fruit: choosing to speak words that build up and to extend kindness, compassion, and forgiveness.

After studying biblical peacemaking, Liu Yang decided to address her strained relationship with her mother. Before this, they frequently clashed over differing opinions. Liu Yang began to consciously speak in a kinder way, asking questions and seeking to understand before criticizing. "After proactively shifting to this model, my conversations with my mom started to grow longer. We went from only being able to stand talking to each other for less than ten minutes at a time to now being able to talk for an hour!" Conscious, compassionate engagement positively impacted their relationship.

Ma Huan and Zhang Li both learned valuable lessons about choosing gentle speech and positive modeling over critical condemnation. As Ma Huan explained, "Because we are God's children, we are to imitate our Father, right? He covered over our mistakes; we also are to cover over others' mistakes." So when her son was in the hospital after a bike accident, Ma Huan brought him his favorite food instead of scolding and reminding him that she had warned him to be careful. Zhang Li began quietly and lovingly helping others do a job correctly instead of verbally berating them. "Think more considerately of others and do your best not to speak useless words. Some words can strike a small spark. You might think nothing of it, but that spark gets buried in the other person's heart." Compassion and kindness—even such a small shift from critiquing to assisting—can change hearts and relationships.

Empathizing with those of an older generation can be particularly helpful in developing an inner willingness to be positive and compassionate. Both Huang Jingjing and Ma Huan developed much-improved family relationships partly due to newly-discovered compassion and empathy.

I [Huang Jingjing] understand [my mother-in-law] better now. . . . [Her son's] marriage to me snatched him away from her; he no longer listens to her. As a result, maybe she no longer has a sense of security, which resulted in hostility toward me. I feel I need to be especially merciful toward her."

Similarly, Ma Huan realized her aging mother is physically struggling. Her previous bitterness, criticism, and blame has turned into "having compassion on her limitations [which] enables me to cool down and change my perspective." For both individuals, a change of perspective and extending of compassion, gentleness, and kindness generated significant change in their relationships. For Ma Huan, grace combined with loving service contributed to her mother becoming a Christian, thus transforming and reconciling their relationship.

Choosing to develop an attitude of compassion over criticism, blame, or condemnation led to kinder responses and improved relationships.

Each one of these stories has a common thread. Choosing to develop an attitude of compassion over criticism, blame, or condemnation led to kinder responses and improved relationships, even despite ongoing conflict. Once again, the fruit of the Spirit leads to changed relationships.

GENTLENESS: CHANGING YOUR COMMUNICATION APPROACH

Putting on the new self with a renewed mind through abiding in Christ also enables the spiritual fruit of gentleness to grow. A new approach to communication can emerge, one that heeds Paul's words to "be completely humble and gentle; be patient, bearing with one another in love" and to "make every effort to keep the unity of the Spirit through the bond of peace" (Eph 4:2–3).

Huang Jingjing's overbearing mother-in-law was the source of significant relational friction between herself and her husband. Changing her approach when discussing his mother's slander of her began to make a big difference in their marriage:

> When his mom would speak badly about me in front of him, I used to complain in disapproval saying, "Look, your mom said that I am [insert criticism]. How can you not say anything or speak up for me?"
>
> Now I have stopped complaining to my husband in this way. Instead, I'll calmly and gently say, "Today your mom said this, and I feel a little sad. What do you think is her reason for saying this? I hope that in the future she doesn't speak like this." Afterwards, my husband was better able to understand my position.

Huang Jingjing changed her approach to discussion with her husband in five productive ways:

1. She spoke in a calm, gentle manner that welcomed dialogue.

2. She stated what happened from her perspective.

3. She shared how she felt in response.

4. She asked a question seeking understanding.

5. She stated her specific desire for change but not in the form of a demand.

Huang Jingjing's gentler communication style resulted in her husband understanding her experience and, in the end, advocating for her with his mom.

Similarly, Wang Jia discovered the power of gentleness in conflict. Previously, in conflicts with her mother, Wang Jia used to react strongly and impatiently saying things like, "Ok, ok, stop talking about it!" She told me, "Now, I am able to have a gentler attitude and say, 'When you say X, I think Y, and I feel Z, so I have a bad reaction.'" Her new approach, similar to Huang Jingjing's, contributed to her mother's more positive response: "If you communicate better with me like this, I can also accept what you have to say."

A gentle, calm, and patient attitude is often paired with talking honestly and expressing one's feelings. As these communication approaches significantly contribute to relationship restoration and biblical peacemaking, we will explore these aspects further in the next chapter.

SELF-CONTROL:
RECOGNIZING EMOTIONS, CALMING DOWN, AND LISTENING

James 1:19–20 instructs us, "My dear brothers and sisters, take note of this: Everyone should be quick to listen, slow to speak and slow to become angry, because human anger does not produce the righteousness that God desires." God calls us to exercise self-control and listen well. In biblical peacemaking, self-control should be one of the first spiritual fruit we seek.

As a conflict erupted between Zhang Jing and a younger, female, Christian colleague, Zhang Jing found herself growing increasingly frustrated when, while trying to talk through the issue together, her colleague repeatedly brought up hurt she had experienced in her childhood. This repetition began to drive Zhang Jing crazy. She could feel her anger increasing, pushing her to escalate the conflict. However, instead of reacting out of her frustration, Zhang Jing exercised self-control:

> A gentle, calm, and patient attitude is often paired with talking honestly and expressing one's feelings.

> A peacemaking principle compelled me to consider: *What does God want me to learn through this?* So, in the middle of that conflict, I took a deep breath and calmed down. I stopped continuously criticizing her in my heart for repeating herself and instead listened, listened, and listened some more. Then, I asked her, "If this situation were to happen again, how would you like me to respond to you?"

As a result of recognizing her emotions and exercising self-control by taking a deep breath, calming down, and reflecting on a peacemaking-focused question, Zhang Jing was able to engage in a positive way with her upset colleague.

Zhang Jing then began praying weekly with this colleague, slowly becoming a better listener in the process: "I learned to ask, 'In our interactions, have there been any times when what I have said has made you uncomfortable?' We would then talk about it." Exercising self-control and listening closely opened up their communication and increased trust.

Taking time to pray together in the moment can also be a great way to recognize and control our emotions. When his five-year-old daughter lied to him, Li Jun felt angry: "Lying is quite serious. In my heart I was praying about how to deal with this situation, so I immediately led her to pray together. Most importantly, the first purpose for praying was that I hoped I could calm down." In this way, Li Jun calmed down and was able to respond with appropriate disciplinary action rather than lashing out in anger.

Li Ailing, an older Christian with a non-Christian husband, described how she learned to follow the James 1:19–20 principles of self-control—shifting from giving an answer before listening to truly listening to her husband before ever responding:

> I often cared for my husband because he was sick, but he was not satisfied with the way I cooked. When my husband would find fault with me and say critically, "You've used too much oil," or "The fire is too high," I would flare up angrily. I used to express my unhappiness by grimacing and ignoring him. I knew that if I argued with him, he would be in even more pain and then I would feel bad for arguing with him and negatively influencing his return to health.
>
> Now, after this peacemaking study, even though I still flare up, I take a moment to control my emotions and examine myself before speaking. From my perspective, I am painstakingly cooking for him and think that what I'm doing is fine. Yet I ask myself, *Have I done anything that is causing him to worry?*

Then I think: *Maybe he thinks I've used too much oil, that I shouldn't put so much oil in this dish, but I think that it's the right amount. But I should still listen to him. And he said the fire was too high; maybe he has a point. I can first accommodate him and use a little less oil and turn the heat down.*" In this way we have slowly, slowly, slowly made it to this day. Now he treats me better and better.

This combination of recognizing and controlling her emotions, practicing self-reflection, and considering her husband's concerns all have contributed to an improved relationship. As the fruit of self-control grows, new approaches to communication can follow. Our normal habits of reacting to others in anger and saying or doing things that enflame a conflict and create distance can begin to change.

CHAPTER WRAP-UP

In China, I frequently witnessed people changing after becoming Christians. After tasting God's forgiveness, receiving new life, and experiencing the joy of reconciliation with God, many of those I interviewed experienced breakthroughs in how they view conflict, apologizing, face, and forgiveness. Isn't it beautiful to see what God makes possible as we abide in Jesus, live by God's Spirit instead of our flesh, and keep in step with Him? We begin to bear the abundant fruit of His Spirit in our lives (John 15:4–9; Gal 5:22–25). Remember, our job is to believe and abide in Jesus, not strive in our own strength to live differently.

Jesus, the one who made reconciliation with God *and changing normal* possible, tells us where to focus instead of relying on ourselves and the status quo:

> Come to me, all you who are weary and burdened, and I will give you rest. Take my yoke upon you and learn from me, for I am gentle and humble in heart, and you will find rest for your souls. For my yoke is easy and my burden is light. (Matt 11:28–30)

When applied to our relationships and peacemaking, I hear Jesus saying something like, "Come to me, all you who are weary of the conflicts in your relationships, who have been taught how to respond to conflict by your family and culture but find that following those rules isn't working for you. You are carrying heavy burdens. You are distanced in your heart from others, even though, on the surface, you are polite and everything looks fine. Come to me; I will give you rest. Walk with me, learn my pace, learn my way of doing things. I will be gentle with you. I am humble and will show you the way to be gentle and humble with others. In this, you will find rest for your souls."

We often wonder why we are tired, cut up, and bleeding from the yoke. We blame God. But the yoke itself is not causing us to bleed. We bleed because we are pushing ahead of Jesus, dragging behind Him, or heading in a different direction altogether, still trying to do things our own way.

When we allow Jesus to gently and humbly lead the way, we begin to think and live differently. As we walk in step with Jesus, learning to love others as He loves, and to forgive as He forgives, we can find rest for our souls. What a gift! It all starts with choosing to be humble and die to ourselves, to receive God's abundance prepared for us in Christ, and to rely on the Holy Spirit. Let's accept being yoked with Christ, confess our striving, learn His ways to face conflict, and step into the rest that Jesus offers.

A PRAYER

Lord, You tell us that what Your Spirit desires is contrary to what my flesh desires; Your Spirit and my flesh are in conflict (Gal 5:16–25). Thank You that I belong to Christ Jesus. My flesh, with its passions and desires, has been crucified. You instruct me to live by the Spirit, to depend on Your Spirit, to keep in step with Jesus' stride, yoked together with Him. The resulting fruit of love, humility, joy, peace, patience, forbearance, kindness, goodness, compassion, faithfulness, gentleness, and self-control will then begin to characterize my life. Thank you!

Lord, when someone speaks in anger or frustration to me, strengthen me with grace by Your Spirit to choose to be gentle, humble, and calm in response; to exercise self-control, listen well, and be patient; and to ask good questions and clarify as needed without defensiveness. Increase my recognition of when I speak with critical, condemning, or attacking words.

I ask for grace to see what loving actions You would have me take to care for those I find hard to love. When I have very different views, priorities, and habits from those around me, help me see how our differences can bring value to our relationship.

Thank you, Lord, for giving me the mind of Christ so that I can be guided by Your thoughts and purposes (1 Cor 2:16). Thank You that Your divine power has given me everything I need for a godly life through my knowledge of You who called me by Your own glory and goodness (2 Peter 1:3). Grow me in my experiential knowledge of You. In Jesus' name I pray, amen.

REFLECTION QUESTIONS

1. Which stories from this chapter encouraged or inspired you? What steps do you feel led to imitate in your personal relationships?

2. Which stories from this chapter challenged or convicted you? What are you going to do with those challenges or convictions?

3. How do you view and approach the differences between you and [your spouse, colleague, church leader, child, etc.]? Do you appreciate the differences? Do you experience them as threatening? Is your response changing as you learn more?

4. Have you found yourself stuck in a pattern of (1) verbally or physically attacking others or (2) ignoring conflict, pretending it doesn't exist, and leaving when there is trouble? If so, what practical actions have you read about that might help you start breaking this pattern?

5. To what degree are you relying on God for help to be gentle and humble in your relationships?

6. Which fruit of the Spirit would you like to see more of in your life and relationships? What might that look like practically speaking?

NINE

INITIATING CONVERSATIONS

IF YOU ARE UNACCUSTOMED to initiating conversations about conflict issues, you might feel nervous, scared, or anxious when considering such an action. Perhaps everything in you cries out, "Leave!" or "Just ignore this." When telling me about his process of praying to determine whether he should stay or leave a church, Li Jun said, "If I were to behave according to my instinct and habitual way of thinking, I would just quit and leave; this is the Chinese way." This is not just the Chinese way, it's the human way!

Initiating a conversation after conflict can be difficult for many of us; it is a muscle that needs to be exercised in order to grow stronger. Wang Jia's story of how her father proactively approached her after an intense conflict illustrates the challenge and need for us to exercise this important muscle.

My dad gets drunk sometimes. During our worst argument ever, I smashed every single bottle of alcohol in the house. The floorboards still bear marks from it. I prayed to God, "I thought you were a righteous God; how could you have given me such a terrible father?"

But in the middle of the conflict, I began to see that my dad is also weak. He's not purposefully trying to treat us this way. I suddenly saw that my own behavior reflected low character. . . . [Looking back], I began to see myself more clearly. My dad actually behaves better toward me in conflict than I do toward him!

After [another] conflict . . . I was angry and spent a lot of time complaining to God, "I can't be the only one who does the work of reconciling! You have to make him change some, too. If you tell me to bear with this, what should I do when I can't bear it?"

At that time, my dad lived with me. The day after I prayed, God did something amazing. My dad called me over. He said, "My meaning yesterday isn't what you imagine it to be. In my heart I really was not thinking like that."

I immediately felt comforted. First, God heard my prayer. Second, I saw how, in conflict, my dad is the one who is willing to make concessions; I'm the one who builds up a wall. I engage in a cold war, give a cold shoulder, and don't value the relationship.

My father . . . demonstrated that he isn't the evil person I had imagined him to be. Also, I saw that I am not the good person that I imagine myself to be. Just like the peacemaking study teaches, "You might be the person with the log in your eye but think you have the splinter."[129] I'm that person. My dad always takes the posture of reconciliation first. Only after he initiates will I examine myself and ask, have I done anything wrong? He has behaved better than I have when it comes to reconciling.

In a situation where Wang Jia would have continued to relationally distance herself in her anger, her father proactively initiated a clarifying conversation which led Wang Jia to see how she had misunderstood him. Even though Wang Jia was the one who prayed, and thus is the person we might expect to initiate a conversation, God showed Wang Jia grace through her dad's initiative. She discovered how much she still needed to grow in this area.

Someone has to take the first step to initiate conversation. For those seeking to reflect God's Face in relationships, let's be the ones doing the initiating. Read on to learn ways to initiate conversation that don't exacerbate a situation.

PRAYER FIRST

Despite being accustomed to initiating difficult conversations, I still tend to feel fearful and anxious when I know I need to go talk to someone. It has gotten easier with practice but not more comfortable. Such feelings drive me, and many of those I interviewed, to prayer. God often enables us to do what feels impossible when we first persevere in praying.

Zhou Na found prayer opened her up to forgive a man whom she despised—her father. At the end of his life, after ten days of caring for him in the hospital, Zhou Na was faced with a choice. When her father called her over to do something for him, in her physical and emotional exhaustion, she prayed, "God, look at this man. He can't do anything. He caused so much suffering to his wife and daughter. How can he glorify you?" God's clear response was amazing:

"It is now time. The time to forgive your father has come."

I thought, "Wait a minute! First, I don't want to forgive him out of pity. Second, I don't want to forgive him just because he is about to die and I don't want to regret not having forgiven him."

God then said, "It's not for these two reasons. *I* want you to do this."

Even though I was quite unwilling, there was an urgent voice in my heart saying, "This bus stop won't come again after you pass this village." Meaning, after this moment, I would never again have the opportunity to have this conversation with my father.

God said, "You choose."

I said, "Okay, I choose to do it."

That night was a very big turning point in my life. I said to my dad, who was in a tremendous amount of physical pain at the time, "I want to say something to you. In Christ, I am choosing to forgive you of all the hurt you have caused me in the past, present, and future."

After saying these words, I cried but not out of pity for myself. No. I cried because I finally felt free.

I had kept such an emotional distance from him prior to that night, so I knew that the ability to speak and forgive him in this way did not come from myself.

Sometimes God keeps graciously nudging our hearts as we pray, gifting us discomfort or a lack of peace until we make things right. Thank God for this nudging so our hearts can be set free and relationships set right.

No matter what kind of conflict you find yourself facing and no matter how overwhelmed, scared, or angry you feel about the idea of initiating conversation with someone else, there is one step you can always take without hesitation: Pray. God hears the prayers of His people, and He will be with you as you place the situation in His hands.

TALKING DIRECTLY WITH THE PERSON

In Chinese culture, when two people are in conflict, it is common to have a third party be a go-between for communication in order to preserve everyone's face. While a go-between is needed in some conflicts, talking directly with the other person, although uncomfortable and counter-cultural, is the better first step in many situations.

For six years, Liu Yang had not spoken to her good friend of forty years. When her friend became a Christian and joined the church's baptism class, they had a natural opportunity to talk again. Being at the same gatherings opened the door to conversation, renewing their communication with one another. Because their attitude toward each other at these times was very gentle, they were willing to set an appointment to talk through the details of the past conflict.

When they finally met up to talk about the conflict issue that had caused the rift in their relationship, they discovered that misunderstanding and misinformation was at the root of the breakdown of trust in their relationship.

> Having this specific time to talk enabled us to bring everything out in the open. . . . We discussed the conflict between us, the hurts, and the areas which needed apologies.

> As we talked, we discovered our mutual friend—who tended to exaggerate, magnify things, and add her own fictional perspective to information she shared—had spread misinformation to each of us, resulting in my friend and I no longer trusting each other. Because I didn't know whether or not she was telling the truth at the time, I distanced myself from her.
>
> We saw how our previous communication had been obstructed. In the end, we completely reconciled.

It was six years before they discovered that misinformation and misunderstanding had hurt their relationship! Yet the relationship would have stayed broken if they had not met up to talk through what had happened those many years ago.

For Wu Chunhua, privately discussing an issue that had come up with her Christian colleague led to them seeing how they also had misunderstood each other:

> I am a kindergarten teacher, and I have a colleague who is a great person. One day, in our class, she said, "Those who are mothers definitely have more experience than those who aren't mothers," meaning those teachers who weren't mothers yet maybe aren't that good of teachers—at least this is what she seemed to be communicating. Well, because I was not a mother yet, I felt like my work had been negated. I was hurt, but I didn't go talk to her directly about it. We saw each other often, but I always felt unhappy. No matter what she did, I felt like she was speaking against me, aiming at me.
>
> Finally, one day I asked her, "Have I offended you in any way?"

She replied, "No," but then shared about a time when she had asked me about my plans to get married and it seemed like I didn't want to answer her. At the time of her question, I was dating but not yet engaged. She felt she was expressing her care for me, yet I was distancing myself from her, so she began to wonder if perhaps our relationship wasn't as close as she thought it was.

I didn't remember this conversation at all! I apologized and reassured her that asking me this question was truly fine. I told her I would have no problem telling her when I will get married because I planned to invite her. In all honesty, I couldn't recall the conversation!

She responded with a surprised, "Oh!"

Then I told her about the time I had felt hurt by her statement that teachers who are mothers have more experience. She replied, "Oh! That wasn't my meaning. I was just making conversation."

I reflected on this and realized she had simply been stating what is true. I had felt negated, rejected as a result of her words, but in certain ways, those who are already mothers do have more experience. When she told me she didn't intend to convey the meaning that I had heard, we prayed together, cried, and were reconciled.

Because Wu Chunhua initiated the conversation and asked directly about offense, her coworker had the opportunity to think back and respond. Thankfully, her coworker was also willing to reflect, speak honestly, and go deeper in conversation, which resulted in clearing up the misunderstandings and developing an even closer relationship.

In both these examples, if one person had not initiated opening up the conversational door, these relationships would have continued with a barrier or may have even drifted further apart until there was no longer any relationship at all. As long as our motivation comes from a godly desire for peace and reconciliation, seeking clarity in relationships is worth the effort.

TALKING HONESTLY: EXPRESSING FEELINGS

Talking honestly about our feelings and thoughts may be uncomfortable and counter-cultural due to an unconscious tendency to preserve face, either ours or the other person's. Yet honesty lays the foundation for increased intimacy. In our interviews, many people described how expressing their feelings or the thinking behind their behavior provided helpful information which led to the other person's increased understanding and empathy.

Following a serious conflict with her husband, Chen Dandan and her husband specifically took time to talk through it using a process they called "clearing out the garbage."

> I just wanted to ignore him. On the second day, we didn't speak to each other. Actually, in my heart I knew what my problem was. I knew I had my part of the problem, and he had his part. But I felt so wronged. I needed to deal with my sense of feeling wronged. He also felt wronged.

> Finally, we used a method called "clearing out the garbage" to talk. Clearing out the garbage refers to a process where I first let him share what bad feelings he has because of the issue. I then apologize for causing those bad feelings. In this situation, I was able to apologize after listening to him. I also shared what made me feel bad, and he apologized for causing me to have those bad feelings. After

we both apologized, we cried together. In fact, my husband had been very distressed. He has a soft heart.

Our reconciliation process also has a condition of glorifying God. We are each committed to asking ourselves: Does what we do glorify God? Whatever in our relationship does not glorify God, we must immediately stop.

In this way, we reconciled and never again brought up the incident. I no longer felt any sense of being wronged. It truly is in the past.

Clearing out the garbage is a process in which both people take turns listening carefully and honestly expressing feelings that surface in response to the other person's behavior. Not only does this process facilitate both party's listening and sharing, but it also helps each person see what they personally need to apologize for. The process moves both individuals toward reconciliation.

Another way to talk honestly with each other is to intentionally "return to the scene," to revisit a particular conversation that ended in conflict. This involves going line by line through the conversation and sharing with each other what you were thinking and feeling both as you spoke and as you listened to the other person speak (and vice versa).

Chen Meizhen described proactively sharing her feelings with her female Christian colleague after an uncomfortable, previous interaction:

One time we went to [name of a ministry location]. She and I were responsible for a small group together. As we were preparing for the small group, she commented about me not doing something well. This made me uncomfortable, but I didn't say anything. We completed our work and returned home; I thought everything was fine. But, after a while, I still felt uncomfortable. Even so, I didn't go talk with her about it. This used to be my standard approach to conflict.

In recent years, I began proactively going to her. For example, the same experience happened again last year. This time I went to her and asked if she had time to talk. She said yes. I told her I wanted to share something from that day. Then I shared what had happened, how her words seemed a bit critical and left me feeling uncomfortable. In response she said, "Oh, if you didn't tell me, I wouldn't have had any idea my words had that kind of impact." After speaking out about this, my heart felt comfortable again, and our relationship wasn't influenced negatively by what had happened.

I've changed. Now when I feel uncomfortable from a conflict, maybe we haven't even argued face to face, I will still go and speak to the person.

Not only did Chen Meizhen initiate conversation, but she also "returned to the scene" and talked through the specifics of their exchange, expressing how she felt in response to the other person's precise words. Her sharing opened up the possibility for the other person to clarify misunderstanding and make changes.

When telling me about the reconciliation that occurred between her and a Christian colleague, Zhou Na also illustrated the importance of talking through the details of a specific interaction and honestly expressing the impact of the other person's words. As you read, note how both parties listened to each other and shared openly.

My dad had been sick with a serious illness for many years. Most of my work colleagues knew how bad my relationship with my dad used to be and how we now had a restored relationship; I will be sad when my father dies. One day, when several of us who have a good relationship were together, I jokingly said, "After my dad passes away, I will take my mom out to do things."[130]

One of my colleagues said, "Oh my! Zhou Na, don't talk like that! This is such a serious thing."

I replied, "Indeed, it is a serious thing." Our tone was lighthearted and joking.

Suddenly, one of my male colleagues started shaking his head and said with a heavy voice, "You can't talk like that. For a father to hear his daughter speak of his death in this way . . . " He then reprimanded me in front of everyone and the atmosphere suddenly became quite awkward.

Zhou Na and this Christian colleague previously had a good working relationship, but after this exchange, things were strained between them. She felt embarrassed and struggled to find an appropriate way and time to talk with him about the incident. So when he asked her to have a meal together, she understood that his purpose and desire was to talk about the conflict. She was relieved, "His initiation to meet up dissolved the awkwardness that I felt."

Over lunch, he shared what had happened from his perspective. Zhou Na then shared how deeply hurt she felt by his response. She told him how his behavior had affected her feelings and thinking. He then explained what was behind his thinking, why he gave her that advice, and why he had gotten angry. Zhou Na then described to him what her relationship with her parents is like. After they both shared, Zhou Na felt they understood each other much better. Her colleague acknowledged he could now understand why his words felt hurtful. This sharing of behind-the-scenes feelings and motivations, together with the accompanying clarification, paved the way for reconciliation.

Whether you are "clearing out the garbage" or "returning to the scene," being willing to pause, listen for understanding, share your own feelings, take responsibility for hurts you have caused, and forgive all can go a long way to calming the storm in a relationship. Engaging in this type of conversation requires a willingness to be honest and vulnerable with someone else. It also requires acknowledging your own and the other person's emotions and the ways you've fallen short of loving as Christ loves.

Being willing to pause, listen for understanding, share your own feelings, take responsibility for hurts you have caused, and forgive all can go a long way to calming the storm in a relationship.

GIVING AFFIRMATION AND EXPRESSING RESPECT

Sometimes we fear speaking honestly because we know how blunt and harsh we can be or how our words can be misconstrued. Speaking words of affirmation and expressing genuine respect through our tone, posture, and actions, can create the safety needed for others to receive our honesty.

Affirming someone and expressing respect can significantly impact movement toward reconciliation. Zhang Jing told me,

> I used to regularly bring up my older sister's bad habits but would never mention any of the good things she had done. After studying

peacemaking . . . I started telling my older sister the various aspects I admired about her. I also would tell her I saw how tired and hardworking she was. She was then able to receive what I had to say.

Zhang Jing's affirmation of her sister's positive qualities followed by an expression of empathy demonstrated to her sister that Zhang Jing recognized all she did and valued her.

Speaking of a difficult relationship with her teenage daughter, Chen Yuling said, "Through the peacemaking study, I learned how to praise my daughter, express my appreciation of her, use a gentle tone of voice, and respect her." After learning that physical touch is very important in relationships, Chen Yuling also tried various ways to show affection toward her teenage daughter who, at that time, was not interested in a relationship with her. Note the respect Chen Yuling showed her daughter in this process.

Sometimes when walking with her, I would intentionally link arms with her for a short while and then let go because she would feel uncomfortable if I did it for too long. I was afraid of being rejected. Sometimes when she was sitting doing homework, I would stand behind her, speak, and then lightly and briefly place my hands on her back. In this way I let her slowly get used to my expressions of love. Sometimes I would ask her what she would like to eat and rub her head with my hands.

Now our relationship looks so different. My daughter lives in [name of another city], so sometimes when we are at the train station preparing to part ways or when we have just met up, we will hug each other. When others see what we are doing they say, "Wow, look at those two people! What a great relationship!"

As a result of taking small steps in respectful ways and slowly experimenting with different actions to accomplish her goal, Chen Yuling discovered what physical expressions of love her daughter was willing to accept, all of which contributed to their relationship slowly improving.

Chen Dandan had a small conflict with her eighteen-year-old son that ended with a stronger bond of trust forged because of the respectful way she approached the conversation:

> On that night, my son was in his bedroom exercising. I wanted to watch how he was exercising, so I sat next to him. He didn't like me watching him. He got a bit agitated and irritable and said, "I want to sleep. You, you, you . . ." meaning that I was in the way, a hindrance.
>
> When I saw his expression, I felt rather uncomfortable and indignant. I thought to myself, *What's wrong with me sitting here? I'm your mom.*
>
> If I had acted according to my flesh, I would have said in a disapproving tone, "Why don't you let me watch? Your behavior . . ."
>
> In that moment, I didn't express my complaint. I said calmly and caringly, "Okay, if you want to sleep, I'll go," and I went off to wash my face and brush my teeth. After fifteen minutes, I returned, but he hadn't gone to bed. He had finished exercising but was now on his cell phone.
>
> At this time, I said to him with a loving yet direct tone, "Come over here," and called him out to the living room so we could talk outside of his bedroom.

I said, "Just now you didn't like having mom in your bedroom, so you said you were going to bed. I supported you and expressed understanding; if you want to sleep, I will leave. Now I have already finished washing my face and brushing my teeth, but you still haven't gone to bed."

Then he started to hug me saying, "Mom, I'm sorry."

I said, "Okay. In the future, if you don't want me to watch you exercise, all you have to do is say, 'Mom, when I'm exercising, I don't want you to watch,' and I will not watch. You are already a big kid, so I will understand and respect your personal space, not force something. Using a correct way of speaking instead of lying safeguards our relationship. If you lie to drive me out, this isn't right and hurts me. I feel rejected, not welcome. In this case, you weren't really planning on sleeping. You need to speak truthfully. I will understand you."

So, we were able to work through the issue in a great way which kept us from accumulating conflict inside. Now he trusts me more and isn't so defensive. If he wants to say something, he dares to say it knowing I will respond in an appropriate way.

In this story, Chen Dandan illustrates controlling her emotions, engaging calmly rather than aggressively, and proactively initiating a conversation in which she discusses the conflict situation directly, openly, and with an honest expression of her feelings. Woven throughout her story is a clear expression of respect, value for the relationship, care for her son's feelings, and an acknowledgment of her need to approach their relationship differently due to his older age. The way in which she engaged her son caused him to more willingly receive her instruction.

When we start looking at others with an eye to affirm who they are, what they need, and what they desire, our attitudes and perspectives shift. As we verbally and physically affirm relationships with others in a way which supports them, recognizing their needs and values, new patterns begin to form. Relationships have room to deepen. The love of Christ can be seen.

SETTING COMMUNICATION GUIDELINES

In Chen Dandan's conversation with her son, even as she affirmed and respected him, she also openly and honestly expressed a preferred way of communicating (communication guidelines). These guidelines contributed to Chen Dandan having a closer relationship with her teenage son and kept relational conflicts from building up between them. Setting up guidelines in communication can establish a good framework for handling conflicts that do arise and pave the way to avoid future conflict.

In a story involving her older sister-in-law and mother, Liu Yang demonstrates how setting up communication guidelines improved all their relationships:

> My conflicts with my sister-in-law stem from the fact that, in interpersonal relationships, she is the type of person who pays close attention to detail while I am more casual and don't easily notice people's needs. Beginning around last year, my sister-in-law had a lot of negative opinions about me, but her method of expressing them to me was to complain to my mom, who would then share those complaints with me.
>
> Finally, I couldn't stand it any longer. . . . I was deeply upset and sad. Putting my mother in the middle made me feel very angry, like

I was being treated unjustly. Afterwards, I prayed. Because I had just studied the peacemaking principle that says when there is conflict one should talk face to face about it, I struggled as I prayed. I did not want to talk with my sister-in-law because I felt she was too much trouble and had too many opinions. I felt like I couldn't handle it. But deep in my heart, there was a voice that said: *The more you avoid it, the worse it will get.*

Having asked her mom to avoid being a go-between in the relationship (to which she happily agreed), Liu Yang then called her sister-in-law. Speaking with a loving and hopeful tone she suggested, "In the future, if something happens between us, can you directly call me or meet up in person to share the ways I have offended you? I can assure you that I will seriously reflect on what you share, and if I have offended you, I will apologize." Her sister-in-law agreed to do so.

Afterwards, Liu Yang followed up with her mom who thought this approach was a great idea. Her mom was quite tired of listening to her sister-in-law's complaints and never knew what to do in response. Her mom also affirmed her suggestion for in-person communication. Setting up these communication guidelines significantly reduced the issues and improved Liu Yang's relationship with both her older sister-in-law and mother.

Establishing such guidelines, even simple ones, and working out details like this often gets overlooked, and yet such communication guidelines provide needed safety as well as an invitation and permission to bring issues up in healthy ways. They can shape the tone and quality of a relationship.

PRAYING TOGETHER

Sometimes we aren't able to set up communication guidelines, or we find it difficult to directly initiate a conversation about a conflict. Initiating prayer together can be a less threatening first step.

Zhang Jing had hoped to set up communication guidelines to help with addressing conflict that occurred between her and her colleague, but instead she initiated regular prayer together to support each other which brought the needed relational breakthrough.

> This colleague is wonderful, but her way of thinking and looking at things is very different from mine. When conflict happens, she prefers to talk immediately, but I need to go a bit slower. I need some time to prepare.
>
> So, from the very beginning, I kept my distance unless we really needed to communicate about something. We had so many personal differences that caused tension between us. When we interacted with each other, I had feelings, but we couldn't talk about them. So we both just kept them to ourselves.
>
> When I know someone should not be messed with, I hide from them and try my best not to trigger that person. This was my way of peace. After studying biblical peacemaking, I discovered this is not peace. If it wasn't for the Holy Spirit's intense work, we would have just kept on like this.
>
> Finally we began praying together. When we met to pray, we often talked about our differences and then brought those differences to God in prayer together. Little by little I came to understand her better, and she came to understand me better. This resulted in an

authentic peacemaking experience. It wasn't just a one-time peacemaking experience, but something that happened many times.

Smiling with joy and wonder as she told me this story, Zhang Jing said, "How is it possible to connect on a deep level with someone who is so different from yourself? Yet, I have indeed found a way to genuinely experience this type of connection in my life!" What a joyful resolution to what was becoming a troubled relationship.

Zhang Jing also described how praying with her mother was an effective way to indirectly express her hopes for their relationship after a conflict:

> My mom and I are not at the same place spiritually, so we see things differently from each other. Even though she is a Christian, she felt it was fine to give a Buddha wall hanging as a gift to a friend; whereas, I feel extremely uncomfortable doing this. She said that while she personally will not believe in Buddha and will only believe in Jesus, this wall hanging was suitable to hang in her friend's home. She kept disputing this matter with me, so I found it difficult to talk with her.
>
> During a moment of prayer together, I said out loud to the Lord, "Our way of seeing things is different, but please protect us, enable our relationship to not be impacted by this. I know my mom loves me very much. You know I also love my mom very much. So Lord, protect us. Don't let our different viewpoints impact our relationship."
>
> After I finished praying, my mom said, "Right, right, right, our relationship will not be impacted. I still love you; you still love me."
>
> So I was able to return home with a peaceful heart.

The communication that happens both in preparation to pray and in praying together can sometimes facilitate or complete the reconciliation process. Do not underestimate the power of prayer in relationships.

WAITING FOR, SEIZING, OR CREATING THE OPPORTUNITY

In some situations, we need to patiently wait for the right time to initiate a peacemaking conversation. In others, we must seize or create an opportunity to initiate this type of conversation.[131]

> Do not underestimate the power of prayer in relationships.

Zhang Li desired to reconcile with her friend after a significant conflict, but she understood the importance of waiting for the other person's heart to be ready. Zhang Li waited for the right time, praying and preparing all the while: "You have to go step by step; you can't rush. You can't act according to what you think. You need to consider what the other person thinks and go slowly." She observed her friend on a regular basis, and when she noticed a lifting of her friend's countenance, she took advantage of the woman's good mood and greeted her with a genuine compliment: "You permed your hair; it looks so pretty!" This broke the ice and contributed to moving the relationship toward peacemaking and reconciliation.

Yang Lin knew a training was approaching where she would be alone with a colleague and could take advantage of that moment to pursue peace. She prayed and wrestled with her own discomfort and fear of speaking up to apologize for her poor behavior at a previous work event. "As I was driving, I struggled for a long time. Finally . . . I took a deep breath and began my apology, "I am really sorry . . . ”[132] Deliberate planning for an upcoming opportunity led to breakthrough, forgiveness, and reconciliation.

Sometimes we simply need to seize the opportunity of the moment. We might take the opportunity afforded by a communion service to apologize or take advantage of an unexpected meal together to talk. Opportunities will often naturally arise that allow us, if we push through our own reluctance, to seek reconciliation.

Specifically setting up an appointment to create an opportunity to talk with the other party can also be effective. If you are Chinese, you know how culturally common it is to invite others out to a meal as a way to indicate you would like to talk about something. Purposefully creating opportunities for communication that can lead to relational restoration can be quite powerful.

Whether waiting for the opportunity, seizing the natural moment, or going out of your way to plan a conversation, choosing to pursue these conversations instead of avoiding them—despite personal discomfort—can open the door to desired conflict resolution or reconciliation.

PREPARE YOURSELF:
NOT EVERY INITIATED CONVERSATION ENDS POSITIVELY

Even though initiating a conversation is often a positive step in the reconciliation process, not every initiated conversation ends positively. Li Jie told me how discussing a financial matter with his work partner did not change anything:

> Because more of the financial resources were in his hands, and because he had some other ideas, he chose to keep all the profits that he should have split between the two of us. I felt this wasn't right, so

> I talked with him about it. I said, "When we started out, we agreed to . . ." He denied things.

Even though Li Jie tried to address the issues, his work partner was unwilling to negotiate, so the rift in their friendship remained.

For Wang Min, an initial conversation did not result in an improved relationship, but given time and proactive efforts, change did occur. Wang Min and her, now-husband, were in a difficult position. They wanted to start dating but didn't want to hurt another church sister's feelings so they waited a year. Wang Min finally talked with the woman, but she was unable to accept the relationship. She responded by talking behind Wang Min's back and eventually leaving the church.

> I highly valued our relationship, but I didn't know if I should reconcile with her and maintain the previous relationship or accept the state of the relationship as good enough. When I tried to draw close to her, she would open her heart and share her internal struggles which left me in a difficult position. I didn't know how to apply the peacemaking principles. . . . I stopped reaching out, and she didn't reach out to me either.

> For three years, I focused on doing my own internal work, including forgiving what she had said to others about me and being misunderstood. Finally, I initiated reaching out to her to express my regret. I valued our friendship and didn't want it to be like this. When I said this to her, she shared with me that things were already in the past for her, and she felt she could bless us. Now she has slowly returned to church.

Like Wang Min's experience, when we initiate a conversation, the results are sometimes far from what we had hoped. In Wang Min's case, she responded to this disappointment by focusing on her own internal peacemaking work, coming to a place of being able to forgive, and maintaining an openness to relationship. She continued to pray for her friend and waited to see if another time to talk would surface. While the relationship will never be what it was due to the conflict involving emotional ties to Wang Min's husband, a degree of restoration has occurred.

Don't be discouraged if the first time you try to initiate conversation, it fails. Just because someone else refuses to change or isn't following biblical peacemaking principles themselves does not mean God releases us from pursuing peacemaking. You may end up following peacemaking steps but never truly get full resolution—at least on earth—with the other person. And sometimes your peacemaking steps will bear fruit down the road. Believe and follow Jesus, pray for wisdom, and "as far as it depends on you," seek to live at peace (Rom 12:18). God empowers us to live this way in humility and with compassion; we leave the results in His hands.

CHAPTER WRAP-UP

We never know what direction the other person will take in response to our initiating a conversation. Will they be open or closed? Will they soften or be defensive? Will they respond honestly to our honesty? Will they also openly share their feelings or stay at the surface level? Will they listen or misunderstand? How will they respond to our attempts to set communication guidelines? We have no way to answer these questions because we can't control their responses. But we do know what God calls us to do.

Romans 12:10–12 says, "Be devoted to one another in love. Honor one another above yourselves. Never be lacking in zeal, but keep your spiritual fervor, serving the Lord. Be joyful in hope, patient in affliction, faithful in prayer." The alternatives to not attempting God's peacemaking ways include remaining distanced, frustrated, disappointed, bitter, resentful, or upset. Don't let another's possible rejection or unresponsiveness keep you from obeying God and pursuing peace.

At the same time, be patient and wait for God's timing. Sometimes we need further healing and strengthening of our own hearts before we can initiate a conversation with someone, especially if they have been difficult to talk to in the past or harmed us. Be gentle with yourself and intentional about pursuing this heart healing when you realize you need it. Healing can take a long time. Sometimes we don't even realize we need healing, especially if we have been socialized to "pursue reconciliation" in ways that are harmful to ourselves, which may then cause further damage.

Above all, persevere in prayer, hope, and love. In response to prayer and initiated conversations, God often works in amazing ways in our hearts to bring conviction, responsiveness, and clarity when misunderstanding and hurt has occurred.

A PRAYER

Lord, thank You for proactively initiating conversation with me, for being gentle yet honest and direct with me. I know that I don't always respond to You the way You hope for. Even so, You are ever-patient with and ever-loving to me. You always keep an open posture toward me. You don't give up on me.

I ask for the grace and strength to relate to [insert name of person] in the same way. Give me the grace to initiate needed conversations and the wisdom to discern the best timing. Strengthen me to be devoted in love as You are devoted in love to me. When I am unsure about the way forward in a relationship, give me the grace to be patient in affliction, faithful in prayer, and joyful in hope.

Lord, show me what honoring [insert name of person] could look like. Thank You that Your divine power has given me everything I need for a godly life through my knowledge of You who called me by Your own glory and goodness (2 Peter 1:3). In Jesus' name I pray, amen.

REFLECTION QUESTIONS

1. What has your experience of praying to God when in conflict been like?

2. In what ways have you experienced God work in your heart when in conflict?

3. Do you initiate conversation after conflict has occurred? Have you had any positive results?

4. Which actions would you like to experiment with incorporating into your conversations (talking directly with the other person; talking honestly; expressing your feelings and the thoughts behind your behavior/words; giving affirmations; expressing respect; setting communication guidelines; praying together; waiting for, seizing, or creating an opportunity to pursue peacemaking)?

5. If you have you tried to initiate a conversation that bombed, what personal internal work (such as working through anger, discovering what other feelings are present and why, dealing with resentment and bitterness, coming to the place of forgiving, more fully recognizing and receiving God's grace and love, etc.) might help you move forward in your peacemaking efforts?

TEN

FINDING AND BEING A HELPFUL CONFLICT COMPANION

TOWARD THE BEGINNING OF MY RESEARCH, I started noticing that many of those I interviewed not only mentioned the need for God but also the need for someone to come alongside them, especially when they felt stuck or were struggling in conflict. I started referring to this type of person as a *companion* (陪伴者 *peibanzhe*). Li Jun aptly described this companion need:

> Especially among Chinese people, even among Christians, there are not many who can truly reconcile with one another, who are willing to act according to biblical principles to resolve a conflict. Many people feel lonely, weak, and helpless. They feel very uncomfortable when in conflict, but they don't know what to do.

Many Chinese people realize or know they are in conflict, but they don't know what happened to cause the conflict or how to face it. Furthermore, they might not have the spiritual life or strength to deal with it. Why? Satan's power, his vestigial strength, is still quite strong, right?

Looking at it from this point of view, we truly need a lot of prayer, we need to study, and then we also need a companion to come alongside us.

Supportive relationships help us keep swimming through the crashing waves of conflict to calmer ocean waters. If we have gotten tangled up in seaweed, a companion can help us get untangled. If we're struggling against the current, a companion whose feet are planted firmly on the ocean floor can hold us steady and keep us going.

Chen Dandan expressed the deep human need for a helpful conflict companion when facing a conflict:

Whenever there is conflict, everyone feels hurt. That's a problem. If those involved haven't been able to come out of the conflict and are unwilling to face or resolve it, they need someone else to come alongside them.

Sometimes those in conflict are not willing to move forward, but other times they feel unable to move forward. They may be willing, or say that they are willing, to be reconciled, but when they feel they have no ability to do so, they hope someone can come and help them out; they need someone.

There are times when we need someone else's help just *to be willing* to resolve a conflict. At other times, we may be willing, but need help because we feel *unable* to face the conflict.

Warning! Not every person who tries to help is actually helpful. Some cause us to get tangled up even further instead. We'll look at examples of that type of so-called help later in the chapter. As you read on, I invite you to reflect on the following questions:

- Has anyone come alongside you as a companion during a conflict?
- If yes, in what ways has a conflict companion helped you?
- What type of companion are you to others when they are in conflict?

BENEFITS OF A HELPFUL CONFLICT COMPANION

Ecclesiastes illustrates how many benefits come from having companions in life: "Two are better than one because they have a good return for their labor: If either of them falls down, one can help the other up. . . . Though one may be overpowered, two can defend themselves. A cord of three strands is not quickly broken" (4:9–10, 12). Life companions lead to more productive and profitable work. They help us stand back up after falling or failing. A good companion can be an advocate and help when we are attacked. They give us strength to persevere. And when we are caught up in conflict, helpful companionship from other people— a close friend, a pastor, a counselor, or a small group—can broaden perspectives, be positively enabling, provide a role model, and improve the quality of our communication.[133]

Gaining a Broader Perspective

A helpful companion often provides a broadened perspective or clarity regarding a conflict issue. With their assistance, our limited thinking gets expanded. As seen in the following stories, companions also help us see the potential consequences of our conflict-response choices and find motivation to make changes.

Getting beyond Limited Thinking

Wang Lei noted, "Some people need companionship because their thinking has limitations. When they think about the conflict situation, they find it impossible to think broadly. If a friend comes alongside, the friend helps by sharing some ideas, then the person can go pursue reconciliation." It is easy to develop tunnel vision when in a conflict, but in reality, there may be many ways to look at a situation. We simply need help to see them.

Liu Yang had a friend whose comments helped her take a fresh approach to interpreting someone else's behavior:

> God provided a friend who was a lot like me to comfort me. When the other person opposed me, my friend would say, "I don't think she is opposing you. I have the same opinion as her." Through my friend's comments, some balance entered the picture: Some people will have the same perspective as me, others will have a different perspective. It's okay; it doesn't necessarily mean they are opposing me. If we have similar thoughts, then I can share more. If we have different thoughts, I will focus on showing respect.
>
> For a long time, I was unable to look this woman in the face because I felt she was opposing me. In the end, I was able to get to the place of looking her in the eye when face to face in the same group.

A helpful, confidential companion can redirect our thinking, giving us needed balance and new perspective.

Seeing Consequences

For some of us, as in Huang Jingjing's case, a companion can provide needed reminders of consequences, motivating us to change:

> Sometimes I understand what the problem is but don't want to do anything about it. It feels too difficult for me; I feel I have been treated too unjustly. But then someone will remind me: "This is the only right path. If you feel you must take that road, more people will be hurt. There will be a bad result." I need someone to tell me what the correct way is, what an effective way is. I can then try to change; it makes changing a little easier. There is a lot of love in it all.

How often are we blinded to the bigger picture of the consequences our choices might have? Huang Jingjing's companion lovingly and compassionately spoke with her about potential consequences if she acted according to her current way of thinking.[134] A little bit of trustworthy, compassionate, outside perspective can open our eyes to the greater impact of our conflict and responses.

Positive Enabling

Talking to a companion can enable us to do something we thought was too difficult or to say something we did not know how to say. Through the help of a godly companion, many people have experienced breakthroughs in facing personal limitations, forgiving, overcoming internal resistance to apologizing, and gaining courage. Frequently, those breakthroughs may not have happened without that companion. The next few stories show real-life examples of such breakthroughs occurring.

Facing Personal Limitations

Wang Min's Christian supervisors gently pushed her to stretch and grow:

> When my ministry colleague and I had some conflicts, I typically was proactive in communication while she was avoidant. Our relationship was rather tense as a result. But we had assistance from our older supervisors to sort things out. One teacher even encouraged me to room with my colleague to pursue some life breakthrough, so I did. In that process, my supervisors helped me face some of my own limitations and grow.

These companions made suggestions to take personal growth steps beyond what Wang Min would have pursued if on her own. They also provided a supportive environment in which she could take those risks.

Forgiving

For Zhang Jing, having the support of trusted companions helped her to forgive:

> They didn't facilitate the restoration of the relationship, but they did come alongside and help me let go of my bitterness, my unwillingness to forgive, my retaliation against her, and my punishing behavior. I was then able to move to a place of forgiveness.

This type of companionship can be particularly helpful when forgiving has been difficult because the hurt was deep. Sometimes we just need someone to listen and listen again, to help us acknowledge and process a painful experience. Prior to this type of processing, we may feel unwilling or unable to forgive.

Overcoming Internal Resistance

Wang Fang was resistant to the idea of apologizing to her coworker but became willing to resolve the conflict after participating in her job's daily, required, morning devotional. Through this daily time with companions, she established a relationship with God, relinquished a previously held position, and took a new peacemaking step: "Because they were there caring for me and listening to my situation, I gained the ability to proactively apologize to my coworker." Gentle, loving forces surrounding us can break down our resistance to peacemaking.

> A companion can help us become willing and able to face conflict, see more clearly what God calls us to do, and stay on God's path even when it's difficult.

Gaining Courage

As Li Qiang pointed out to me, hearing from others can affect our decision-making and contribute to gaining the courage we need to face a situation:

> When we experience conflict, whether we feel offended or have offended someone else, internally we assess ourselves: was I right or wrong? If I think I was right, then I won't apologize. If I think I was wrong, maybe I will want to apologize, but I need some courage.
>
> If others are present and I discuss the situation with them, they function like balancing scales in my heart. If one of them comments on my situation, it's like he has either gotten on or off the scale. His words add some weight to one aspect and may change the result. It's not determinative, but it provides some assistance.

A companion can help us become willing and able to face conflict, see more clearly what God calls us to do, and stay on God's path even when it's difficult. A helpful companion often provides a listening ear and conversation space to bring up issues and process painful situations which can then empower us with courage to apologize or forgive.

Role Modeling

A helpful companion can also serve as a role model. Wang Jia gained hope for her own relationships after hearing the testimony of a fellow Christian who had experienced successful reconciliation despite an all-but-impossible relationship. "I thought to myself: *This sister and the others here are all just people. God gives the same grace to all of us. God gave this sister ability. If she can do it, why can't I? I can!*" Wang Jia went on to say, "Feeling your way in the dark by yourself might result in a lot of detours. Having a role model can give great encouragement and powerfully change your thoughts in this way!"[135]

Similarly, Li Qiang's peacemaking couples' small group also provided encouraging companionship and hopeful role modeling:

> Because I knew the other couples present had also experienced arguments similar to my wife and mine, I stopped thinking, "I'm so unique; others are unable to understand my suffering" when I looked at my marriage problems.
>
> When I see other couples who have experienced arguments, yet through using a peacemaking method reconciled successfully, I feel greatly encouraged to be able to resolve my own issues.

Never underestimate the role modeling power of testimony. When someone who struggles in a similar manner to us tells their story of how they relied on God to pursue peacemaking, their stories can provide much needed connection, encouragement, and hope.

Improved Quality of Communication

The following stories demonstrate how a third person's presence, when working through a conflict with someone, can improve the quality of the conversation, better allowing for relational breakthrough. This person can facilitate conversation that limits or prevents arguments and empowers both people to share more deeply, increasing mutual understanding.

Prevents Arguments or Stops Conflict from Growing in Intensity

When speaking of his relationship with his wife, Liu Haifeng said, "Many times when the two of us have had conflict, we sought out [the name of a couple] who mediated for us. When a third party is present, out of consideration for face, we won't start arguing as easily which has been helpful."

Zhang Min shared a similar sentiment: "If a conflict arises and there is a third person present, it will keep our conflict from growing in intensity, from going from bad to worse." A mediating companion's presence can help us refrain from saying things that will intensify a conflict or lead to arguments.

Share More Deeply, Increasing Mutual Understanding

A companion can also facilitate a conversation, enabling each individual to say more than they would if alone with the other person. This companion can draw each person out and provide a neutral, open space to share more deeply on vulnerable or difficult topics. As hearts open, greater mutual understanding happens.

Zhang Yong described how a counselor friend's facilitation of conversation between him and his girlfriend (now wife) enabled them to voice everything that normally would go unsaid. She guided them into greater clarity and mutual understanding:

> During the time we were dating, I didn't understand my girlfriend very well, and she didn't understand me very well. There were some things I didn't know how to tell her. Through facilitated conversation, I learned we have some differences and some conflicts that I didn't even know were problems. I also discovered I have some problems that I didn't know I had.
>
> Another person, if they have experience, can guide others through issues. Our friend guided each of us to speak out a lot of things. In this way, we learned so much about each other and ourselves. I feel this guidance is very important.

Another person's presence and guidance can increase openness leading to self-awareness, more honest sharing, and stronger relationships.

PRAYERFULLY SEEK OUT A COMPANION

Whom we seek out for companionship in conflict significantly impacts us. Not every person who tries to help is actually helpful. To those I interviewed, some of the most important qualities in a helpful, godly companion are

- being a confidential, safe, and understanding listener
- providing comfort
- guiding and reminding but not telling what to do[136]

Yang Lin expressed that a helpful companion also "empathizes with me, uses principles from the Bible, and helps me get out of the conflict."

Wang Fang described her supportive companion as someone who did not give her advice, rather, "She said I need to decide for myself and that if I go talk to my work colleague about the issue, she will pray for me."

Describing her conflict companion, Zhang Jing said, "She often connected with me, comforted me, and engaged in some activity with me." Such positive qualities in our companions can greatly encourage us to pursue reconciliation.

Differentiating between Helpful and Unhelpful Qualities

While there are numerous benefits from having a companion when facing conflict, I advise heeding wisdom when choosing someone. The quality of help a companion provides is critically important. Many Christians sincerely desire to help others and are simply blind to the ineffectiveness of their current methods. Unhelpful assistance might look like criticizing, judging and advising without first understanding, stirring a person up instead of calming them down, having all the answers, and joining a side instead of staying neutral. Here are examples of qualities to avoid in others and to change in ourselves.

Criticizing

Criticizing someone as a way to "help" them can be a blind spot for many. When describing a fight between her and a good friend, Zhang Jing told me, "A few other people were present at the start of it. They separated us, keeping the conflict from escalating, and we stepped away from each other. But after separating us, one of them immediately admonished me." Obviously frustrated, she reflected, "A lot of mediating includes criticism; the mediator takes the role of a critic. This unhelpful help only scratches the surface. It doesn't address or resolve my heart issues." I honestly think that if we realized the extent to which our criticism of others is unhelpful, we would work harder at changing our methods.

Judging and Advising without First Understanding

Judging and advising too soon has a similar effect to criticism. The judgement of a colleague was not at all helpful to Wang Xiuying:

> When I sought out help from a church colleague due to a conflict I had with our leader, her response was, "Look at how hard our leader has worked, being so tired has caused her current condition." Her excuse for our leader conveyed a message to me: She works so hard and puts out so much effort, you shouldn't be upset with her. You shouldn't be in conflict.
>
> Then she advised me, "If you have conflict, you shouldn't fight. Just keep doing what you are responsible to do." She used her own conflict-response method to guide me, but what she thought was helpful really wasn't helpful.

Instead of taking time to understand the details of the situation and listen carefully with one ear to Wang Xiuying and one ear to the Holy Spirit, this unhelpful companion immediately took sides, made judgments, and gave advice.

Stirring Up Instead of Calming Down

Not only do we try to help by judging and advising, we also sometimes stir a conflict up:

You know, the average person hasn't had any training in conflict resolution. Sometimes a person is already in the process of calming down with the conflict fizzling and dying, but then this so-called help from a friend suddenly pushes them further into the conflict.

When someone needs a calm person's reflections to help them out but the person next to them says things that stirs up instead of calms down, this is repelling. It doesn't help at all.[137]

Calm reflections are needed, not the stirring up of emotions.

Having All the Answers

It's also easy to unconsciously present ourselves as having all the answers. Liu Yang was confused and stressed from one church counselor's approach to helping her:

> The conflicts that my husband and I had spanned a great length of time, so early on I proactively sought out help from a church counselor. This counselor began acting high and mighty, like he had all the answers. He would observe me from his higher position, counseling and reminding me. The pressure was very intense until, finally, I wasn't willing to talk to him about any problems. I was unable to communicate at all with him. Why? Because our relationship was no longer one of equals.

Coming from alongside is needed, not pressure and answers from someone who takes on a superior stance.

Joining a Side Instead of Staying Neutral

A well-meaning friend might end up unintentionally joining one person's side of a conflict instead of staying neutral. Li Jie described the negative effect this has:

If you and I have a conflict, I will most certainly look for a place to vent. I'll go find a friend and pour out my troubles to him. After listening to me, this friend completely sympathizes with me and follows my line of thinking, making critical remarks about you. Through his response, I basically find proof, or evidence, that you are wrong. Instead of staying neutral and encouraging me to pursue reconciliation, he takes a side.

Li Jie needed encouragement to pursue reconciliation not validation of his position.

Don't Lose Heart

We naturally gravitate toward seeking out the help of people we know well. Unfortunately, some of those people don't provide the needed safe listening space, comfort, good questions, gentle Scriptural nudge, or role modeling of God-honoring ways to respond to conflict. Instead of encouraging us to live according to God's reconciling Kingdom-culture, they criticize, admonish, judge, advise without first listening to understand, give unbiblical advice, stir things up, take sides, or talk as if they have all the answers instead of pointing others to God. Hearing these disturbing, unhelpful experiences might put enough fear into someone that they would purposefully avoid seeking out a conflict companion or trying to be one! It's no wonder some people just try to deal with conflict on their own.

Thankfully, among those I interviewed, the positive stories of companions who came alongside in meaningful, helpful ways far outnumbered the negative stories. As you look for a companion, prayerfully seek out those who demonstrate the helpful qualities and keep an eye out for any of these less-than-helpful ones sneaking into conversations. Being forewarned in what to look for can be enough to guide many of us to the right person, even though they may not always be the most instinctive person to whom to turn.

BEING A COMPANION

In light of these unhelpful—and sometimes quite harmful—experiences, we must take seriously the role of coming alongside others who are in conflict. Personally, these stories prompted me to take another look to see if I exude any unhelpful qualities when attempting to help. Here are six keys we can learn from these stories.

First, as one who comes alongside someone else in their conflict, be careful to:

- Come from alongside, not from above
- Refrain from criticizing and admonishing too quickly
- Avoid viewing yourself as someone who has all the answers

Negative examples of unhelpful help remind us that our listening skills, word choice, perspective, and how we position ourselves in relation to the other person can significantly impact their receptivity to our help.

Second, do your best to be a neutral party, not siding with one person or the other.

Endeavor to stay neutral by keeping one ear listening carefully to the Holy Spirit for direction and insight and the other ear listening to the person. Jesus Christ is our best role model for how to accompany others. As Li Jun put it: "Jesus suffered on the cross for the people on both sides of the conflict. He loves the people on both sides of the conflict and won't favor one side over the other. Jesus says: I am with you, side by side. Jesus walks with you."

When coming alongside someone, be aware of the tendency to adopt a negative appraisal of the person who is not in the room. For example, when a spouse shares a marital conflict with you, if you become biased against the spouse who isn't there, this can lead to a very difficult situation for both parties. Keep Proverbs 18:17 in mind: "In a lawsuit, the first to speak seems right until someone comes forward and cross-examines." Remember you have only heard one side of the story; you don't have the full picture. Every time I have the opportunity to hear both sides of a story, the reality that situations are always more complex and nuanced than what I first assume sinks in deeper.

Third, remind yourself that you are not their savior—Jesus is (and breathe a sigh of relief)!

It isn't your job to fix, save, judge, or have all the answers. Rather, with kindness and compassion, help the person encounter God amid their conflict. Ask questions and share in ways that can broaden their perspectives, shift their thinking, and call forth trust in God. Being available to facilitate God-honoring and other-person-honoring conversations can lead both parties to deeper mutual understanding and relational breakthrough.[138]

Fourth, be a learner; becoming a better conflict companion is a process.

Learning how to better help those in conflict in God-honoring ways is a lifelong process. Liu Yang had the negative experience of being lectured by her women's small group after sharing her marital conflict with them. Their lecturing was not from evil intentions but a natural desire to help and teach. She chose to receive this as a learning opportunity for herself and the group members who also desired to help one another:

> Studying biblical peacemaking has helped me grow in becoming a better listener. When you listen to others who are sharing vulnerably, how will you respond? With judgement? A lecture? Advice? After listening to others, one shouldn't immediately respond or the person sharing will feel uncomfortable.
>
> After having this experience multiple times, our small group tried to practice withholding judgment. It was so hard; everyone couldn't help but comment! Through all these years, we have tried to establish a group in which we listen more and comment less. It is so hard, but we keep trying.

Liu Yang and her small group recognized that their way of coming alongside each other created discomfort rather than greater openness. Even though habits are hard to change, they continue to work at growing into better conflict companions.

Fifth, remember that the people we come alongside may have asked for our help, but they aren't always ready or willing to follow what we suggest.

From time to time, I have found myself getting frustrated and impatient with others. I'm embarrassed to say that I have even started taking offense in my self-righteousness, exasperated that someone who asked for *my* help isn't doing what *I* suggested. Micah 6:8 becomes my prayer: "He has told you, O man, what is good; And what does the Lord require of you except to be just, and to love [and to diligently practice] kindness [compassion], And to walk humbly with your God [setting aside any overblown sense of importance or self-righteousness]?" (AMP, *sic*).

Sixth and most importantly, pray.

When coming alongside someone else in their conflict, it is easy to fall into trusting our own past experiences to help rather than listening to and trusting God. Regularly submitting ourselves to God in prayer, asking for wisdom, love, and insight, and declaring that He is God (and we are not), keeps our focus in the right place.

Six Keys to Being a Helpful Companion

1. First, as one who comes alongside someone else in their conflict, be careful to come from alongside.

2. Second, do your best to be a neutral party, not siding with one person or the other.

3. Third, remind yourself that you are not their savior—Jesus is (and breathe a sigh of relief)!

4. Fourth, be a learner; becoming a better conflict companion is a process.

5. Fifth, remember that the people we come alongside may have asked for our help, but they aren't always ready or willing to follow what we suggest.

6. Sixth and most importantly, pray.

CHAPTER WRAP-UP

Li Na described the great benefit she received from a church friend's companionship when in conflict, yet she also said that sometimes one can only rely on God:

> When someone is in a bad relationship or has many relational conflicts, I think that having someone come alongside is very important. But God is the only one you can completely rely on. Sometimes there is no companion in your environment and that's how it is.

Knowing that God is our ever-present companion from whom we can seek help in our conflicts is comforting. We need both God and helpful companions from God's family to encourage, model, guide, and mediate. These safe, supportive relationships help us face ourselves, what is going on in our own hearts, as well as face others.

Perhaps you are thinking, *I don't have any helpful conflict companions in my life, but I need one.* As you pray for God to bring this type of person into your life, God may bring someone to mind. Take the initiative to reach out and see if they are available. Now that technology has made video conferences, internet phone calls, and social media commonplace, you may have more resources available than you realize. Authors of books and podcast speakers have been some of my conflict companions in life, broadening my perspectives, providing godly role models, and teaching me God's Kingdom-culture. These resources haven't replaced the Bible or physical companions, but they have significantly helped. I also encourage you to reach out to any of the organizations listed in the resource section of this book and at my website: jolenekinser.com.

A PRAYER

Lord, as one who comes alongside others in conflict, I recognize that I still have a lot to learn. I acknowledge that those who want to help others don't always help in beneficial ways. Thank You for Your grace toward us.

Teach me Your way of coming alongside in humility, grace, and love. Grow me in my ability to ask questions that get to the heart of issues. Develop my ability to listen carefully and compassionately. I ask for the wisdom that comes from heaven to fill my heart and mind as I come alongside others. I desire Your wisdom that is pure, peace-loving, considerate, submissive, full of mercy and good fruit, impartial and sincere (James 3:17). Your Word declares that "peacemakers who sow in peace reap a harvest of righteousness" (James 3:18). I want to be a peacemaker!

Lord, I also could use someone to help me navigate my conflict with [insert name]. Sometimes my fear or pride gets in the way of seeking help. Grant me wisdom and discernment in looking for someone who will help and not hinder. Give me the courage and humility to ask for help. In Jesus' name I pray, amen.

REFLECTION QUESTIONS

1. Have you ever sought out a companion to help you deal with a conflict? Why or why not?

2. In what ways have conflict companions in your life been helpful? Unhelpful?

3. What keeps you from seeking out godly help with your conflicts?

4. What kind of conflict companion have you been to others? Describe the characteristics of your help to others.

5. Do you see any of the unhelpful characteristics in your way of coming alongside others in conflict?

6. In what ways would you like to grow as a helpful companion to others in conflict?

ELEVEN

CULTIVATING AN ENVIRONMENT OF PEACE

WALLY YEW, FORMER MINISTRY AMBASSADOR for Chinese Christian Mission, candidly points out that many people resist change: "Most of the time, we change because we have to, we need to, or we are forced to."[139] In many instances, we become willing to change how we relate to others only after realizing a relationship is broken and we start crying out to God. Yew continues saying, "The reality is, we want progress, but we resist change. We want progress within our comfort zone. We want progress but we want to maintain our status quo. We want progress at our speed and at our convenience."[140] We want to keep using our standard conflict response for relating to others, but we also want to see conflicts disappear.

Most of us have an intensely strong aversion to feeling uncomfortable. Yet discomfort stirred by the Holy Spirit can motivate us to reflect before God, repent, learn, and take new actions.[141] As family, church, and organization leaders, we must be willing to not only face our aversions but also remind ourselves to intentionally welcome the discomfort of change. When we push through discomfort and take Holy Spirit-prompted action, we gain internal peace and can have new relational experiences. Only then can we lead the way forward in cultivating an environment of peace and change the conflict culture in our spheres of influence.

The previous chapters have described God's reconciling Kingdom-culture; emphasized the importance of abiding in Christ, believing God's Word, and trusting God for change; and outlined the kind of companion that we can be and want to encourage others to find or be themselves. While many mindset shifts have been introduced, this last chapter highlights five more shifts that, when embraced, can contribute to being able to respond to conflict with godly, Kingdom-culture based actions. If you want to cultivate an environment of peace in your sphere(s) of influence, modeling, training, and teaching in these areas will be critical.

DOWNLOADING NEW INPUT FOR MINDSET CHANGE

When conflict happens, we all make decisions in two key areas: (1) Who will I turn to for help or guidance? (2) How will I respond to this conflict? Surveys conducted among adults in the United States reveal that the average person reads between fifteen to eighteen minutes per day.[142] Another survey reveals Bible reading habits to be at two extremes. The majority report never reading the Bible, while the second largest group say they read it every day. Of those who read the Bible, 23% spend one hour or more and 17% spend less than 15 minutes. The rest fall somewhere in between.[143] Extrapolating from these statistics, we learn that many Americans do not turn to the Bible for guidance when in conflict.

Although I don't have statistics, anecdotal evidence suggests that Christians and non-Christians alike tend to either not turn to anyone at all for help, relying on whatever they have absorbed from sources around them, or turn to family members, friends, and thought leaders on social media for help or guidance, some of whom are Christians. Whether we realize it or not, who we look to for guidance and help directly impacts how we view conflict and choose to respond.

Check out the night and day difference between Scenario #1, which summarizes the impact of looking to our usual sources and responding to conflict in our usual ways, and Scenario #2, which summarizes the impact of mindset shifts resulting from learning a God-honoring approach to conflict.

Scenario # 1: My Standard Conflict Approach	
No new godly input (no new positive experiences, knowledge, or expanded perspectives)	
View conflict as:	Bad; dangerous; a threat; something to fear and avoid
Input/guidance comes from:	No one; family members, friends, leaders; secular books, TV/movies, podcasts, social media, online searches
Conflict response is guided by:	Cultural norms and practices modeled by family and the social environment; personal habits; past experiences
Typical conflict responses:	Avoid, attack, blame, protect face; apologize with actions only; apologize insincerely; give surface-level forgiveness
Common relational outcomes resulting from these actions:	Worsened relationships; surface-level or insincere reconciliation; conflict issues remain unaddressed; continued tension beneath the surface

Scenario #2: God's Kingdom-Culture Conflict Approach	
New input (an introduction to the biblical peacemaking principles of God's Kingdom-culture, new positive experiences, community support)	
View conflict as:	An opportunity to honor God and others; an opportunity to grow personally and relationally
Input/guidance comes from:	God; the Bible; godly companions; sources of biblically based, spiritual input: sermons, podcasts, books
Conflict response is guided by:	God's Kingdom-culture norms; prayer; the Holy Spirit; Christ's abiding presence; practices modeled in the Bible and by godly examples in a Christian community or family
Typical conflict responses:	Cry out to God for help; intentionally pursue peace; examine oneself; die to self; proactively communicate; respond with the fruit of the Spirit; listen; take responsibility; give confession-apologies; genuinely forgive from the heart
Common relational outcomes:	An improved or restored relationship; heart-level reconciliation; internal and external peace; the beginning of a renewal of trust

Without the influence of any new biblical input to shift our mindsets, we tend to respond to conflict according to the cultural norms we've been shaped by. The resulting relational outcomes are predictably bad. We need to learn God's peacemaking principles.

Li Jun's thoughts on why many Chinese people are unable to apologize or resolve conflict illustrate why using our standard conflict approach instead of turning to God for help, is such a problem:

> Many Chinese people don't understand what an authentic apology is, so they are unable to genuinely apologize. In the same way, they

don't understand what conflict is or what has caused the conflict; therefore, they don't know how to face or resolve the conflict.

Many people think that conflicts start because people have differences, but differences do not inevitably cause conflict. Differences cause conflict when they collide with each other and offense is taken. So many Chinese people work hard to put differences aside and avoid talking about them, thinking that is the answer.

Li Jun proposed that if people understood the root causes of conflict and the components of an authentic apology, they would be better able to face and resolve conflicts. We gain the resources and strength we need to choose peacemaking conflict-responses more frequently when we turn first to God for the transforming of our heart and renewing of our mind (Rom 12:1–2).

Mindset Shift 1:
Valuing and Teaching Biblical Peacemaking Concepts

A key mindset shift involves teaching and using biblical peacemaking often enough that we begin turning to Scripture first when in conflict. Many who have been through a peacemaking study will recall a peacemaking principle when in the middle of a conflict, which then impacts how they relate to the other person.

While still caught in the emotions of a conflict, Huang Jingjing remembered the verse, *"No matter what you do, do it all for the glory of God* [1 Cor 10:31 paraphrased]." As a result, she recognized her problem: "My behavior [yelling] did not glorify God's name, so I decided to apologize to my husband." This led to their closer relationship despite the conflict.

Li Ailing recounted the despair she felt when it seemed there was no way to continue in her marriage. After studying biblical peacemaking, when experiencing the same situations as before, she would review the principles. She was then immediately able to release all those things that she previously felt unable to let go of, like it was nothing. Valuing and remembering biblical peacemaking principles can have an immediate impact on our hearts and actions, even decreasing conflict as we learn to apply these concepts.

Mindset Shift 2:
Viewing Conflict Differently

A second essential mindset change involves seeing conflict as normal rather than as something to fear.[144] Su Lijuan explained that, even after salvation, she did not understand this. Only through studying peacemaking did she learn that "conflict is an opportunity. Don't twist conflict, misunderstand it, or fear it. For two people to have conflict is normal."[145]

After a similar learning experience, Chen Yuling told me, "Conflict has its benefits: Through the rubbing and friction we can understand each other better, learn and grow together, and become more united." Conflict itself should not be feared; it is a natural, potentially even positive aspect of life.

Couples have also experienced the benefits of this mindset shift: "We truly see and hear each other now. Prior to studying biblical peacemaking, most of our conflicts were never truly resolved."[146] Some couples are now able to recognize which conflicts are caused by their differences and no longer fear or try to cover up these conflicts: "These conflicts no longer grow or cause more conflict because we understand each other better now and show tolerance and forgiveness."[147] What a difference a change of perspective makes! When conflict is viewed as normal and beneficial when worked through, individuals and groups can move through their fear of conflict and choose to face challenging issues instead of avoiding them.

Mindset Shift 3:
Valuing Relationships Differently

A third, significant mindset change involves valuing all relationships and not just some. As illustrated by Liu Haifeng, when some people do not like another person, they are not motivated to improve the relationship:

> If you care about that person you want to make peace with him. But suppose there is someone that I hate, someone I really don't like. I might intentionally create some conflict so that he won't like me either and will stay far away from me. The best thing would be if I never see him. Conversely, if I go apologize, it most certainly is because I love her. I want to maintain a good relationship.

We face a sobering reality: Many times we choose not to pursue peacemaking or to love as God loves because we do not value the relationship to the degree that God values it.

Knowing how deeply all people (you, me, and the people we dislike) are loved by God can make a pivotal difference in valuing others. Chen Yuling confessed that, "Before I believed in Jesus, if I had an affinity for you and found you easy to get along with, I would spend more time with you. If I didn't think much of you, I simply would not spend time with you." After believing in Jesus, she no longer behaves that way. Even so, as she leads a small group at her church, Chen Yuling sometimes gets annoyed by some of the women. In those moments, she has to focus on

Jesus in her heart to shift her thinking and be willing to love them:

> I say to myself, "Does Jesus see me as lovable? Am I very lovable? Can I call myself someone who is worthy of Jesus' love? Jesus loves this woman just as He loves me; she is God's precious one. I cannot use my type of love to scrutinize her."

Peacemaking discipleship rooted in experiencing God's love instills in us the same value that God places on relationship—even relationships with strangers. As a result, we are more likely to have the motivation to address conflict issues instead of avoiding them.

Mindset Shift 4:
Viewing Questions Objectively, Not as Personal Attacks

Viewing questions and differing views as an opportunity to learn and grow rather than as a competition, a threat, or a personal attack can revolutionize our communication with others. But as Wally Yew points out about church groups, our desire to maintain control makes it difficult to take this approach:

> Unfortunately, the "we" of the young are not the same group of people as the "we" of the not so young; the "we" group of the English-speaking is not the same as the "we" group of the Cantonese-speaking group which in turn is not the same as the "we" group of the Mandarin-speaking and Taiwanese-speaking. . . . With so many different "we" groups in Chinese churches, how can we make progress so that all can benefit? How can we let another group of people, who are so different from us but are in the same church, prosper and multiply without seeing it as competition or loss of control? More positively, how can we actively support and encourage another group of people so

that they can prosper, multiply and mature in their own way?[148]

Far too often, we fail to separate our own sense of well-being from the issues that we care about. When other people bring up ideas or suggestions that counter our own, our default internal interpretation might be to perceive disrespect or a personal attack.

I saw this default interpretation in action at a church's missions committee meeting where the church budget was being discussed. During the meeting, one of the committee members raised a question: "The budget seems to be misleading. If no explanation is given, the congregation will think our missions budget is running a deficit when it is not. Can we clarify this information in the budget?" The immediate response from a senior member of the church was, "Don't attack the treasurer!" He then defended the treasurer vigorously. Rather than viewing the committee member's question objectively as an issue to address, he interpreted it as a personal attack on the hard-working treasurer. As a result, the question was never addressed.

When someone confronts an issue or raises a question, we need to be careful not to automatically interpret their words or actions as condemning, disapproving, or dishonoring. I know this is far easier to say than to do. The impulse rises within us to defend ourselves or someone else because we naturally tend to assume the comment or question was an attack on our position or a judgement of our work and thus an assault on our pride, our face, or our sense of self. However, once we recognize this tendency in ourselves, we can consciously pause, take a deep breath, and shift our mindset to viewing the other person's different ideas or questions as issue-oriented not as hostile or personally judgmental.

Even if the other person's tone is angry, exasperated, impatient, or judging, we can choose to sift through their emotions, focus on the issue they are raising, and seek to understand their perspective or concern. This approach can take the conversation in new, sometimes surprisingly good, directions. Seeing expressed differences as opportunities rather than threats can help us communicate in open and inviting ways rather than closed and intimidating ones. Giving each other the benefit of the doubt goes a long way in cultivating an environment of peace.

Returning to the missions committee conversation, an alternate response to defense of the treasurer might have included seeking clarity on what was being asked, repeating back what was heard, listening to the specifics of the concern, providing explanation and clarification, and confirming that everyone understood each other. In short, focusing on the issue and not on an assumed slight.

Mindset Shift 5:
Creating Conversation Spaces

In New Testament times, there were social and religious consequences if a Jewish man talked to a Samaritan woman, entered a Gentile's home, or touched someone who was bleeding. Yet Jesus frequently broke these social and religious norms by talking to or touching people that He shouldn't have. Jesus did not prioritize gaining social acceptance; He prioritized introducing God's reconciling Kingdom-culture to everyone willing to receive it.

Today's social and cultural environments also provide guidelines for what is considered socially acceptable and respectable behavior. Social expectations dictate who can speak and who needs to remain silent in communication and decision-making: whose voices should be heard? Living by God's Kingdom-culture norms will lead us into previously unexplored communication territory—new conversation spaces—that may be counter-cultural.

The Archbishop of Canterbury Justin Welby wrote, "Peace is not found by avoiding conflict but by disagreeing well."[149] Creating new conversation spaces allows us to dialogue about differing ideas, opinions, critiques, disappointments, or resistance to plans. We can focus on understanding each other's interests rather than on whose position is right or wrong. We can't disagree well if we don't have spaces that welcome the conversation.

Building Conversation Spaces

Some people hesitate to create these types of conversation spaces because socially it's just not done. Some fear that emotions will run high or the conversation will get out of control, resulting in more damage. For others, no one has modeled creating this type of conversation space, so they're not sure where to start.[150] Don't let a lack of modeling keep you from trying to create conversation spaces in your spheres of influence. It may feel challenging and uncomfortable at first; you may need to experiment a bit, but creating a welcoming communication environment over time can be possible. Leading out in authenticity and humility will make a big difference.

You can begin by deciding that taking time to learn about, understand, and appreciate the other "we" groups in your social sphere is critically important. If you are wary of cultivating conversation space because of past negative experiences, you may need to establish some conversation guidelines about mutual respect and listening in order to safeguard the conversations and keep them God-honoring. You may also find that, at times, you need to seek out a helpful third party to create the needed conversation space to address an issue.

Acknowledging and Appreciating Differences

Part of creating conversation spaces involves acknowledging differences that disappoint and moving toward appreciating them. Whether young or old,

- Remember that those around you are most likely expressing love in the best way they know how, even if their expression of love falls short of what you want and doesn't touch on your heart-level needs.

- Recognize that many of those around you have grown up in a different generation or social environment than you which has shaped them.

- Acknowledge that those around you also have interests (needs, concerns, desires, fears, limitations, values, and preferences) that they care deeply about and are worth understanding.

- Take time to listen to other people's stories. Ask questions to learn about their life-shaping experiences and values.

- Be patient, gentle, and compassionate with those who are not willing to share their stories with you. Some people find the painful, traumatic experiences of their past too difficult to share with others. Don't pursue a story just to satisfy your own curiosity if the other person is hesitant to share.

- Stretch yourself to learn different ways of communicating using God-honoring words and methods that those who are older, younger, or of a different "we" group than you can more easily receive.

Docking in an Ocean Bay

Without safe places to share perspectives and learn from one another, conflicts are often exacerbated. A conversation space functions like an ocean bay. An ocean bay is a place where the water is safe and boats can dock. A wave that has crashed on the shore has a relentlessly strong undertow of water which pulls everything and everyone in its path back to sea; unaddressed issues can also knock a relationship off its feet and keep it pinned under the water, drowning it in the chaos of conflict. We need ocean bays where we can dock and experience the waters of conflict in safety. Creating these conversation spaces is valuable and should not be neglected by those sincerely pursuing biblical peacemaking and reconciliation.

MINDSET CHANGE CAN LEAD TO CULTURE CHANGE

A group's conflict culture begins to change after enough individuals personally choose to live according to God's Kingdom-culture norms. In this way, individual mindset change can lead to culture change. Culture change is "a change of knowledge and attitude, and therefore of design—of ideas about behavior. Culture change is the process by which new ideas regarding social behavior are generated and interpreted."[151] When leaders in a group recognize and affirm living out God's Kingdom-culture norms, and when structures are aligned with those norms, we begin to see noticeable change.

Speaking about facilitating change in general, Yew describes the responsibility of church leaders:

The challenge of the Chinese church, or any church, lies mostly with the people in leadership positions. In order to make progress, leaders should allow, better yet, actively encourage and initiate changes knowing full well that there are risks involved. With every change, there is potential discomfort, disagreement and tension. Further, changes, if not handled properly, may result in confusion, contention and conflict. And conflict, if prolonged, may result in division and hurt. But there are risks involved even without change. Without change, we run the risk of becoming irrelevant and eventually dying a natural death.[152]

Individuals of higher status or position have the greater opportunity (and dare I say responsibility) to facilitate conflict-culture change. And don't forget: We all have relationships and spheres of influence in which we are the person in positional power and have the best opportunity to provide modeling and discipleship.

Someone who has made the shift from behaving according to their original cultural norms to following God's Kingdom-culture might say things like:

- I used to view conflict, apologizing, and reconciliation as . . .

- I used to behave in _____ ways during conflict.

- My relationships were . . .

- Now I view conflict, apologizing, and reconciliation as . . .

- Now I behave in _____ ways when conflict happens.

- Now my relationships are . . .

Families, churches, and organizations can all experience conflict-culture change. The change starts with individual mindset shifts, heart change, and behavior change. But one day you might overhear someone in your family or group telling someone else, "My [kids, parents, team members] used to view conflict as _____. We used to respond to conflict by _____. Now when conflict happens, we _____."

One day you might hear someone on your church board say, "We used to argue and fight at our church board meetings. Now we listen respectfully and patiently discuss decisions." Or alternatively, "We used to be silent in board meetings and just nod in agreement but didn't support final decisions with our actions because in our hearts we disagreed. Now we have enough individual pre-meetings where people feel comfortable to give their honest input, so decisions made in our meetings are fully supported after the meeting has ended as well."

When you hear testimonies such as these, you will know that conflict-culture change has taken place in your family or group. What a joyful day that will be!

CHAPTER WRAP-UP

The old saying that more is caught than taught holds true for peacemaking discipleship. Those around you are watching how you live and lead. As a parent or leader, the consistency between what you say (your instructions, sermons, text messages, and off-hand comments) and do (your actions, tone of voice, and body language) can have a profound impact on those around you. By persevering in growing as a peacemaker yourself, you are better positioned to cultivate an environment of peace in your spheres of influence. And be encouraged: If you are the younger one in a relationship, your peacemaking behavior still has the potential to impact the conflict culture.

Ultimately, teaching for heart and mindset change is also necessary. Yet when we haven't personally mastered biblical peacemaking in our own relationships (and who truly masters such a topic), we often hesitate to teach others, thinking we aren't qualified. We want to leave the teaching to people who have successfully handled every conflict and reconciled every relationship, but such people don't exist. Once when I was questioning my qualification to teach something I had just learned, my team leader told me, "If you know 10% more than others on a subject, you are qualified to teach it. Just stay humble, have accountability, acknowledge your mistakes, and be a learner as well." My perspective on teaching shifted that day.

Of those I interviewed, many were still learning how to be peacemakers, but some, like Li Jun, committed themselves early on to begin discipling others in peacemaking. Throughout the five months in which a serious church conflict issue developed, Li Jun was simultaneously teaching Corlette Sande's *The Young Peacemaker* to the church's children.[153] He could have easily thought, *How can I teach these kids when I myself am in the middle of conflict?* Instead, because he persevered in teaching others, he was constantly reminded to ask himself how to glorify God, build others up, and be more like Jesus. He felt teaching the children was great preparation for facing these big conflicts. As we teach others, we continue learning and maturing as well.

Be encouraged. Dive in. Others are already swimming ahead of you. God makes *changing normal* possible. Embrace the discomfort of change and experiment with creating safe conversation spaces to have the difficult, awkward, and challenging conversations that your family, church, organization, or team needs to have.

Embracing change will most likely be hard, perhaps one of the hardest things you have done in a long time. You may feel as if your attempts at change increase, not lessen, the intensity of the crashing ocean waves. Seek out companionship to help you keep going. Don't swim these waters alone. Remember, not everything you try will work. Keep abiding in Christ, persevering in humility and love, and giving your relationships time. And keep working your way toward the ocean bay, the calmer waters where conversations can happen.

A PRAYER

Lord, I ask for the grace and humility to embrace the discomfort of change and to recognize when my discomfort comes from Your Spirit's nudging to take a step out of my comfort zone into new peacemaking territory. I admit that it is easy to see the need for others to change, but when it comes to seeing my own personal need for mindset shifts, I struggle. I have blind spots. Shine Your light in my heart. Reveal to me those relationships in which I haven't valued and loved others in the same way that You value and love me. Open my eyes to see when I have viewed questions and differing views as competition or a threat instead of as God-given diversity to be appreciated and explored.

Cultivate in me a deeper biblical understanding and new attitude toward conflict, apologizing, forgiveness, and reconciliation. Fill me with courage to try out new Holy Spirit-empowered communication practices that are proactive, gentle, listening-oriented, and lovingly honest.

By Your grace, I choose to not be conformed to the pattern of this world—where face trumps all and my status determines how I relate to others—but to be transformed by the renewing of my mind, resulting in mindset shifts in line with Your will (Rom 12:2). I will not think of myself more highly than I should, but humbly recognize that I am now in Christ, have been reconciled to You, and have been given the message and ministry of reconciliation as Your ambassador (Rom 12:3; 2 Cor 5:17–20). Guide me regarding how to create a new conversation space at home, at church, or in our organization this week and in the weeks ahead. In Jesus' name I pray, amen.

REFLECTION QUESTIONS

1. Use the chart below to record to what degree (never, sometimes, or often) you and/or those around you study, teach, and/or model the topics presented throughout this book.

    a. Does my own personal Bible study include these topics? (never, sometimes, often)

    b. Does my family's study and discussion together include these topics? (never, sometimes, often)

    c. Do my church's discipleship materials for children, youth, and adults include these topics and application practice?

    d. Does my organization's staff or team development program include these topics and application practice?

Prayerfully consider prioritizing further personal Bible study as well as group study in some of these areas in the near future.

Chapter in book	Topic	Personal	Family	Church or Organization
	To what degree (never, sometimes, often) do you and/or those around you study, teach, and/or model the topics presented throughout this book?			
		NEVER (N)	SOMETIMES (S)	OFTEN (O)
1, 2	Example: What keeps us stuck in conflict?	N	O	S
1, 2	What keeps us stuck in conflict?			
2	Understanding the root causes of conflict			
3	God's provision for our reconciliation with Him and for our reconciliation with each other			
3	Biblical forgiveness			
3	Loving each other as God loves us when we are in conflict			
3	God's call to be peacemakers and ambassadors of reconciliation			
3	Being the family of God to all believers			
4	A theology of face			
4	The role of dying to self			
4	The characteristics of a face-safe community			
5	Navigating status and power differences when conflict happens			
5	Understanding when conflict involves abuse and what to do when this happens			
5	Setting communication guidelines, boundaries, and accountability when needed			

Chapter in book	Topic	Personal	Family	Church or Organization
		NEVER (N)	SOMETIMES (S)	OFTEN (O)
5	The impact of our cultural lens on our behavior, conflict response, perception of others, and biblical interpretation			
6	The practicalities of caring for Christ's interests, others' interests, and your own interests			
6	Effective listening			
6	Developing observation skills			
7	The importance of verbal, authentic confession-apologies			
8	Abiding in Christ, living by the Spirit, and bearing the fruit of the Spirit when in conflict with someone			
8, 9	Proactive, honest, and loving conversations			
10	Finding and/or being a helpful conflict companion			
11	Responding to conflict according to God's Kingdom-culture ways			
11	Viewing conflict as an opportunity			
	Viewing differences objectively			
11	Valuing relationship with others in the same way that God values relationship with us			

FINAL THOUGHTS

WHEN TAKING A TRIP, WE USUALLY have to make a choice between different routes. Do we take the scenic route that is slower but more visually enjoyable, or do we take the fastest, most direct route? After choosing a route and heading out, we (well, some of us) closely follow our GPS and hope we have chosen the best time of day and the route with the least amount of traffic.

As we travel, we might begin to doubt our choice or our GPS, especially if an accident happens slowing traffic down, forcing us to take a detour. Or perhaps the scenery we expected has changed or there is road construction. Maybe we miss a sign along the way. Or night changes the look of everything. Panic might set in: Am I headed in the right direction? Did I choose the best route? But then we see a sign that reassures us our path will lead to our destination, and we exhale a breath of relief; we'll get there eventually.

In contrast, we generally don't use a GPS device for our everyday travel to school, work, and church. We have our usual routes and many of us travel on autopilot. One day, when driving home from church, I decided to take a different route and discovered it was so much better! I wondered why I hadn't tried it earlier. I had been stuck in my usual rut.

It was only by changing my normal behavior that I found an improved path to take.

Throughout *Changing Normal*, we have seen from Scripture how God's Kingdom-culture way of responding to conflict and relational engagement looks quite different from ours; it's an entirely new relational route. We've been taking our usual relationship paths, traveling on autopilot, but God has a much better route. This route, however, requires us to rely on our GPS: the Bible and Christ within. When we choose God's way of addressing conflict, we have to stick to our GPS for the most accurate directions to our final destination—a God-honoring, restored and reconciled relationship. What joy we experience when we reach that destination!

Yet because reconciliation requires willingness from both parties, not every relationship will be reconciled this side of heaven, and there will be times when we get confused along the way. Am I on the best route? Am I headed in the right direction? Memorizing the directions (Scripture) can help when we are suddenly faced with an unexpected fork in the road. We'll know which way to turn, even if it doesn't feel right. Pursuing reconciliation can be slow and often requires courage, compassion, perseverance, and even repeated conversations. Trust God's GPS and stick to His route. Praise God that changing normal in our relationships is possible because we are in Christ and Christ is in us.

Perhaps you are just beginning to learn what it means to be a peacemaker; this book is your first exposure to God's reconciling Kingdom-culture and God's cultural norms related to conflict. I am excited for you as you step out in faith—relying on God—to apply what you are learning.

Or perhaps you are somewhere on the peacemaking discipleship journey already, but relationships have been rough, and you needed to hear testimonies reminding you of what is possible and where to find strength as you stick to God's route. Be encouraged; God has a way forward for you. Be intentional about applying, modeling, and, yes, teaching biblical principles to others.

Whatever your situation, I pray that you will accept the challenge to begin cultivating an environment of peace in your spheres of influence. "May the God of hope fill you with all joy and peace as you trust in Him, so that you may overflow with hope by the power of the Holy Spirit" (Rom 15:13) as you follow God's lead in your relationships and peacemaking discipleship. Take heart—God is with you!

WHAT'S YOUR NEXT STEP?

If you would like to lead others through discussing this book, you can access next step resources at https://jolenekinser.com/.

For guidance as you practice applying principles learned here, join a workshop. Find information at https://jolenekinser.com/.

I'd love to hear your changing normal experiences and mutually encourage one another along the way. You can share your stories with me at https://jolenekinser.com/contact/.

ACKNOWLEDGEMENTS

It won't be possible to acknowledge every person whose fingerprint is on this book, but here's a start:

I am indebted to my thirty-one Chinese brothers and sisters in Christ who so openly told me their conflict stories. Thank you for permitting me to share your experiences with others.

Thank you to the many people who have been through peacemaking trainings. Our discussions have helped me better understand the nuances and challenges of living out biblical peacemaking in Chinese cultural contexts. I continue to learn from you.

Thank you to the countless friends and relatives, my SGVAC family, the SPA district staff, and other leaders who have spiritually and financially supported me over the years, particularly throughout my PhD studies and this season of writing. You have been present on difficult days, believing these long months of writing will bear peacemaking and reconciling fruit in many lives.

Thank you to my Monday/Thursday peacemaking prayer groups: Andrea Childs, Christine Ho, Sai Wang, Monica Mac, Jude Brown, Becky Sappington, Mom, and Linea Theiss. You prayed me through the entire book writing process—I couldn't have done this without you.

Linda Roberts helped me keep focusing on Jesus, break out of "analysis paralysis," and figuratively speaking, step out of one room, make my way down a long hallway, and step over the threshold into another larger, more spacious room. You have been so faithfully present. I thank God that He brought you into my life to help me along this journey.

Jeff and Julie Su, Gordon and Lilian Gong, and Kip Schnackenberg provided quiet places to live enabling me to focus on writing. Thank you for your incredible generosity.

Some of the peacemaking mentors and pioneers who have gone before me, invested in me, and made materials accessible for Chinese believers include: Anne Bachle-Fifer, Brian Noble, Cecilia Yau, Chip Zimmer, Gary Friesen, Karl Dortzbach, Ken and Corlette Sande, Rick Stein, and Roger Duerksen. Thank you for continuing to share your wisdom, experience, and time with me.

Leanne Dzubinski, my dissertation chair at Biola University, expertly guided me to complete the research and dissertation that made this book possible. Jamie Sanchez and Tom Steffen served on my dissertation committee, strengthening the final product. Thank you for your academic investment and encouragement throughout that six-year journey.

My beta-readers: Alan Chow, Brent Fulton, Cissy and Vincent Yu, Dan Allen, Eunice Chuang, Michael Wu, Pao Hwa Lin, Rick Stein, Tim Fung, Vicki Chui, and Yvette Wu. Thank you for reading the longer version and giving valuable input for making the content more accessible.

Deep thanks goes to each one who poured countless hours into this book making it technically possible for *Changing Normal*'s message to get out into the world:

- Hanna Lyons, my editor, who greatly encouraged this first-time author, working with me every step of the way. *Changing Normal* communicates far more clearly and compellingly thanks to your work.

- My dear friends, Linda and Vince Hucks, at Azure Seas Publishing who have supported this vision from inception. You helped me see what could be and brought it to fruition.

- The ZDL Books team who translated and published the Chinese versions.

Lastly, my parents, Ken and Cheryl Kinser, have been my biggest cheerleaders in life and ministry. You have never wavered in encouragement or support. I can't say thank you enough for wholeheartedly loving God, loving others, and entrusting me to God.

APPENDIX A: FEELINGS REFERENCE GUIDE

The following list of feelings is not intended to be a comprehensive list, but rather a starting point to help you gain awareness of your inner experience. Used with permission from NVC Academy. Copyright 2005 by Center for Nonviolent Communication. Website: www.cnvc.org. Email: cnvc@cnvc.org.

BASIC HUMAN FEELINGS WHEN OUR NEEDS ARE FULFILLED

Absorbed	Curious	Fondness
Adventurous	Cushy	Friendly
Affectionate	Dazzled	Fulfilled
Alert	Delighted	Gay
Alive	Eager	Giddy
Amorous	Ecstatic	Glad
Animated	Ebullient	Gleeful
Appreciative	Effervescent	Glorious
Amazed	Elated	Glowing
Amused	Electrified	Grateful
Aroused	Enchanted	Gratified
Astonished	Encouraged	Grief
Astounded	Energetic	Happy
Awake	Engrossed	Helpful
Awed	Enlivened	Hopeful
Blissful	Enthralled	Humbled
Breathless	Enthusiastic	Inquisitive
Buoyant	Exalted	Inspired
Calm	Excited	Interested
Carefree	Exhilarated	Intrigued
Comfortable	Expansive	Invigorated
Confident	Expectant	Involved
Contented	Exuberant	Joyful
Cozy	Fascinated	Joyous

Jubilant	Rapturous	Startled
Liberated	Refreshed	Still
Loving	Reinvigorated	Stimulated
Mellow	Rejuvenated	Stunned
Merry	Relaxed	Surprised
Mirthful	Relieved	Tender
Moved	Renewed	Thankful
Optimistic	Rested	Thrilled
Overwhelmed	Restored	Tickled
Passionate	Revived	Tranquil
Peaceful	Safe	Touched
Perky	Satisfied	Upbeat
Pleased	Secure	Uplifted
Proud	Serene	Warm
Puzzled	Shocked	Zestful
Quiet	Spacious	
Radiant	Spellbound	

BASIC HUMAN FEELINGS WHEN OUR NEEDS ARE NOT FULFILLED

Afraid	Chagrined	Distant
Aggravated	Cold	Distraught
Agitation	Concerned	Distressed
Alarmed	Confused	Disturbed
Aloof	Cool	Doubtful
Angry	Contrite	Downcast
Anguish	Cross	Downhearted
Animosity	Dejected	Dread
Annoyance	Depressed	Dull
Anxious	Despair	Edgy
Apathetic	Despondent	Embarrassed
Appalled	Detached	Embittered
Apprehensive	Diffident	Enraged
Ashamed	Disappointed	Envious
Aversion	Disconnected	Exasperated
Awful	Discouraged	Exhausted
Bad	Disenchanted	Exposed
Beat	Disgruntled	Fatigued
Bewildered	Disgusted	Fearful
Bitter	Disheartened	Fidgety
Blah	Disinterested	Forlorn
Blue	Dislike	Frightened
Bored	Dismayed	Frustrated
Breathless	Displeased	Furious
Brokenhearted	Disquieted	Gloomy

Grief	Melancholy	Sour
Guilty	Miserable	Spent
Hate	Mopey	Spiritless
Heavy	Morose	Startled
Horrible	Nervous	Surprised
Hostile	Overwhelmed	Suspicious
Hot	Pain	Tense
Humdrum	Panicky	Terrified
Hurt	Passive	Tired
Impatient	Perplexed	Troubled
Incensed	Pessimistic	Uncertain
Indifferent	Puzzled	Uncomfortable
Indignant	Rancorous	Uneasy
Infuriated	Regretful	Unglued
Inquisitive	Reluctant	Unhappy
Insecure	Remorseful	Unnerved
Intense	Repelled	Unsteady
Irate	Resentful	Upset
Irked	Restless	Uptight
Irritated	Revolted	Vengeful
Jealous	Sad	Vexed
Jittery	Scared	Vulnerable
Lazy	Sensitive	Weary
Lethargic	Shaky	Withdrawn
Listless	Shocked	Woeful
Lonely	Skeptical	Worn out
Mad	Sleepy	Worried
Mean	Sorrowful	

APPENDIX B: UNIVERSAL HUMAN NEEDS

The following list is used with permission from Inbal, Miki and Arnina Kasthan, of the Bay Nonviolent Communication group. Copyright 2014, https://baynvc.org/list-of-needs/. Email: nvc@baynvc.org. Phone: (510) 433-0700.

This list builds on Marshal Rosenberg's original needs list with categories adapted from Manfred Max-Neef. Neither exhaustive nor definitive, it can be used for study and discovery about each person's authentic experience. These needs are without reference to specific people, time, actions, or things.

SUBSISTENCE & SECURITY

Physical Sustenance
Air
Food
Health
Movement
Physical Safety
Rest / Sleep
Shelter
Touch
Water

Security
Consistency
Order/Structure
Peace (external)
Peace of mind
Protection
Safety (emotional)
Stability
Trusting

FREEDOM

Autonomy
Choice
Ease
Independence
Power
Self-responsibility
Space
Spontaneity

Leisure/ Relaxation
Humor
Joy
Play
Pleasure
Rejuvenation

CONNECTION

Affection
Appreciation
Attention
Closeness
Companionship
Harmony
Intimacy
Love
Nurturing
Sexual expression
Support
Tenderness
Warmth

To Matter
Acceptance
Care
Compassion
Consideration
Empathy
Kindness
Mutual recognition
Respect
To be heard, seen
To be known, understood
To be trusted
Understanding others

Community
Belonging
Communication
Cooperation
Equality
Inclusion
Mutuality
Participation
Partnership
Self-expression
Sharing

MEANING

Sense of Self
Authenticity
Competence
Creativity
Dignity
Growth
Healing
Honesty
Integrity
Self-acceptance
Self-care
Self-connection
Self-knowledge
Self-realization
Mattering to myself

Understanding
Awareness
Clarity
Discovery
Learning
Making sense of life
Stimulation

Meaning
Aliveness
Challenge
Consciousness
Contribution
Creativity
Effectiveness
Exploration
Integration
Purpose

Transcendence
Beauty
Celebration of life
Communion
Faith
Flow
Hope
Inspiration
Mourning
Peace (internal)
Presence

APPENDIX C: APOLOGIZING FAQS

The following questions and complications surface for some people as they begin incorporating apologizing into their lives. While there are more questions and lots more that could be said, this provides a place to start.

1. Why is it awkward to respond when someone apologizes to me?

When being apologized to, we may suddenly feel uncomfortable, awkward, and even embarrassed. We may find ourselves averting our eyes, avoiding making eye contact, and brushing off or minimizing the apology by saying things like, "You don't need to apologize," "It's okay," "It didn't bother me," "Why are you apologizing for such a small thing? It was nothing." No matter the words, our voice might communicate that we feel they shouldn't be apologizing to us. Our tone might even be a bit disapproving or judgmental. Even if we really were hurt and did secretly or subconsciously want them to apologize, we sometimes still communicate the opposite. Why is it so hard for us to look someone in the eye and genuinely receive their apology? Below are a few of my personal reflections to consider.

First, if apologizing is not common and hasn't been modeled in your social context, then how to appropriately respond to an apology most likely hasn't been modeled well either. You may find yourself taken off guard, shocked even, when someone apologizes to you. This is normal. Thankfully, learning how to respond to an apology is relatively easy (see FAQ #2).

Second, at a deep unconscious level, I think we don't want others to know that they have the capability to hurt or offend us. We would like to think we are strong, and we don't allow other people to hurt us. But the reality is, most of us have times when we do get hurt and offended, even by small things. Then our pride rises up and we don't want to let on that we were hurt. Acknowledging and receiving an apology from someone else means that we are admitting that we are vulnerable. For this reason, it often takes humility and courage to receive an apology, just like it takes humility and courage to apologize.

2. How should I respond when someone apologizes to me?

When someone apologizes to you, it's important to remember that it might have taken a lot of humility and courage for this person to take this sometimes difficult step. So you want to ask yourself how you can respect and honor the person who has just apologized to you. I have found that looking the person in the eye and genuinely saying a simple, "Thanks," "I accept your apology," or "Thanks for apologizing. I appreciate that," can express an acknowledgement of receiving the apology instead of brushing it off. You can take it a step further by saying something like, "Thanks, I did feel hurt by what you said earlier, and I forgive you." Acknowledging that you felt hurt, if true, and verbally expressing forgiveness can be personally healing and freeing as well.

If the person seems to be giving an artificial apology, it probably feels a lot harder to accept it. Be gracious and receive the apology. Perhaps their future actions will demonstrate the genuineness of their regret and you misread their apology. Or perhaps their heart will change further over time. Or perhaps they really didn't mean the apology or didn't know what they were apologizing for but were simply trying to smooth things over or normalize the relationship. You might feel sad, disappointed, and angry when this happens. You might need to confront this behavior in a God-honoring way at some point in time. No matter what, keep focusing on doing your part as a peacemaker.

3. **How should I respond when someone apologizes to me, but I don't feel the apology was necessary?**

Sometimes someone apologizes to us about something that we had completely forgotten about or didn't feel hurt by to begin with. In that moment, our pride might puff up and we'll take offense that this person thought they had hurt us or thought we would be offended by such behavior. When that happens, we need to let humility and our respect for the other person rise up instead. Keep a kind, sincere tone of voice, even if you are surprised. Stay away from any disparaging or judgmental responses.

In a situation like this I have said something like, "Oh, thanks! I really appreciate that you cared enough to apologize. Actually, I don't even remember the incident. You can rest assured that I haven't been harboring anything in my heart against you over this." If it's relevant, I might even ask them to tell me what I had done or said that made them think I had been hurt. I can then share what was going on in my heart at the time (if I remember and if I think it would help us relationally).

4. **What should I say if someone apologizes to me, but I am still angry and not ready to forgive them?**

I once experienced a Chinese friend apologizing to me for not telling me about an important decision in her life that we had previously prayed about and discussed at length together—I found out two months after her wedding that she had met and married someone. When she heard me express how disappointed and sad I felt because she had not told me earlier, she genuinely apologized for the hurt she had caused. Even though she had apologized, I still felt angry and unable to forgive immediately. The force of my emotions had surprised me; I needed some time to process the reasons why I felt hurt and to discover the source. So, in the moment I said, "Thank you for apologizing. I will forgive you; it's just hard to do so right now. I need some time to process this news because, you're right, I do feel hurt."

If you need some time to process their apology, it's fine to express that. You may discover that, as part of your healing and forgiving process, you would like to talk further about the situation and the reasons why you felt hurt or offended. If that is the case and if you are able, end the conversation by setting up another time to get together to talk further. In this way, you let the other person know that you still want to be in relationship, or at least bring closure to things, even if you don't feel like it at the moment.

5. **What if someone does not accept my apology? Or, what if someone says they have accepted my apology but remains distant—what should I do?**

Unfortunately, we can't see into other people's hearts to know what's going on. At times we need to wait patiently as we entrust the relationship to the Lord and faithfully love the other person with God's love. Listen to God to see if there is anything else He would have you do. Is there some form of restitution you need to complete? Any particular actions to rebuild trust? Do you need to further change any behavior? Perhaps God will point something out that you still need to do to make things right. Stay sensitive to the Holy Spirit in this regard.

Sometimes we like to say to ourselves, "I've apologized; I've done my part; it's up to them now," and wash our hands of any further responsibility. To some degree, this is true. If we have done all that God has prompted us to do, our hearts can be at peace. We need to trust God regarding the timing of the other person's responsiveness to God's work in their heart.

At the same time, it's important to stay sensitive to anything else God might prompt you to do in the coming days, months, or years. Someone I know (Person A) was prompted by God to apologize to Person B a number of times for the same thing over the course of a few years. Prior to Person A's final apology, Person B had heard a sermon on forgiveness. While Person A didn't know this, the Holy Spirit did. Even though, technically speaking, Person A had already done their part years earlier, because of their obedience to the Holy Spirit's prompting to sincerely apologize once again, the relationship was able to be restored. The time had come. Like Person A, you might also find God speaking to your heart over time to take further action. Keep your heart open to the nudging of the Holy Spirit.

6. **Should I keep apologizing even if I'm the only one who is apologizing and the other person should be as well?**

The following concerns have come up for some people who are proactively living out biblical peacemaking:

1. If I always apologize, will it cause the other person to take me less seriously or to not think highly of me?
2. Will the other person, who should also be apologizing but doesn't, start to view as habitual my apologizing for my 2% of the problem? Should I apologize less?
3. If we apologize often to our child, will that make her think too highly of herself?

There's no doubt about it, continuing to apologize to someone for your contribution to a conflict when the other person doesn't take responsibility for their contribution is quite difficult. First, it's important to remember that your reason for apologizing to the other person is to take responsibility for your part and heal any hurt. This motivation honors God. Second, instead of apologizing less, you might need to exercise an additional communication muscle.

You may have done the hard work of apologizing for your inappropriate words or behavior but avoided having a vulnerable and boldly loving conversation in which you discuss how the other person's words or behavior impact you. In some situations, apologizing is only one part of the communication that needs to happen. The other person might not have realized or is refusing to acknowledge their contribution to the problem. Sometimes people need you to initiate this conversation. Having this type of conversation creates an opportunity for the other person to also apologize and make changes if they are willing.

APPENDIX D: RESOURCES

There are many excellent books, small group studies, courses, seminars, and retreats that teach Christ-followers how to respond to conflict in God-honoring ways. Some organizations provide reconciliation services and teach individuals how to address conflict in their personal relationships, how to coach and mediate, or how to respond to community and societal level conflicts.

Note: Listing an organization, book, or article here does not mean I necessarily endorse all views and teachings of that organization or author.

Check out my website: www.jolenekinser.com for regularly updated postings of organizations, books, and article recommendations.

BIBLICAL PEACEMAKING ORGANIZATIONS

United States

- Alliance Peacemaking: https://cmalliance.org/our-work/church-ministries/developing-people/peacemaking/
- Ambassadors of Reconciliation: https://www.aorhope.org/
- Love & Conflict 爱与冲突: https://www.loveandconflict.org/
- Metanoia Ministries: https://www.restoringthechurch.org
- Peacemaker Ministries: https://www.peacemakerministries.org/
- Relational Wisdom 360: https://rw360.org/
- ReconciliAsian: https://www.reconciliasian.org

Taiwan

- 3R: https://three3r.weebly.com

Australia

- Peacewise: https://peacewise.org.au

HIGH CONFLICT SITUATION RESOURCES

- The High Conflict Institute https://www.highconflictinstitute.com/what-is-high-conflict

SUPPORT FOR ABUSE SURVIVORS & RESOURCES FOR HELPERS

- American Bible Society: Trauma Healing Institute https://trauma-healinginstitute.org/
- Living Waters of Hope: https://www.livingwatersofhope.org
- Tahrir Alnisa Foundation: https://www.tahriralnisa.org/
- The Allender Center: https://theallendercenter.org/

BOOKS & ARTICLES

Abuse & Trauma:

Allendar, Dan B. *The Wounded Heart: Hope for Adult Victims of Childhood Sexual Abuse.* Colorado Springs, CO: NavPress, 2008.

Menakem, Resmaa. *My Grandmother's Hands: Racialized Trauma and the Pathway to Mending Our Hearts and Bodies.* Las Vegas, NV: Central Recovery Press, 2017.

Van der Kolk, Bessel A. *The Body Keeps the Score: Brain, Mind, and Body in the Healing of Trauma.* New York, NY: Penguin Books, 2014.

Church Conflict:

Langberg, Diane. *Redeeming Power: Understanding Authority and Abuse in the Church.* Grand Rapids, MI: Brazos Press, 2020. Kindle.

Poirier, Alfred. *The Peacemaking Pastor: A Biblical Guide to Resolving Church Conflict.* Grand Rapids, MI: Baker Books, 2006.

Van Yperen, Jim. *Making Peace: A Guide to Overcoming Church Conflict.* Chicago, IL: Moody Publishers, 2002.

Yew, Wally, and Cecilia Yau. 教會衝突的處理與重建 [Managing Church Conflicts]. Petaluma, CA: CCM Publishers, USA, 2002.

- Look here for other titles on church conflict management: https://www.libraryofbook.com/books/understanding-managing-redeeming-church-conflict

Communication:

Silk, Danny. *Keep Your Love On: Connection Communication and Boundaries.* United States of America: Loving On Purpose, 2013.

Culture:

Shin, Benjamin C., and Sheryl Takag Silzer. *Tapestry of Grace: Untangling the Cultural Complexities in Asian American Life and Ministry*. Eugene, OR: Wipf & Stock, 2016.

Face & Shame:

Flanders, Christopher L. *About Face: Rethinking Face for the 21st-Century Mission. American Society of Missiology Monograph*. Eugene, OR: Wipf and Stock Publishers, 2011.

Thompson, Curt. *The Story of Shame: Retelling the Stories We Believe About Ourselves*. Downers Grove, IL: InterVarsity Press. 2015.

Wu, Jackson, and Ryan Jensen. *Seeking God's Face: Practical Reflections on Honor and Shame in Scripture*. Houston, TX: Lucid Books, 2022.

Forgiveness:

Linn, Matthew, and Sheila Fabricant Linn, and Dennis Linn. *Don't Forgive Too Soon: Extending the Two Hands That Heal*. Mahwah, NJ: Paulist Press, 1997.

Volf, Miroslav. *Free of Charge: Giving and Forgiving in a Culture Stripped of Grace*. Grand Rapids, MI: Zondervan, 2005.

Grief & Loss:

Boss, Pauline. *Ambiguous Loss: Learning to Live with Unresolved Grief*. Cambridge, MA: Harvard University Press: 1999.

Sittser, Jerry. *A Grace Disguised: How the Soul Grows Through Loss*. Grand Rapids, MI: Zondervan, 2004.

Wright, H. Norman. *Experiencing Grief*. Nashville, TN: B&H Publishing Group, 2004.

INTERGENERATIONAL ISSUES/IMMIGRANT FAMILY ISSUES

Wally Yew:

Immigrant Families 1: Three Basic Conflicts within the Family
https://ccmusa.org/u2u/u2u.aspx?id=198702-2

Immigrant Families 2: Most Important Relationship within a Family
https://ccmusa.org/u2u/u2u.aspx?id=198703

Immigrant Families 3: Favoritism
https://ccmusa.org/u2u/u2u.aspx?id=198704

Immigrant Families 4: Communicating with Teens
https://ccmusa.org/u2u/u2u.aspx?id=198705-2

Immigrant Families 5: If You Are Not the Favored Child
https://ccmusa.org/u2u/u2u.aspx?id=198710-2

Immigrant Families 6: Solving the Classic In-law Conflict
https://ccmusa.org/u2u/u2u.aspx?id=198711

Immigrant Families 7: Honor Your Parents
https://ccmusa.org/u2u/u2u.aspx?id=198712

Immigrant Families 8: Successful Parenting
https://ccmusa.org/u2u/u2u.aspx?id=198801-2

The Power of Reconciliation
https://ccmusa.org/u2u/u2u.aspx?id=200010

Chinese Church, Asian Church, Community Church
https://ccmusa.org/u2u/u2u.aspx?id=200004

Practical Peacemaking:

Eddy, Bill. *It's All Your Fault! 12 Tips for Managing People Who Blame Others for Everything*. HCI Press, 2009.

Lederach, John Paul. *Reconcile: Conflict Transformation For Ordinary Christians*. Harrisonburg, VA: Herald Press, 2014.

Love, Rick. *A Peace of the Bible: Following the Prince of Peace into a World of Conflict*. Arvada, CO: Rick Love Publications, 2014.

Noble, P. Brian. *The Path of a Peacemaker: Your Biblical Guide to Healthy Relationships, Conflict Resolution, and a Life of Peace*. Grand Rapids, MI: Baker Books, 2019.

Noble, P. Brian. *Living Reconciled: 7 Ways to Bring Peace to Your Most Difficult Relationships*. Grand Rapids, MI: Baker Books, 2022.

Sande, Ken. *The Peacemaker: A Biblical Guide to Resolving Personal Conflict*. Grand Rapids, MI: Baker Books, 2004.

Sande, Ken, and Kevin Johnson. *Reconciling Everyday Conflict*. Grand Rapids, MI: Baker Books, 2011.

APPENDIX E: CONVERSATION SPACE IDEAS

BELOW ARE SOME QUESTIONS that require vulnerability and courage to ask but can reveal a goldmine of information for you to prayerfully consider if you are willing. Such questions can get a conversation going about what is considered respectful and loving behavior in your family, church, or organization as it relates to discussion, meetings, and disagreement. The goal of the discussion is to better understand each other's interests, not to determine whose ideas are better, right, or wrong. In your discussion, be sure to have each person respond to the questions and share their views, perceptions, and experiences.

1. Do you experience me as someone who wants you to speak up and say something if you disagree with me? (If yes, what types of things do I say or do that give you this impression?)

2. When we have a conversation or meeting, do you think I expect you to show support of what I am saying by just agreeing and

not saying anything, even if you disagree with me? (If yes, what types of things do I say or do that give you this impression?)

3. Is there anything I do that causes you to be fearful to speak up and say something? (If yes, share an example.)

4. Do you sometimes feel hurt or disrespected by my words or actions? Can you share an example? (Discuss what would be some appropriate ways for them to let you know in the future that they felt hurt or disrespected by you.)

5. Do you feel like I sometimes talk too much? Interrupt you? Cut off dialogue? How well do I listen? Please share examples.

6. What can I do differently to improve our communication? (Ask for specific examples.)

After listening to the other person's response to your question, a great follow up is to repeat back what you heard, "I heard you say . . . Is that correct?" Allow for the other person to ask questions or to clarify.

As a parent, find a relaxed time to have a conversation with your teenage or adult children. Or as an elder or pastor who leads board or committee meetings, deliberately set aside time to gather to discuss the communication dynamics of your meetings. Both types of conversations might sound something like this:

"I have realized that I'm not always the best communicator or listener. I've been reading about expectations and assumptions in relationships and am wondering how you experience me. I would also like to share how I experience you. I hope we can both share as honestly as possible without getting defensive. My purpose for talking about this is to better understand each other, not to determine who is better, right, or wrong. I'd like to improve how we communicate with one another. I believe that taking time to understand each other honors and pleases God and will help our communication."

Then initiate a conversation using some of the suggested questions. Make sure everyone has the opportunity to share their expectations and experiences (including you) and discuss whether making changes to better understand each other would be helpful.

I designed these questions with the person of higher position in mind: parent to an adult/older child, pastor to a church member, boss to an employee. Often someone of lower position won't give upward feedback if the conversation space isn't created by the superior in the relationship. The person initiating will need a certain level of emotional and spiritual maturity to guide the conversation. Additionally, to have this kind of discussion, there needs to be a level of pre-established safety and trust in the relationship. If safety has been an ongoing issue in a relationship, then more should be done to rebuild safety before trying to ask these questions.

To initiate requesting this type of personal feedback is counter-cultural to most of us and can feel a bit scary. Even so, I invite you to consider trying it as you seek to develop a face-safe community. Choose a time and place where no one will be rushed. Also, choose a time when no one's emotions are running high due to a recent conflict. And if you need a third party present to facilitate the conversation, seek out that kind of help as it might make all the difference.

ENDNOTES

Preface

1. Check out my May 16, 2008 pingshu performance at a Performing Arts Exhibition in Beijing here: https://www.youtube.com/watch?v=hU5Yqy-iOd-g. For more information about pingshu storytelling, check out this website: https://english.visitbeijing.com.cn/article/47OO2n4FkX6.

Introduction

2. L. Samovar, R. Porter, and E. McDaniel, *Intercultural Communication: A Reader*, 11th ed. (Thomas/Wadsworth, 2006), 10.

3. Samovar, Porter, and McDaniel, *Intercultural Communication*, 98.

4. Politeness practices within cultures change over time, so these may or may not still be practiced.

5. Samovar, Porter, and McDaniel, *Intercultural Communication*, 10.

6. One could even argue that the references to these thirteen different churches from three different cities in China cannot be considered one cultural context. I acknowledge this.

    My interview participants came from three first-tier cities in China's southwest, south-central, and eastern regions. The participants, twenty-three women and eight men, had an age range that spread across six decades, with the majority being in their 30s, 40s, and 50s.

    All participants in my research study minimally had a junior high education, with the large majority having either a three-year technical academy degree, a bachelor's degree, or a master's degree. While eleven participants grew up in the countryside, all but one of those completed higher education of some kind.

7. See the Resource List for references to works on face and facework in other contexts.

8. All Chinese language references are to Mandarin Chinese.

9. Hui-Ching Chang and G. Richard Holt, "A Chinese Perspective on Face as Inter-Relational Concern," in *The Challenge of Facework: Cross-Cultural and Interpersonal Issues*, ed. Stella Ting-Toomey, *Suny Series in Human*

Communication Processes (Albany, NY: State University of New York Press, 1994), 95–132.

10   Chung-Ying Cheng, "The Concept of Face and Its Confucian Roots," *Journal of Chinese Philosophy* 13, no. 3 (1986): 329–48.

11   Kwang-Kuo Hwang, *Foundations of Chinese Psychology: Confucian Social Relations*, ed. Anthony J. Marsella, *International and Cultural Psychology* (Book 1) (New York, NY: Springer, 2012), 342.

12   David Yau-fai Ho, "On the Concept of Face," *American Journal of Sociology* 81, no. 4 (1976): 867–84.

13   Xiaohong Wei and Qingyuan Li, "The Confucian Value of Harmony and Its Influence on Chinese Social Interaction," *Cross-Cultural Communication* 9, no. 1 (2013): 60–66.

14   Li Jie, author interview, pseudonym used and location undisclosed for privacy purposes, 2019. To protect the privacy of those interviewed, all interview quotes will follow this same format of anonymity throughout the rest of the book.

15   For a more full explanation of my limitations and research bias explanation, see my dissertation: Jolene Kinser, "Factors Impacting Relational Reconciliation in a Mainland China Faith-based Context: A Qualitative Study" (doctoral thesis, Biola University, 2020), 66–67, https://www.researchgate.net/publication/346573669_Factors_Impacting_Relational_Reconciliation_in_a_Mainland_China_Faith-based_Context_A_Qualitative_Study.

Chapter 1

16   Chen Dandan, interview, 2019.

17   Wang Xiuying, interview, 2019.

18   Micheal Hyatt, "The Difference Between a Sin and a Mistake," *Full Focus*, 2022, accessed August 8, 2022, https://fullfocus.co/the-difference-between-a-sin-and-a-mistake/. *Merriam-Webster*, s.v. "mistake," accessed August 8, 2022, https://merriam-webster.com/disctionary/mistake.

19   See also Romans 8:31–39. All Scripture references are from the NIV unless otherwise specified.

Chapter 2

20 The battle may have started in one person's heart, but often there is a problem in both hearts.

21 Bertice Berry, "Changing Your Outcomes by Shifting Your Focus," October 18, 2021, video podcast, 2:17, https://www.youtube.com/watch?v=Rpcoo-ZUIS8s.

22 Conflict Research Consortium Staff, "Summary of 'The Dynamics of Conflict Resolution: A Practitioner's Guide,'" *Moving Beyond Intractability* (MBI), 2003-2022, accessed August 30, 2021, https://www.beyondintractability.org/bksum/mayer-dynamics.

23 Based on Hocker and Wilmot's definition of conflict: "An expressed struggle between at least two interdependent parties who perceive incompatible goals, scarce resources, and interference from others in achieving goals." This definition emphasizes that interpersonal conflict is an expressed struggle. However, behind every externally expressed struggle is a conflict that first arose either within oneself or the other person (intrapersonal conflict), which lines up with the description in James 4:1–3. Joyce L. Hocker and William W. Wilmot, *Interpersonal Conflict* (New York: McGraw-Hill Education, 2018), 3.

24 Hocker and Wilmot, *Interpersonal Conflict*, 3–4.

25 Bernard Mayer, *The Dynamics of Conflict: A Guide to Engagement and Intervention*, 2nd ed. (San Francisco, CA: Jossey-Bass, 2012), 5.

26 According to Yu, depending on the intensity of the conflict, other terms such as fenqi (分歧, "disagreement") or chongtu (冲突, "clash") are also used, but maodun is used the most broadly. In the training I conducted in China, we primarily used the term chongtu to translate the English word conflict. Traditionally, maodun was similar in meaning to "contradiction, mutually opposed, or logically incompatible." At the time of this research, Mao Zedong had expanded the meaning of the term to something much closer to the western meaning of conflict. The term now includes differences, problems, difficulties, and antagonism in interpersonal or group situations. Xuejian Yu, "The Chinese 'Native' Perspectives on Mao-dun (Conflict) and Mao-dun Resolution Strategies: A Qualitative Investigation," *Intercultural Communication Studies*, 7(1) (1997–1998): 63–79, https://web.uri.edu/iaics/files/04-Xuejian-Yu.pdf; Guo-Ming Chen and William J. Starosta, "Chinese Conflict Management and Resolution: Overview and Implications," *Intercultural Communication Studies*, 7(1) (1997-1998): 3. Retrieved from https://digitalcommons.uri.edu/cgi/viewcontent.cgi?article=1015&context=com_facpubs.

27 Yu, "The Chinese 'Native' Perspectives on *Mao-dun* (Conflict) and *Mao-dun*," (1997–1998): 72. Stella Ting-Toomey, "Toward a Theory of Conflict and Culture," in *Communication, Culture, and Organizational Process*, eds. W. B. Gudykunst, L. P. Stewart, and S. Ting-Toomey (Beverly Hills, CA: Sage, 1985), 71–86.

28 Chung-Ying Cheng, "Toward Constructing a Dialectics of Harmonization: Harmony and Conflict in Chinese Philosophy," *Journal of Chinese Philosophy* 33 (2006): 31.

29 Cheng, "Toward Constructing a Dialectics of Harmonization," 44–45.

30 Ibid., 31.

31 Li-Li Huang, a professor of indigenous Chinese psychology, described how being in conflict negatively impacts oneself: "In a conflict, a person drops to a morally inferior position, maintains a losing stance emotionally and rationally, and pays a high price in personal, societal, and survival aspects." Li-Li Huang, "Interpersonal Harmony and Conflict for Chinese People: A Yin–Yang Perspective," *Frontiers in Psychology* 7 (2016): 4.

32 Marjorie Kagawa-Singer and Rena J. Pasick, "Cultural Norms," *Encyclopedia of Public Health*, Encyclopedia.com, accessed May 10, 2022, https://www.encyclopedia.com/education/encyclopedias-almanacs-transcripts-and-maps/cultural-norms.

33 The cultural norms listed here are by no means limited to Chinese culture, but as my research only focused on Chinese culture, I can't make statements broader than these. And while anecdotal evidence indicates these cultural norms are widespread, the limited nature of my doctoral study research only confirms their influence in mainland China among the Christians that I interviewed. From an academic or research perspective, further study is needed to determine how prevalent these cultural norms are throughout Chinese cultures in general. See what resonates with you.

34 Li Qiang, author interview, location undisclosed, 2019. Confucian Relationalism is the technical term that defines a number of social relationships in China. Confucian values and their accompanying ethical system dictate the intimacy or distance of a relationship as well as the superior or inferior status of each party in a relationship. Confucian Relationalism, which establishes seniority and authority, determines who has power: "The hierarchical structure of particularistic relationships ascribes the ruler (supervisor), father, husband, and older brother with authority to receive more power or control over their counterparts." Hwang, *Foundations of Chinese Psychology: Confucian Social Relations*; Guo-Ming Chen and William J. Staros-

ta, "Chinese Conflict Management and Resolution: Overview and Implications." *Intercultural Communication Studies* 7, no. 1 (1997–1998): 7; Kinser, "Factors Impacting Relational Reconciliation," 38.

35 See chapter three for an analysis of surface-level reconciliation.

36 Many factors contribute to conflict, making it complex to study. Mayer's book, *Dynamics of Conflict*, identifies factors such as group dynamics, cognitive styles, gender, and external events that also affect conflict. And there are four more variables that cut across the sources of conflict: culture, power, personality, and how data or information is handled (p. 18). But Mayer highlights the above-mentioned factors as being of critical importance to look at when helping people determine where they have gotten stuck in conflict, what insight is needed, and what opportunities are present.

Ting-Toomey and Oetzel, who have conducted extensive intercultural research on facework and communication, developed a culture-based situational conflict model in which they identify four groupings of factors that determine the results of intercultural conflict negotiation: one's primary orientation (cultural value patterns, personal attributes, conflict norms, and face concerns), situational features (ingroup/outgroup perceptions, relationship parameters, conflict goal assessments, conflict intensity and resources), conflict process factors (conflict interaction styles, emotional expressions, facework behaviors, and conflict competence skills), and conflict competence criteria and outcomes (appropriateness, effectiveness, satisfaction, and productivity). While Ting-Toomey and Oetzel created this model to help individuals see how people from different cultures may have differences in these areas, this model might also be useful in a mono-cultural setting. Stella Ting-Toomey and John G. Oetzel, *Managing Intercultural Conflict Effectively, Communicating Effectively in Multicultural Contexts* (Thousand Oaks, CA: SAGE Publications, Inc, 2001), Book.

37 E. Janet Warren, "(Mis)Understanding Submission, Sin, and Self-Esteem: A Theological and Psychological Perspective," *Priscilla Papers* 36, no. 1 (2022): 23-24.

Prideful thinking can take many forms, a few of which are exhibited by:

- Personal self-hatred that leads to comparison with others
- Perfectionistic behaviors resulting from believing we can control what others think
- A prideful belief of being longsuffering which causes some people to continue to accept abuse from others

38 Mayer, *Dynamics of Conflict*, 11.

39 See Mayer's book, *The Dynamics of Conflict*, and Toomey and Oetzel's, *Managing Intercultural Conflict Effectively*.

Chapter 3

40 For our purposes, we are focusing in on the religious and interpersonal uses of the term.

41 As de Gruchy says, "Reconciliation is a way of dealing with and overcoming past alienation, enmity and hurt. But it is also a way of relating to the 'other' in the present, and a goal that is always ahead of us in the future however much we may experience it here and now." John W. de Gruchy, *Reconciliation: Restoring Justice* (Minneapolis, MN: Fortress Press, 2002), chap. 1, sec. 2, Kindle.

42 de Gruchy, *Reconciliation*, chap. 1, sec. 2, Kindle.

43 Surface-level reconciliation in Chinese: 表面上的和好 (biaomian shang de hehao)

44 Li Jie, interview.

45 Huang, "Interpersonal Harmony and Conflict," 4.

46 Heart-level reconciliation in Chinese: 发自内心的和好 (fazi neixin de hehao)

47 Huang, "Interpersonal Harmony and Conflict," 4.

48 Hocker and Wilmot, *Interpersonal Conflict*, 324.

49 Peter Rowan, *Proclaiming the Peacemaker: The Malaysian Church as an Agent of Reconciliation in a Multicultural Society* (Eugene, OR: Wipf and Stock, 2012), 16.

50 See de Gruchy, *Reconciliation*, chap. 1, sec. 1, Kindle.

51 Paul is writing to Gentiles who were not physically circumcised. Based on Old Testament Law, they were unable to be in covenant relationship with God. Jews, however, were physically circumcised which was the God-given, outward, Old Testament sign of being in covenant relationship with God. Here however, Paul is referring to an inner circumcision, the cutting off of the sinful nature, or state, into which all human beings are born.

52 Miroslav Volf, *Free of Charge: Giving and Forgiving in a Culture Stripped of Grace* (Grand Rapids, MI: Zondervan, 2005), 130.

53 People living in a culture influenced by Confucian thought typically prioritize the father/son relationship above the other primary relationships as the most intimate. Due to the beliefs about origin of life coming from one's ancestors instead of from a transcendent creator, an individual's life is viewed as the continuation of one's parents', which explains why a high emphasis is placed on filial piety. It is generally understood that, in all relationships, one must first favor those who are more intimate (i.e., family) and superior. See Hwang, *Foundations of Chinese Psychology*.

54 de Gruchy's book, *Reconciliation: Restoring Justice*, goes into much more detail about these types of situations and what is needed for forgiveness and reconciliation to be possible.

55 The five stages of grief a dying person passes through: denial ("I'm not really sick"), anger ("It's the doctors' fault"), bargaining ("God, I'll stop smoking if you let me live"), depression ("Why didn't I get a checkup sooner?") and acceptance ("I really am going to die and I can accept it"). As presented in Dennis Linn, Sheila Fabricant Linn, Matthew Linn, *Don't Forgive Too Soon: Extending The Two Hands That Heal* (Mahwah, NJ: Paulist Press, 1997), 28.

56 Ibid., 29.

57 There is so much more about forgiveness that could be included here. For a deeper understanding of forgiveness, especially if you are wondering if or how to forgive someone who has caused you great harm or been abusive in any way, consider reading Miroslav Volf, *Free of Charge*.

58 Hocker and Wilmot, *Interpersonal Conflict*, 348–349.

59 See Ephesians 1:3–14; Colossians 1:15–23.

Chapter 4

60 Chang and Holt, "A Chinese Perspective on Face," 95–132; Cheng, "The Concept of Face," 329–48. Interestingly, the American sociologist Charles Horton Cooley similarly described how our perceptions of how others view us impact our view of ourselves: "Society is an interweaving and interworking of mental selves. I imagine your mind, and especially what your mind thinks about my mind, and what your mind thinks about what my mind thinks about your mind." The modern-day version, attributed to Cooley, says, "I am not who you think I am; I am not who I think I am; I am who I think you think I am." Charles Horton Cooley, *Life and the Student: Roadside Notes on Human Nature, Society, and Letters* (New York, NY: Alfred A Knopp, Inc, 1927), 201–202.

61　Christopher L. Flanders, *About Face: Rethinking Face for the 21st-Century Mission*, American Society of Missiology Monograph (Eugene, OR: Wipf and Stock Publishers, 2011), 189. Chris Flanders researched face in Thai culture—obviously a broader cultural context than Chinese but with many cross-overs.

62　I highly encourage you to read chapter eight in Flanders' book, *About Face*, for the full treatise on "a theological framework to orient face."

63　Flanders cites William Ury's book, *Trinitarian Personhood: Investigating the Implications of a Relational Definition* (Eugene, OR: Wipf and Stock Publishers, 2002).

64　Flanders, *About Face*, 191.

65　Flanders, *About Face*, 193.

66　Flanders, *About Face*, 191.

67　Flanders, *About Face*, 192.

68　Flanders, *About Face*, 192.

69　Flanders says this anxiety then produces fear, guilt, and shame. Flanders, *About Face*, 193. Check out Edward Tronick's fascinating work on the importance of face attachment. Mindyour class, "Still Face Experiment Dr. Edward Tronick," March 25, 2016, video, 2:49, https://www.youtube.com/watch?v=YTTSXc6sARg. And for more on the child development, psychology, and neuroscience aspects of this, check out Daniel Siegel, *The Developing Mind: How Relationships and the Brain Interact to Shape Who We Are*, 3rd ed. (New York: Guilford Press, 2020).

70　Flanders, *About Face*, 194.

71　Flanders, *About Face*, 196.

72　Flanders, *About Face*, 197.

73　See chapter five for further information regarding situations where power differentials or relational abuse are present.

74　Khiok-Khng Yeo, ed. *From Rome to Beijing: Symposia on Robert Jewett's Commentary on Romans* (Lincoln, NE: Kairos Studies, 2013), Kindle Loc 282. For descriptions of the Jewish and Roman culture of Jesus' day see the following works: David deSilva, *Honor, Patronage, Kinship & Purity: Unlocking New Testament Culture* (Downers Grove, IL: InterVarsity Press, 2000); Bruce J. Malina, *The New Testament World: Insights from Cultural Anthropology*, Third ed. (Louisville, KY: Westminster John Knox Press, 2001).

75 *Raca* is a term of severe insult in Aramaic.

76 Chapter nine gives examples of how individuals have successfully, proactively gone to talk with others.

77 Li Qiang, interview.

78 See the Feelings Reference Guide in Appendix A for help with pinpointing your emotions.

79 See the Universal Human Needs List in Appendix B for help with pinpointing your needs, longings, and desires.

Chapter 5

80 Diane Langberg, *Redeeming Power: Understanding Authority and Abuse in the Church* (Grand Rapids, MI: Brazos Press, 2020), Kindle. 3.

81 Ibid.

82 Ibid., 5.

83 Guanxi is generally translated into English as "relations, relationship, connections, or social connections." This means that if you have a particular type of relationship with someone—such as being a relative, being from the same town, or attending the same school—you automatically have guanxi with that person. One's guanxi with someone else can be used as a social resource. In many Chinese contexts, success in life not only depends on personal hard work but also on having a well-connected family and having attended school with the right people, all of which gives one the needed guanxi to get things done. Guanxi is also something that one can develop with others over time through a reciprocal relationship built on the giving and receiving of favors and gifts. Hui-Ching Chang and G. Richard Holt, "A Chinese Perspective on Face as Inter-Relational Concern," in The Challenge of Facework: Cross-Cultural and Interpersonal Issues, ed. Stella Ting-Toomey, *Suny Series in Human Communication Processes* (Albany, NY: State University of New York Press, 1994), 106; Wei and Li, "The Confucian Value of Harmony and Its Influence on Chinese Social Interaction," 64.

84 Langberg, *Redeeming Power: Understanding Authority and Abuse in the Church*, 7-9. Referenced by Daniel Teater, "Managing Power Imbalances and Abuse," audio of workshop, Sowing Peace RW360 Conference, Billings, MO, September 10, 2021, https://qubc5lbqub-flywheel.netdna-ssl.com/wp-content/uploads/2021/10/Managing-Power-Imbalances-and-Abuses-9_10_21-2.41-PM.mp3.

85   Langberg, *Redeeming Power: Understanding Authority and Abuse in the Church*, 7–9.

86   Langberg, *Redeeming Power: Understanding Authority and Abuse in the Church*, 4.

87   Eric H.F. Law, *The Wolf Shall Dwell with the Lamb* (St. Louis, MO: Chalice Press, 1993).

88   Teater, "Managing Power Imbalances and Abuse."

89   Dacher Keltner, *The Power Paradox: How We Gain and Lose Influence* (New York, NY: Penguin Books, 2017), 23.

90   Ibid., 100–110, 27–31.

91   South Dakota Coalition Ending Domestic & Sexual Violence, "Is it Domestic Violence, Abuse, Conflict, Violence, or Battering?" *South Dakota Coalition Ending Domestic & Sexual Violence*, 2022, accessed June 1, 2022, https://www.sdcedsv.org/information/domesticviolenceinformation-1/.

92   Teater, "Managing Power Imbalances and Abuse," workshop handout, accessed August 3, 2022, https://rw360.org/2021acrc/.

93   Upstream Investigations, "Conflict and Abuse. What's the Difference," *Upstream Investigations*, accessed June 1, 2022, https://www.upstream-investigations.com.au/conflict-and-abuse-whats-the-difference/.

94   Kristen Milstead, "Abusive Behavior vs. Normal Behavior: What's the Difference?," *Healthy Place*, February 14, 2019, https://aws.healthyplace.com/blogs/verbalabuseinrelationships/2019/2/abusive-behavior-vs-normal-behavior-whats-the-difference.

95   Abuse includes physical, verbal, sexual, or spiritual. Examples of abusive behaviors include but are not limited to threats, using intimidation, bullying, stalking, being financially or physically manipulative, or being coercively controlling.

96   Teater, "Managing Power Imbalances and Abuse."

97   Read the following article for more on why giving the benefit of the doubt and believing someone is so important: NSVRC, "False Reporting," National Sexual Violence Resource Center, 2012, https://www.nsvrc.org/sites/default/files/2012-03/Publications_NSVRC_Overview_False-Reporting.pdf. However, if you discover that someone is actually lying to you, that person needs your compassionate, loving, and listening ear just as much. Something that needs God's healing touch is motivating their deceptive behavior.

98 Bob Smietana, "Millions Wanted to 'Save Saeed.' Few Wanted to Help His Abused Ex-Wife," *The Roys Report*, https://julieroys.com/millions-save-saeed-few-help-abused-ex-wife/.

99 Teater, "Managing Power Imbalances and Abuse."

100 Smietana, "Millions Wanted to 'Save Saeed.'"

101 Smietana, "Millions Wanted to 'Save Saeed.'"

102 See Appendix D for some learning opportunities.

103 When someone is from a minority culture, being in conflict with a peer from the dominant culture can be equally difficult to navigate.

104 See chapter ten for examples of what to look for and what to avoid when seeking a companion or coach to help you navigate a conflict.

105 Benjamin C. Shin and Sheryl Takag Silzer, *Tapestry of Grace: Untangling the Cultural Complexities in Asian American Life and Ministry* (Eugene, OR: Wipf & Stock, 2016), 109.

106 Hwang, Foundations of Chinese Psychology. Note: sometimes "friend to friend" gets replaced by "elders to juniors" as one of the five primary or cardinal relationships.

107 Chen and Starosta, "Chinese Conflict Management and Resolution," 7.

Hierarchy refers to "how people fit into a whole and also how they are categorized by age, status, and gender." Shin and Silzer, *Tapestry of Grace: Untangling the Culutral Complexities in Asian American Life and Ministry*, 108.

108 Hwang, Foundations of Chinese Psychology, 123–124.

109 Yuling Pan, *Politeness in Chinese Face-to-Face Interaction* (Stamford, CT: Ablex Publishing Corporation, 2000), Kindle Reader, Chapter 4, Gender, Age, and Rank in the Official Setting, para. 2. Because of these structured relationships, regardless of situation, Chinese people intuitively and unconsciously walk through four steps when deciding how to communicate with someone else:

(a) identify the situation and setting

(b) recognize the hierarchical order, the social distance, and the social relationship

(c) identify who has power in this setting, determining what factors (age, gender, rank) are important in the power relation

(d) apply face strategies according to the social relation and power hierarchy

110 Though the context of this book is limited to Chinese culture, there are similarities in conflict-response practices in several Asian cultures due to a shared Confucian (as well as Buddhist, Taoist, and Shamanist) influence. For an excellent summary of literature describing how Confucianism impacts Korean Christians, Korean church culture, and native-born Korean missionaries, read Hannah Kyong-Jin Cho, *Understanding Burnout Recovery among Native-Born Korean Missionaries, Evangelical Missiological Society Monograph Series 3* (Eugene, OR: Pickwick Publications, 2020), 64.

111 For a more extensive description of Confucian principles that foster hierarchical structure as well as Confucian relationships and Scripture, see Shin and Silzer, *Tapestry of Grace: Untangling the Cultural Complexities in Asian American Life and Ministry*, 138–50.

112 LuLu Wang, "The Farewell," (United States: A24, 2019).

113 Read Joshua 22 for a biblical example of looking at actions and misinterpreting motives. Some of the Israelite tribes almost went to war with other tribes over misinterpreted motives. Thankfully they took time to communicate and clarify intentions before acting on their plan to fight.

114 Shin and Silzer, *Tapestry of Grace: Untangling the Cultural Complexities in Asian American Life and Ministry*, 109.

115 For further help discovering what is going on in your own heart, read chapter five, "Conflict Starts in the Heart," of Ken Sande's book *The Peacemaker* (Grand Rapids, MI: Baker Books, 2004).

Chapter 6

116 To understand more about what happens physically in the brain when experiencing conflict, check out resources such as: Maggie Holland, "Emotional Flooding: Symptoms, Examples, & How to Cope," *Choosing Therapy*, March 10, 2023, https://www.choosingtherapy.com/emotional-flooding/ or Taylor Wendt, "Amygdala: What to Know," *WebMD*, September 1, 2022, https://www.webmd.com/brain/amygdala-what-to-know.

117 See Appendix A for a sample list of feelings and emotions.

118 See Appendix B for a sample list of universal human needs.

Chapter 7

119 Hyatt, "The Difference between a Sin and a Mistake," 2022. In 1 John 1:9, the Greek word (ὁμολογωμεν), translated as confession in English and 认 (ren) in Chinese, literally means "to speak the same word."

120 Lynne Fox, "The Biblical Meaning of Confession," BibleGrapes: Biblical Resources for Everyday Life," March 29, 2019, accessed August 8, 2022, https://biblegrapes.com/the-biblical-meaning-of-confession/.

121 Those I interviewed had learned the Seven A's of Biblical Confession found in Ken Sande's book, The Peacemaker. This specific list was pulled from RW360, "Seven A's of a Biblical Confession — Get the Log Out of Your Eye," accessed December 17, 2021, https://rw360.org/seven-as-of-a-biblical-confession/.

122 Huang Jingjing, interview. Sande, *The Peacemaker*.

123 Zhang Yong, interview.

124 Zhao Cheng, interview.

125 Liu Yang, interview.

Chapter 8

126 Faithfulness includes being reliable, dependable, loyal, and devoted.

127 Ibid. If I had explored her interests with her, she may have discovered that beneath her anger was a desire for respect and/or a desire to be responsible. Recognizing our underlying desire(s) can help us be more aware of our anger triggers in the future and mindful of how we respond.

128 Notice how Li Min's change from being critical in her text interaction with her husband to simply expressing the difficult position that she found herself in gave him the opportunity to respond to her heart rather than needing to respond to an attack.

Chapter 9

129 Matthew 7:3–5, "Why do you look at the speck of sawdust in your brother's eye and pay no attention to the plank in your own eye? How can you say to your brother, 'Let me take the speck out of your eye,' when all the time there is a plank in your own eye? You hypocrite, first take the plank out of your own eye, and then you will see clearly to remove the speck from your brother's eye."

130 In Chinese culture, it is disrespectful to talk about someone's upcoming death.

131 See 1 Samuel 25:14–24 for an excellent biblical example of seizing the opportunity to apologize. In Abigail and David's story, Abigail proactivity seized the opportunity and apologized on behalf of her husband—explaining the situation—which led to David's calming down, praising God, and no longer bringing retaliation upon Abigail's home.

132 Yang Lin, interview. The Seven A's: **A**ddress everyone involved. **A**void *if*, *but*, and *maybe*. **A**dmit specifically. **A**cknowledge the hurt. **A**ccept the consequences. **A**lter your behavior. **A**sk for forgiveness.

Chapter 10

133 A companion can help in more ways than listed here; however, these four ways specifically surfaced during my dissertation research.

134 Note: These same words could have been spoken in a judging, admonishing tone, which more often leads to resistance than receptivity.

135 Wang Jia, interview.

136 To receive training and practice in how to biblically guide someone without telling them what to do, I highly recommend participating in a training course on conflict coaching. Many of the peacemaking organizations listed in Appendix D provide such training.

137 Zhang Wei, interview.

138 I highly recommend conflict coaching training and mediation training for individuals in any level of leadership. If people regularly come to you seeking help with their conflict situations, you can strengthen your ability to help by attending these trainings. Many of the peacemaking organizations listed in Appendix D provide opportunities to learn how to come alongside others in effective, God-honoring ways.

139 Wally Yew, "Chinese Church, Asian Church, Community Church," Challenger, April 2000. CCMUSA, https://ccmusa.org/u2u/u2u.aspx?id=200004.

140 Ibid.

141 Alternatively, discomfort resulting from ego-protection or face vulnerability might prompt us to justify and defend our own position; to act self-righteously and increasingly judge others; or to condemn ourselves.

142 Amy Watson, "Average Daily Time Spent Reading Per Capita in the United States from 2014 to 2022 (in hours)," Statista, June 22, 2023, https://www.statista.com/statistics/622525/time-reading-us/.

143 Amy Watson, "Average Amount of Time Spent Reading the Bible among Adults in the United States from 2013 to 2017," *Statista*, August 9, 2019, https://www.statista.com/statistics/299981/time-spent-reading-the-bible-usa/. In daily Bible reading, 23% of adults surveyed spend one hour or more, 6% spend 45–59 minutes, 29% spend 30–44 minutes, 23% spend 15–29 minutes, and 17% spend less than 15 minutes.

Chapter 11

144 Note: Differences of opinion are normal and to be expected. Conflict often results from poor responses to those differences. While also normal, conflict can be lessened as we grow in responding to our differences in God-honoring ways.

145 Su Lijuan, interview.

146 Liu Haifeng, interview.

147 Li Jie, interview.

148 Yew, "Chinese Church, Asian Church, Community Church."

149 Justin Welby, *The Power of Reconciliation* (London, UK: Bloomsbury Continuum, 2022), 13. Just before this sentence Welby wrote, "I write about peacebuilding and reconciliation in the sense of seeking relationships at all levels of human life that are resilient enough to have disagreement without destruction, victory without triumphalism, concessions without degradation. Reconciliation is the long drawn-out process, extending sometimes over generations, which seeks to achieve that end."

150 See Appendix E: Conversation Space Ideas, for specific exploratory conversation starter ideas.

151 Louis Luzbetak, *The Church and Cultures* (Maryknoll, NY: Orbis Books, 1988), 294.

152 Yew, "Chinese Church, Asian Church, Community Church."

153 Corlette Sande, *The Young Peacemaker* (Wapwallopen, PA: Shepherd Press, 2002).

BIBLIOGRAPHY/REFERENCES

Chang, Hui-Ching, and G. Richard Holt. "A Chinese Perspective on Face as Inter-Relational Concern." In *The Challenge of Facework: Cross-Cultural and Interpersonal Issues*, edited by Stella Ting-Toomey. *Suny Series in Human Communication Processes*, 95–132. Albany, NY: State University of New York Press, 1994.

Cheng, Bor-Shiuan, Li-Fang Chou, Tsung-Yu Wu, Min-Ping Huang, and Jiing-Lih Farh. "Paternalistic Leadership and Subordinate Responses: Establishing a Leadership Model in Chinese Organizations." *Asian Journal of Social Psychology* 7, no. 1 (2004): 89–117.

Cheng, Chung-Ying. "The Concept of Face and Its Confucian Roots." *Journal of Chinese Philosophy* 13, no. 3 (1986): 329–48.

———. "Toward Constructing a Dialectics of Harmonization: Harmony and Conflict in Chinese Philosophy." *Journal of Chinese Philosophy* 33 (2006): 25–59.

Cho, Hannah Kyong-Jin. *Understanding Burnout Recovery among Native-Born Korean Missionaries*. Evangelical Missiological Society Monograph Series 3. Eugene, OR: Pickwick Publications, 2020.

Cooley, Charles Horton. *Life and the Student: Roadside Notes on Human Nature, Society, and Letters*. New York: Alfred A. Knopp, Inc, 1927.

de Gruchy, John W. *Reconciliation: Restoring Justice*. Minneapolis, MN: Fortress Press, 2002.

deSilva, David. *Honor, Patronage, Kinship & Purity: Unlocking New Testament Culture*. Downers Grove, IL: InterVarsity Press, 2000.

Flanders, Christopher L. *About Face: Rethinking Face for the 21st-Century Mission*. American Society of Missiology Monograph Eugene, OR: Wipf and Stock Publishers, 2011.

Ho, David Yau-fai. "On the Concept of Face." *American Journal of Sociology* 81, no. 4 (1976): 867–84.

Hocker, Joyce L., and William W. Wilmot. *Interpersonal Conflict*. New York: McGraw-Hill Education, 2018.

Huang, Li-Li. "Interpersonal Harmony and Conflict for Chinese People: A Yin–Yang Perspective." *Frontiers in Psychology* 7 (2016).

Hwang, Kwang-Kuo. *Foundations of Chinese Psychology: Confucian Social Relations*. *International and Cultural Psychology* (Book 1). Edited by Anthony J. Marsella. New York: Springer, 2012.

Keltner, Dacher. *The Power Paradox: How We Gain and Lose Influence*. New York: Penguin Books, 2017.

Langberg, Diane. *Redeeming Power: Understanding Authority and Abuse in the Church*. Grand Rapids, MI: Brazos Press, 2020. Kindle.

Law, Eric H. F. *The Wolf Shall Dwell with the Lamb*. St. Louis, MO: Chalice Press, 1993.

Linn, Dennis, Sheila Fabricant Linn, and Matthew Linn. *Don't Forgive Too Soon: Extending The Two Hands That Heal*. Mahwah, NJ: Paulist Press, 1997.

Luzbetak, Louis. *The Church and Cultures*. Maryknoll, NY: Orbis Books, 1988.

Malina, Bruce J. *The New Testament World: Insights from Cultural Anthropology*. Third ed. Louisville, KY: Westminster John Knox Press, 2001.

Mayer, Bernard. *The Dynamics of Conflict: A Guide to Engagement and Intervention*. 2nd ed. San Francisco, CA: Jossey-Bass, 2012.

Pan, Yuling. *Politeness in Chinese Face-to-Face Interaction*. Stamford, CT: Ablex Publishing Corporation, 2000. Kindle Reader.

Rowan, Peter. *Proclaiming the Peacemaker: The Malaysian Church as an Agent of Reconciliation in a Multicultural Society*. Eugene, OR: Wipf and Stock, 2012.

Sande, Corlette. *The Young Peacemaker*. Wapwallopen, PA: Shepherd Press, 2002.

Shin, Benjamin C., and Sheryl Takag Silzer. *Tapestry of Grace: Untangling the Cultural Complexities in Asian American Life and Ministry*. Eugene, OR: Wipf & Stock, 2016.

Smietana, Bob. "Millions Wanted to 'Save Saeed.' Few Wanted to Help His Abused Ex-Wife." *The Roys Report*. October 16, 2021. Accessed June 1, 2022. https://julieroys.com/millions-save-saeed-few-help-abused-ex-wife/.

South Dakota Coalition Ending Domestic & Sexual Violence. "Is it Domestic Violence, Abuse, Conflict, Violence, or Battering?" *South Dakota Coalition Ending Domestic & Sexual Violence*. 2022. Accessed August 21, 2023, https://www.sdcedsv.org/domestic.

Teater, Daniel. "Managing Power Imbalances and Abuse." *Worship for Sowing Peace RW360*. Conference filmed in Billings, MO. September 10, 2021. https://qubc5lbqub-flywheel.netdna-ssl.com/wp-content/uploads/2021/10/Managing-Power-Imbalances-and-Abuses-9_10_21-2.41-PM.mp3.

Ting-Toomey, Stella. "Toward a Theory of Conflict and Culture." In *Communication, Culture, and Organizational Process*. Edited by W. B. Gudykunst, L. P. Stewart, and S. Ting-Toomey, 71–86. Beverly Hills, CA: Sage, 1985.

———, and John G. Oetzel. *Managing Intercultural Conflict Effectively*. Thousand Oaks, CA: SAGE Publications, Inc, 2001.

Upstream Investigations. "Conflict and Abuse. What's the Difference," *Upstream Investigations*. Accessed June 1, 2022, https://www.upstreaminvestigations.com.au/conflict-and-abuse-whats-the-difference/.

Wang, LuLu. *The Farewell*. A24, 2019.

Warren, E. Janet. "(Mis)Understanding Submission, Sin, and Self-Esteem: A Theological and Psychological Perspective." *Priscilla Papers* 36, no. 1 (2022): 21–30.

Wei, Xiaohong, and Qingyuan Li. "The Confucian Value of Harmony and Its Influence on Chinese Social Interaction." *Cross-Cultural Communication* 9, no. 1 (2013): 60–66.

Welby, Justin. *The Power of Reconciliation*. London: Bloomsbury Continuum, 2022.

Yu, Xuejian. "The Chinese 'Native' Perspectives on Mao-dun (Conflict) and Mao-dun Resolution Strategies: A Qualitative investigation." *Intercultural Communication Studies*, 7(1) (1997–1998): 63–79. https://web.uri.edu/iaics/files/04-Xuejian-Yu.pdf.

Yeo, Khiok-Khng, ed. *From Rome to Beijing: Symposia on Robert Jewett's Commentary on Romans*. Lincoln, NE: Kairos Studies, 2013.

Yew, Wally. "Chinese Church, Asian Church, Community Church." *Challenger*, April 2000. CCMUSA, https://ccmusa.org/u2u/u2u.aspx?id=200004.

ABOUT THE AUTHOR

Jolene Kinser is an author, trainer, speaker, and ICC Peace Certified Christian Conciliator who specializes in global Chinese peacemaking ministry development.

Between 1997–2020, Jolene spent much of her time either working or studying in China. A pioneer at heart, in 2010 she started Step Up Educational Consulting in Wuhan as well as began conducting conflict resolution and peacemaking trainings. Fluent in Mandarin and well-traveled beyond China, Jolene works with Chinese and multicultural leaders to introduce culturally appropriate biblical peacemaking in their contexts.

Jolene holds a PhD in Intercultural Education from Biola University (2020), an MA in Intercultural Studies from Fuller Seminary (2002), and BAs in Linguistics and Religious Studies from UC Davis (1997). Though she travels worldwide for training, graduate-level teaching, and ministry development, Jolene currently lives in southern California, serving as a peacemaking specialist with the South Pacific District of The Christian and Missionary Alliance.

Visit

JoleneKinser.com

to

- *Discover the latest resources written or recommended by Jolene*

- *Sign up for a workshop with Jolene*

- *Subscribe to Jolene's newsletter*

Jolene Kinser